BRITTEN AND BRÜLIGHTLY

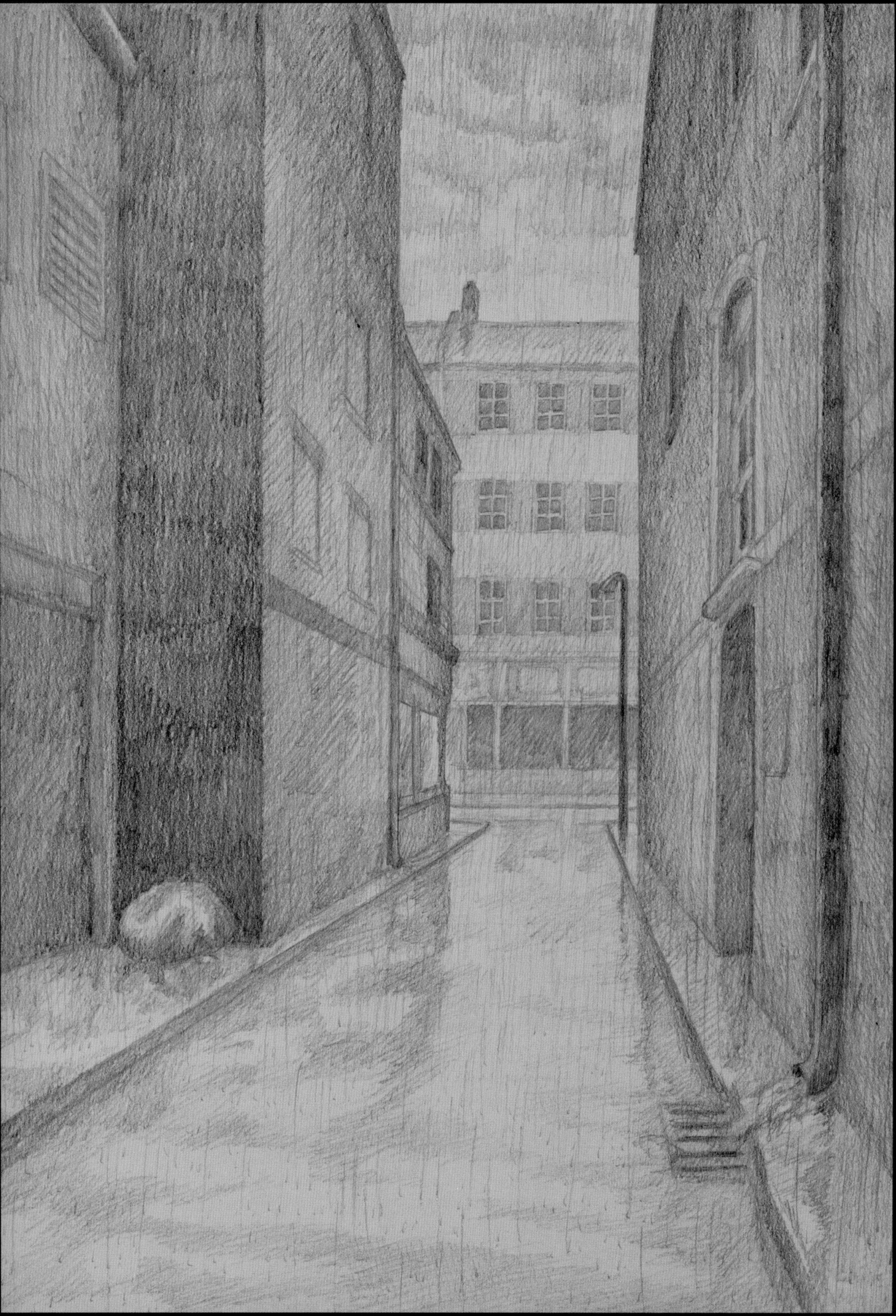

BRITTEN
AND
BRÜLIGHTLY

HANNAH BERRY

Metropolitan Books

Henry Holt and Company   New York

Metropolitan Books
Henry Holt and Company, LLC
Publishers since 1866
175 Fifth Avenue
New York, New York 10010
www.henryholt.com

Originally published in the United Kingdom in 2008 by Jonathan Cape, London

Berry, Hannah, 1982–
    Britten and Brülightly / Hannah Berry.—1st U.S. ed.
        p. cm.
    ISBN-13: 978-0-8050-8927-1
    ISBN-10: 0-8050-8927-6
    1. Graphic novels.   I. Title.
    PN6737.B47B75 2009
    741.5'973—dc22   2008023133

Henry Holt books are available for special promotions and premiums.
For details contact: Director, Special Markets.

First U.S. Edition 2009
Printed in China
1 3 5 7 9 10 8 6 4 2

For
Nan and Granddad,
'Bita y 'Bito

BRITTEN AND BRÜLIGHTLY

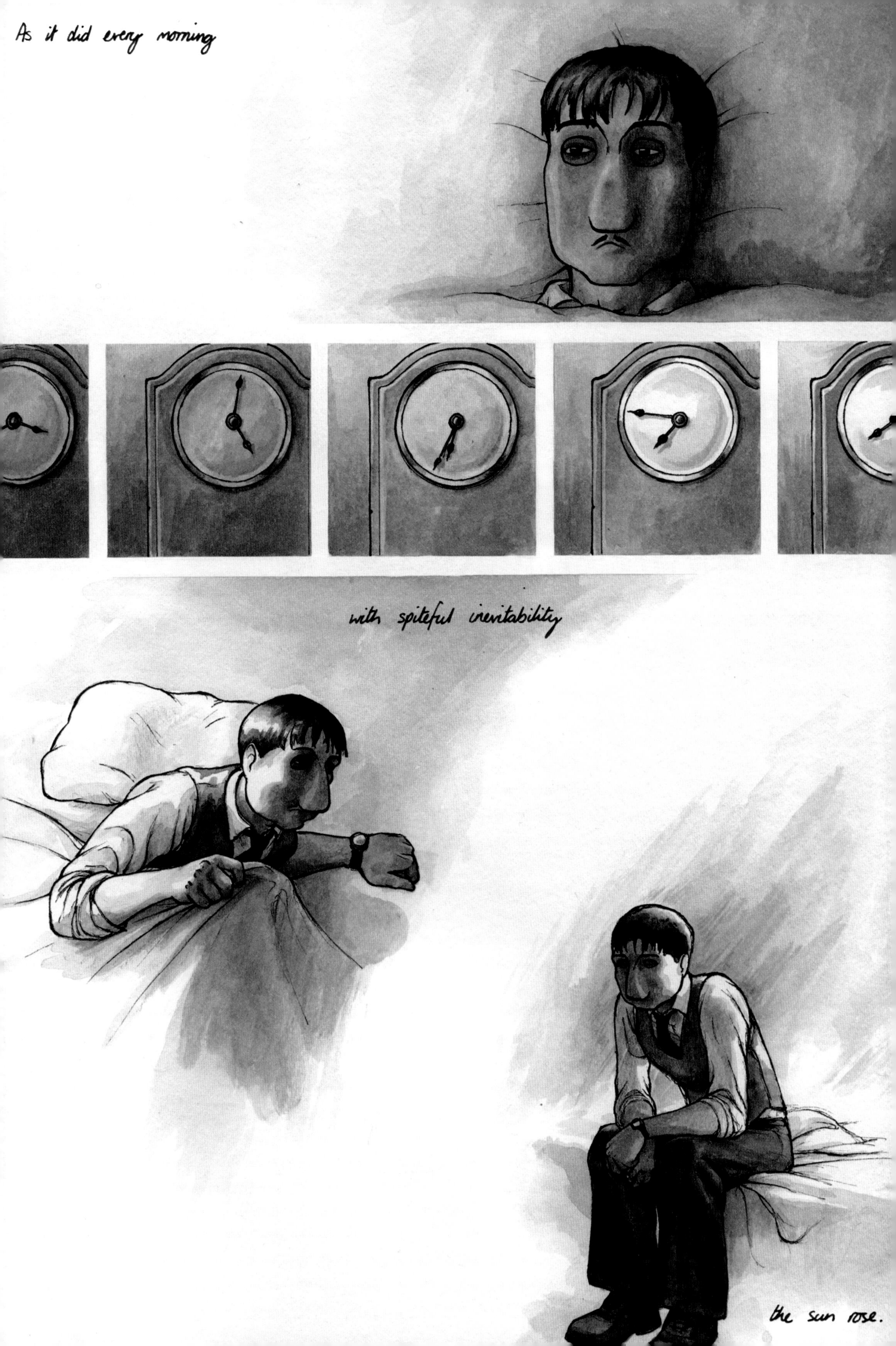
As it did every morning
with spiteful inevitability
the sun rose.

It rose in a sky that was bruised and tender to look at, if you could see it through the weather. The view from the window changed so rarely that I didn't bother to look at it any more.

It rose in a sky that was bruised and tender to look at, if you could see it through the weather. The view from the window changed so rarely that I didn't bother to look at it any more.

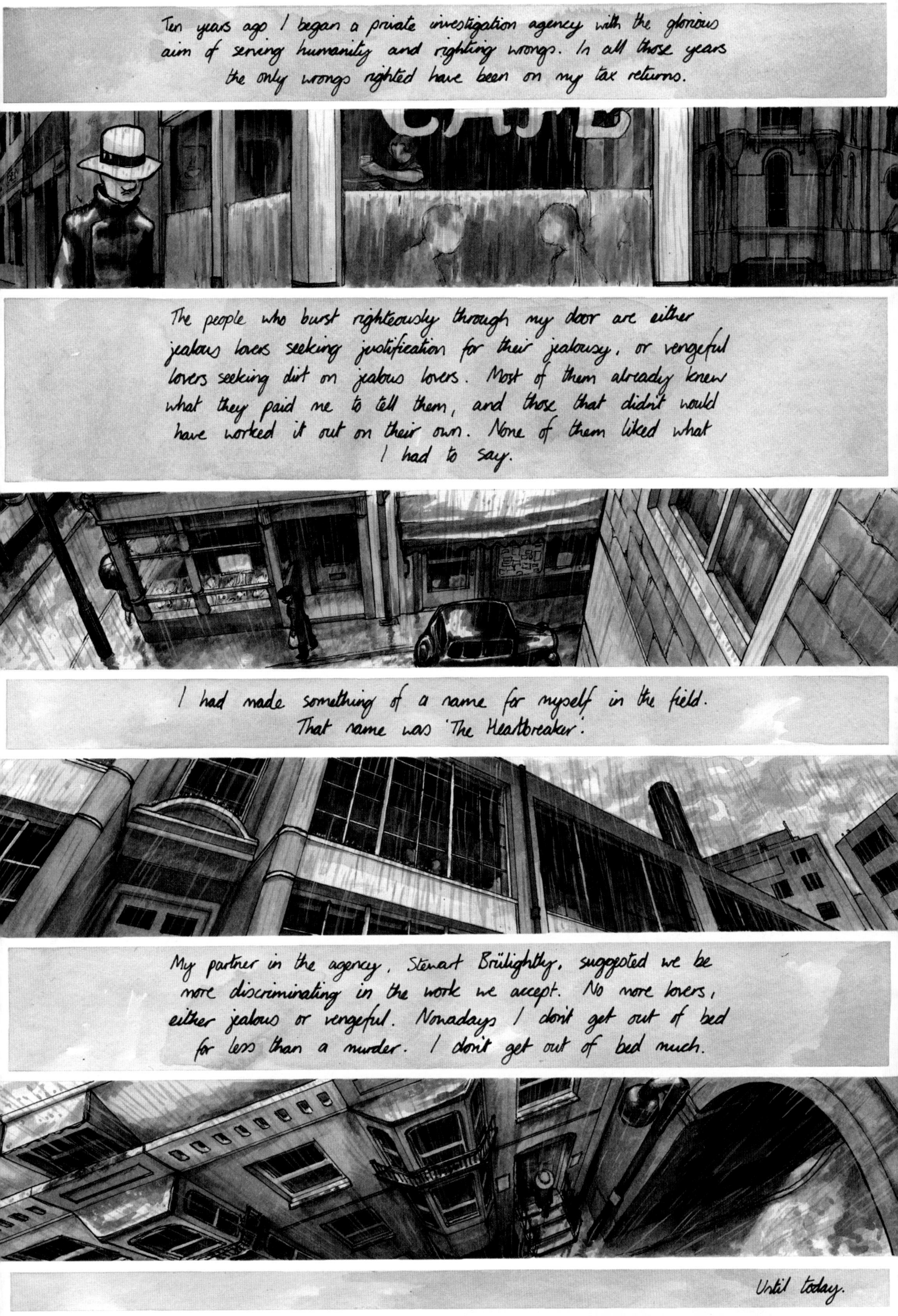
Ten years ago I began a private investigation agency with the glorious aim of serving humanity and righting wrongs. In all those years the only wrongs righted have been on my tax returns.
The people who burst righteously through my door are either jealous lovers seeking justification for their jealousy, or vengeful lovers seeking dirt on jealous lovers. Most of them already knew what they paid me to tell them, and those that didn't would have worked it out on their own. None of them liked what I had to say.
I had made something of a name for myself in the field. That name was 'The Heartbreaker'.
My partner in the agency, Stewart Brülightly, suggested we be more discriminating in the work we accept. No more lovers, either jealous or vengeful. Nowadays I don't get out of bed for less than a murder. I don't get out of bed much.
Until today.

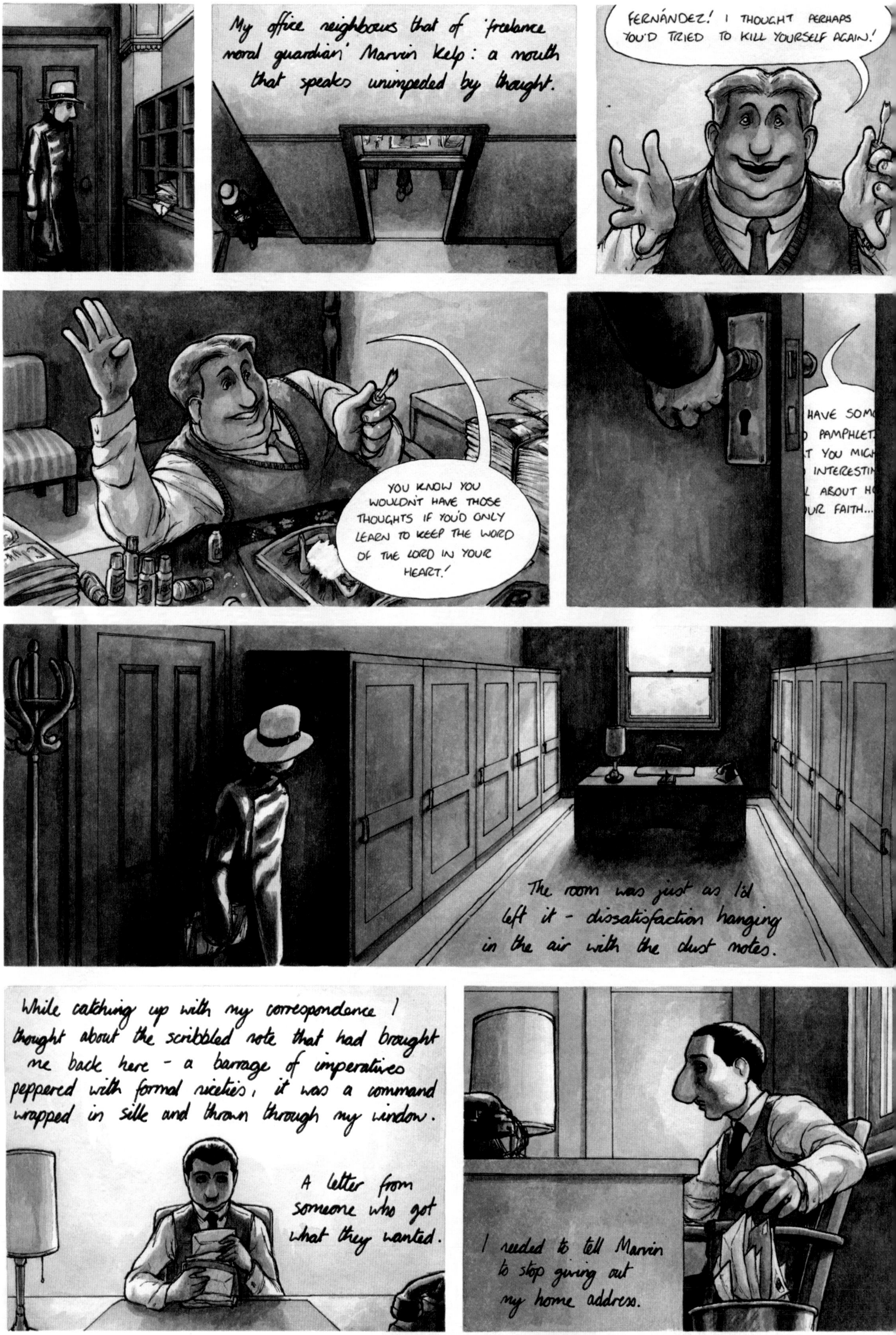
My office neighbours that of 'freelance moral guardian' Marvin Kelp: a mouth that speaks unimpeded by thought.
FERNÁNDEZ! I THOUGHT PERHAPS YOU'D TRIED TO KILL YOURSELF AGAIN!
YOU KNOW YOU WOULDN'T HAVE THOSE THOUGHTS IF YOU'D ONLY LEARN TO KEEP THE WORD OF THE LORD IN YOUR HEART!
HAVE SOM
PAMPHLET
T YOU MIGH
INTERESTIN
L ABOUT HO
UR FAITH...
The room was just as I'd left it - dissatisfaction hanging in the air with the dust motes.
While catching up with my correspondence I thought about the scribbled note that had brought me back here - a barrage of imperatives peppered with formal niceties, it was a command wrapped in silk and thrown through my window.
A letter from someone who got what they wanted.
I needed to tell Marvin to stop giving out my home address.

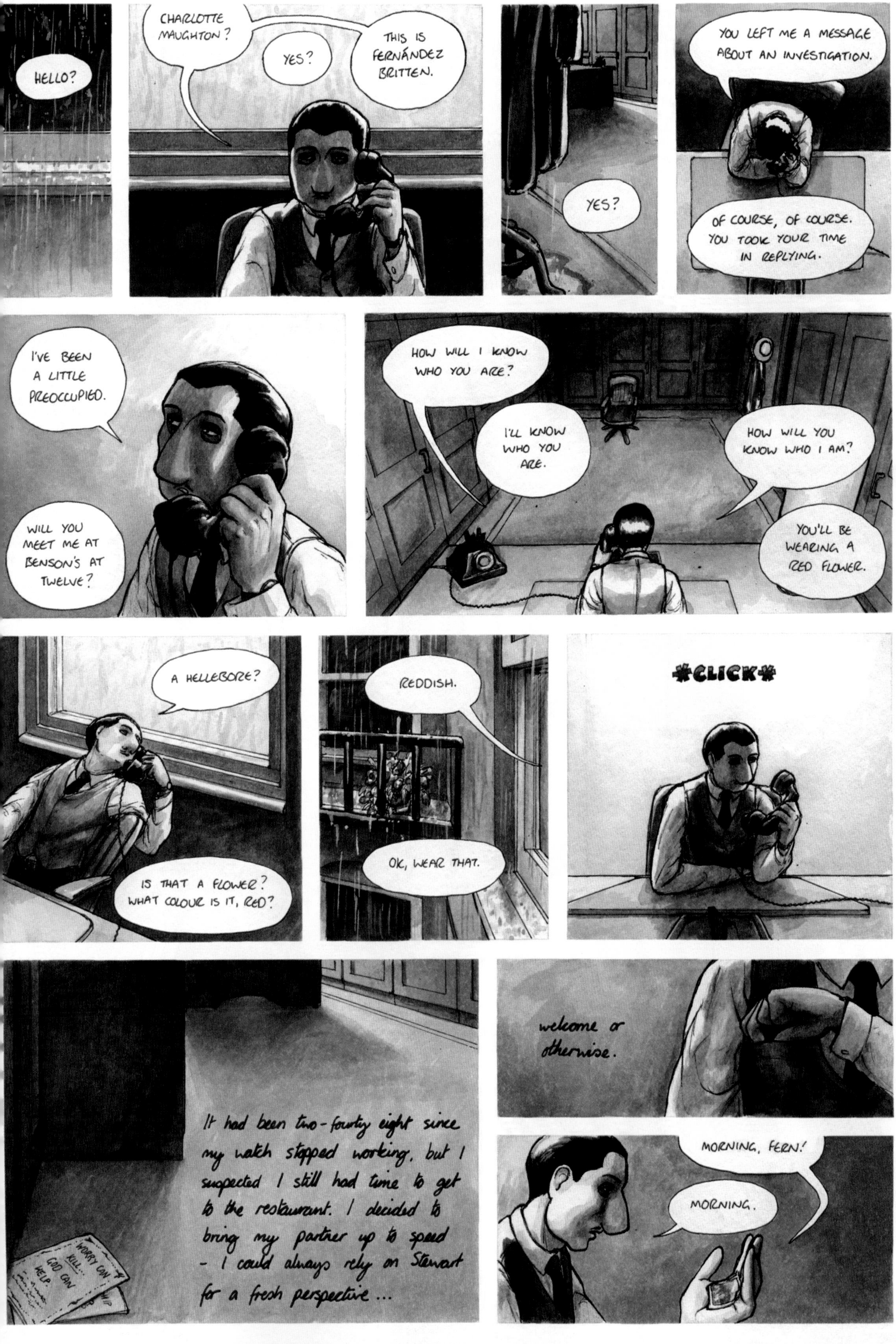
HELLO?
CHARLOTTE MAUGHTON?
YES?
THIS IS FERNÁNDEZ BRITTEN.
YOU LEFT ME A MESSAGE ABOUT AN INVESTIGATION.
YES?
OF COURSE, OF COURSE. YOU TOOK YOUR TIME IN REPLYING.
I'VE BEEN A LITTLE PREOCCUPIED.
WILL YOU MEET ME AT BENSON'S AT TWELVE?
HOW WILL I KNOW WHO YOU ARE?
I'LL KNOW WHO YOU ARE.
HOW WILL YOU KNOW WHO I AM?
YOU'LL BE WEARING A RED FLOWER.
A HELLEBORE?
IS THAT A FLOWER? WHAT COLOUR IS IT, RED?
REDDISH.
OK, WEAR THAT.
CLICK
WORRY CAN KILL... GOD CAN HELP.
It had been two-fourty eight since my watch stopped working, but I suspected I still had time to get to the restaurant. I decided to bring my partner up to speed - I could always rely on Stewart for a fresh perspective ...
welcome or otherwise.
MORNING, FERN!
MORNING.

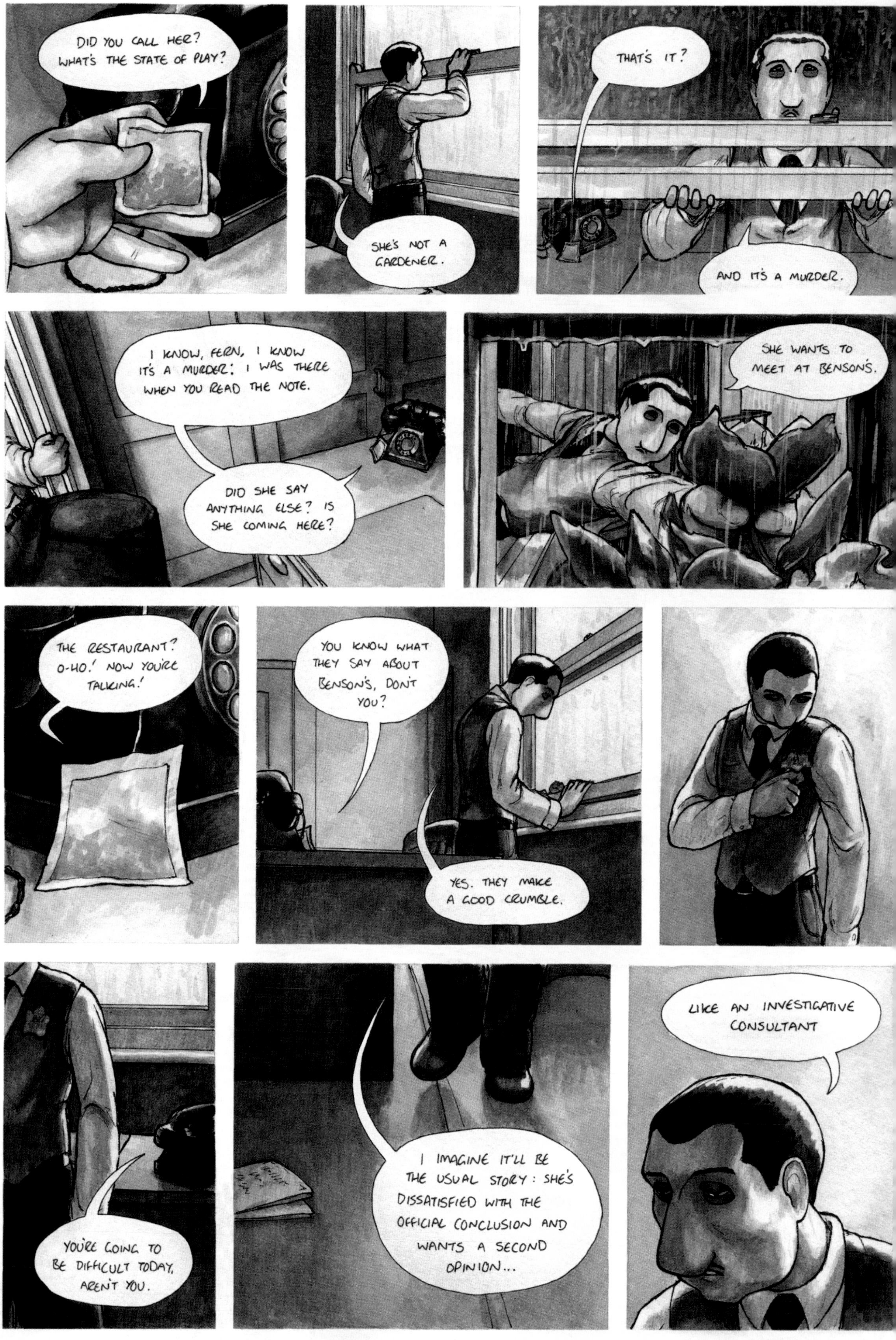
DID YOU CALL HER? WHAT'S THE STATE OF PLAY?
SHE'S NOT A GARDENER.
THAT'S IT?
AND IT'S A MURDER.
I KNOW, FERN, I KNOW IT'S A MURDER: I WAS THERE WHEN YOU READ THE NOTE.
DID SHE SAY ANYTHING ELSE? IS SHE COMING HERE?
SHE WANTS TO MEET AT BENSON'S.
THE RESTAURANT? O-HO! NOW YOU'RE TALKING!
YOU KNOW WHAT THEY SAY ABOUT BENSON'S, DON'T YOU?
YES. THEY MAKE A GOOD CRUMBLE.
YOU'RE GOING TO BE DIFFICULT TODAY, AREN'T YOU.
I IMAGINE IT'LL BE THE USUAL STORY: SHE'S DISSATISFIED WITH THE OFFICIAL CONCLUSION AND WANTS A SECOND OPINION...
LIKE AN INVESTIGATIVE CONSULTANT

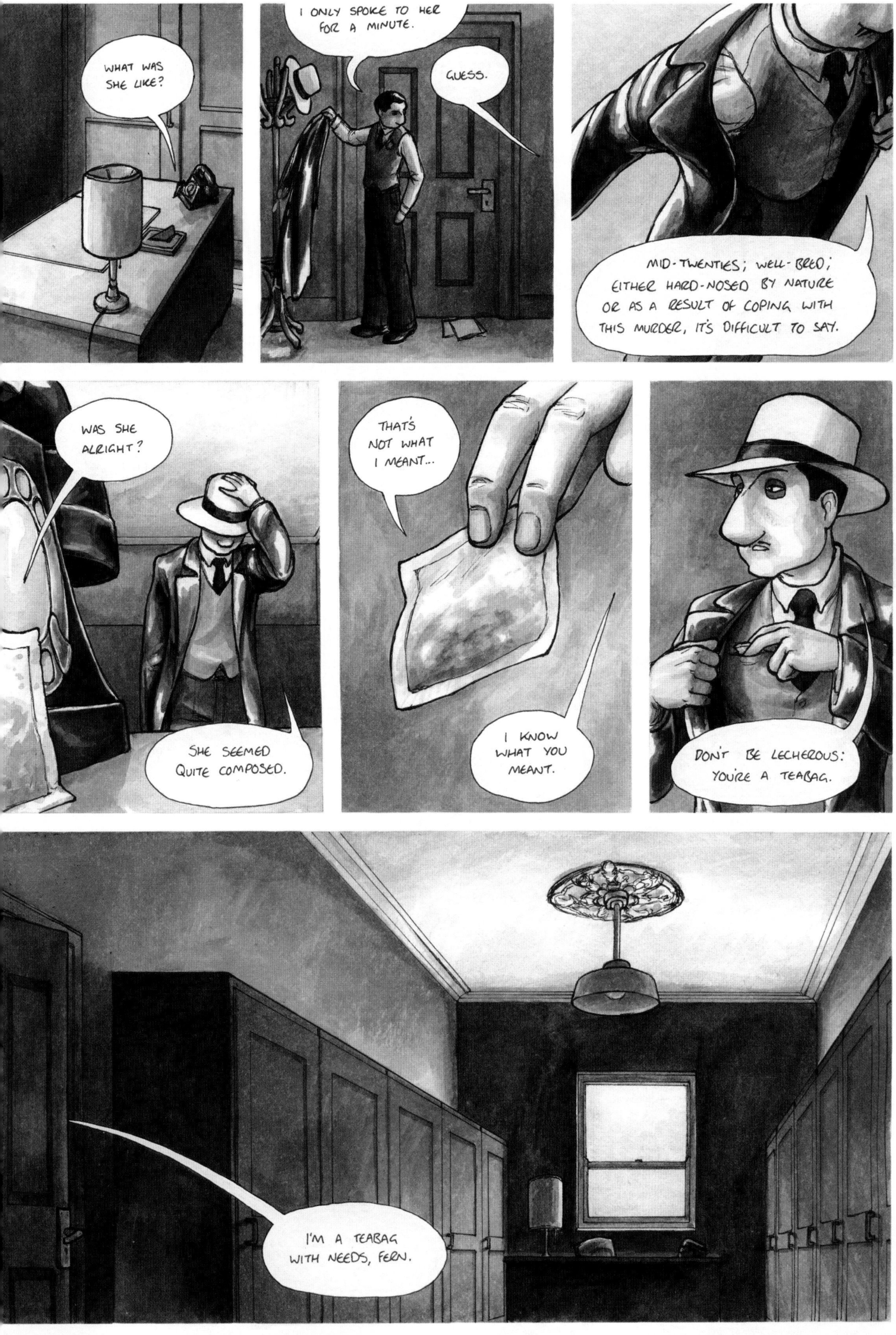
WHAT WAS SHE LIKE?
I ONLY SPOKE TO HER FOR A MINUTE.
GUESS.
MID-TWENTIES; WELL-BRED; EITHER HARD-NOSED BY NATURE OR AS A RESULT OF COPING WITH THIS MURDER, IT'S DIFFICULT TO SAY.
WAS SHE ALRIGHT?
SHE SEEMED QUITE COMPOSED.
THAT'S NOT WHAT I MEANT...
I KNOW WHAT YOU MEANT.
DON'T BE LECHEROUS: YOU'RE A TEABAG.
I'M A TEABAG WITH NEEDS, FERN.

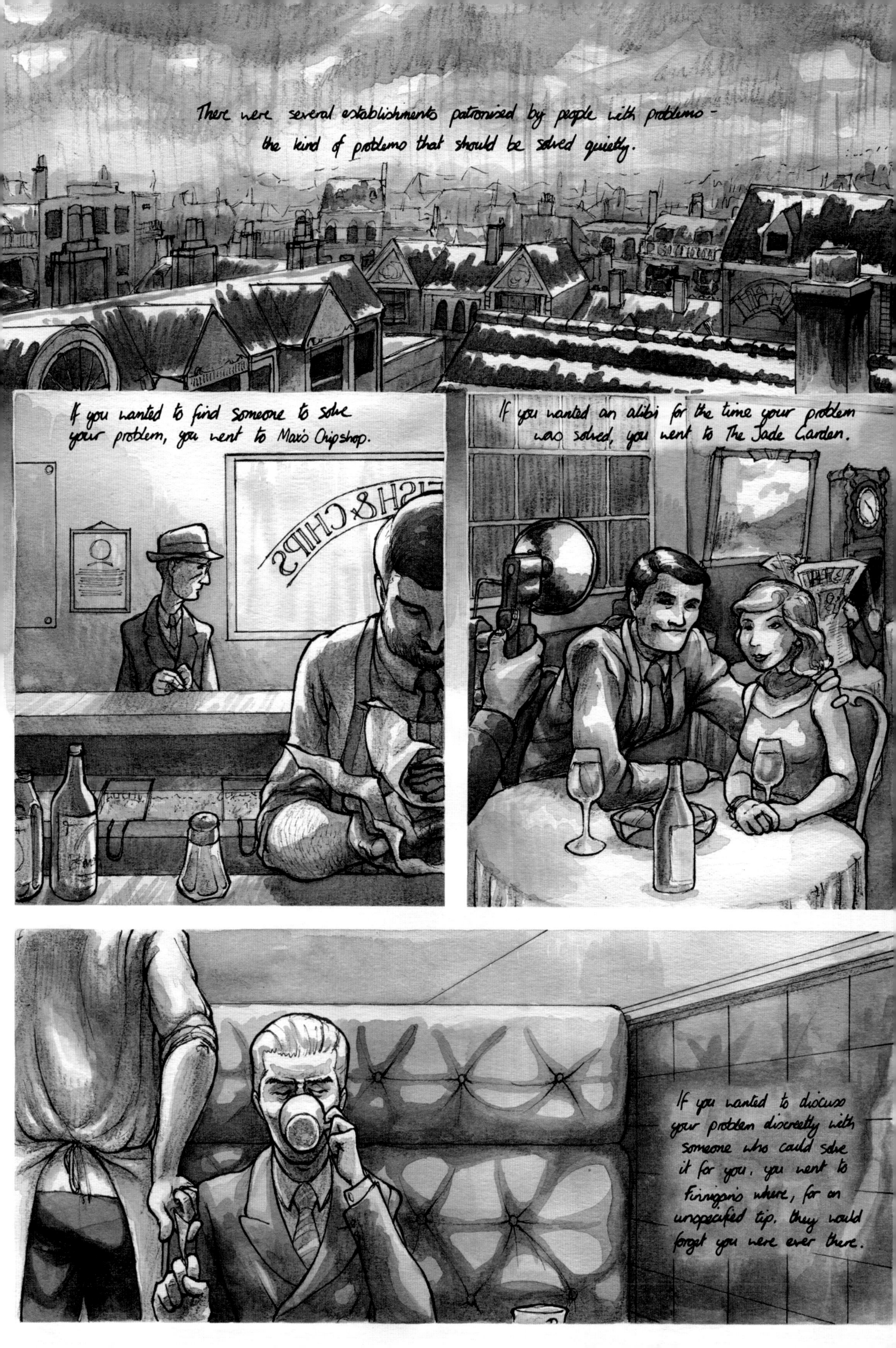
There were several establishments patronised by people with problems - the kind of problems that should be solved quietly.
If you wanted to find someone to solve your problem, you went to Max's Chipshop.
FISH & CHIPS
If you wanted an alibi for the time your problem was solved, you went to The Jade Garden.
If you wanted to discuss your problem discreetly with someone who could solve it for you, you went to Finnigan's where, for an unspecified tip, they would forget you were ever there.

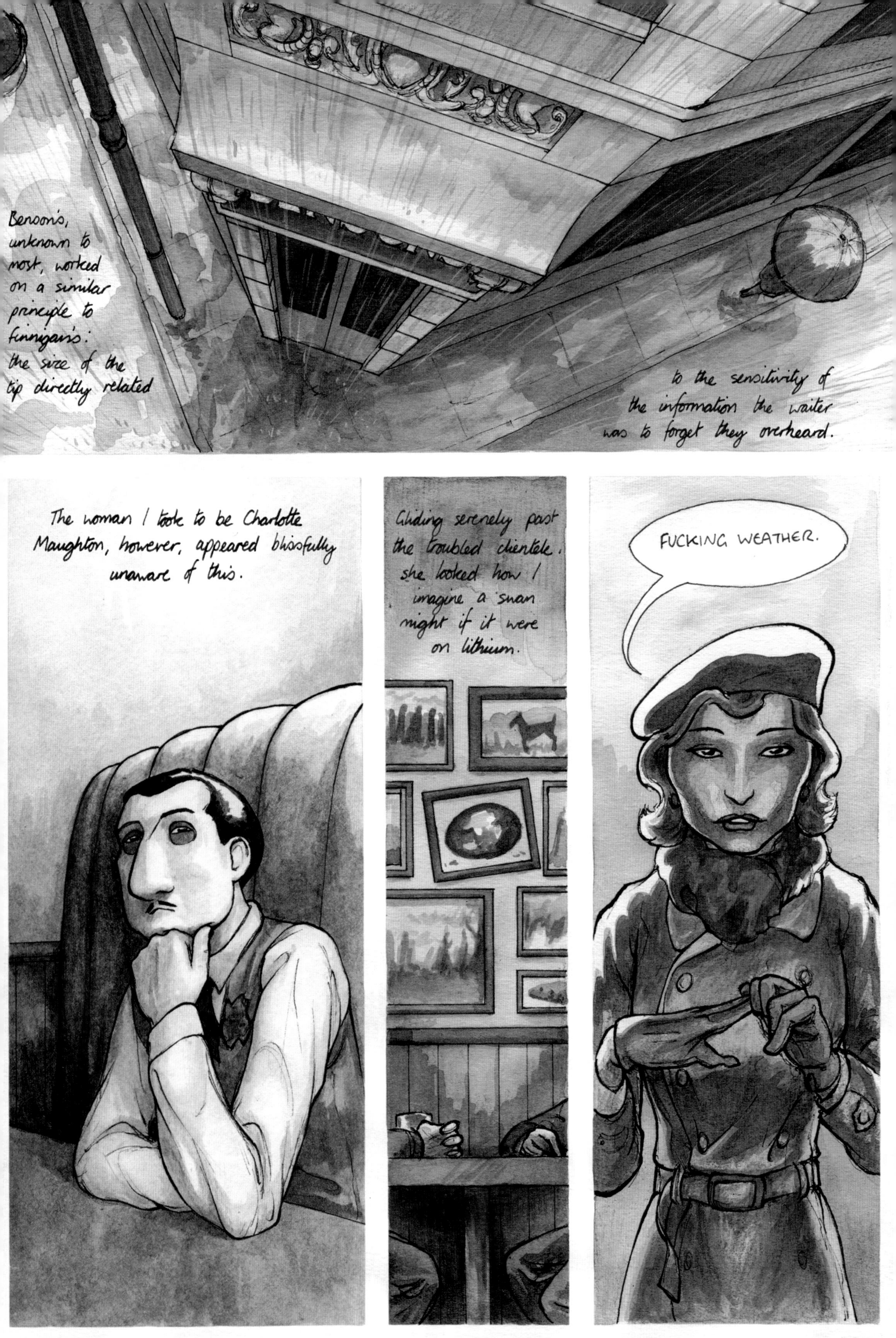
Benoon's, unknown to most, worked on a similar principle to Finnigan's: the size of the tip directly related
to the sensitivity of the information the waiter was to forget they overheard.
The woman I took to be Charlotte Maughton, however, appeared blissfully unaware of this.
Gliding serenely past the troubled clientele, she looked how I imagine a swan might if it were on lithium.
FUCKING WEATHER.

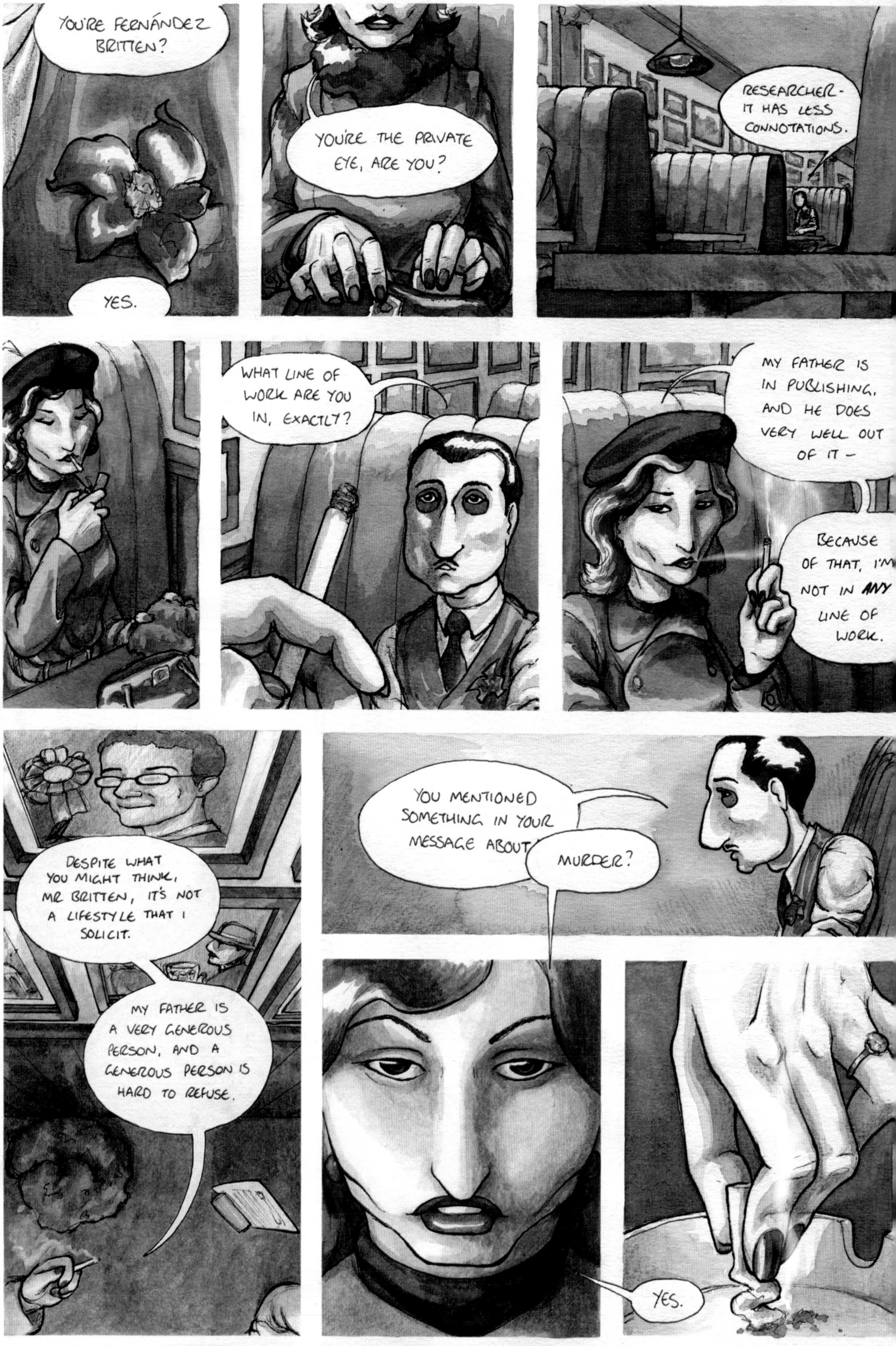
YOU'RE FERNÁNDEZ BRITTEN?
YES.
YOU'RE THE PRIVATE EYE, ARE YOU?
RESEARCHER- IT HAS LESS CONNOTATIONS.
WHAT LINE OF WORK ARE YOU IN, EXACTLY?
MY FATHER IS IN PUBLISHING, AND HE DOES VERY WELL OUT OF IT -
BECAUSE OF THAT, I'M NOT IN **ANY** LINE OF WORK.
DESPITE WHAT YOU MIGHT THINK, MR BRITTEN, IT'S NOT A LIFESTYLE THAT I SOLICIT.
MY FATHER IS A VERY GENEROUS PERSON, AND A GENEROUS PERSON IS HARD TO REFUSE.
YOU MENTIONED SOMETHING IN YOUR MESSAGE ABOUT...
MURDER?
YES.

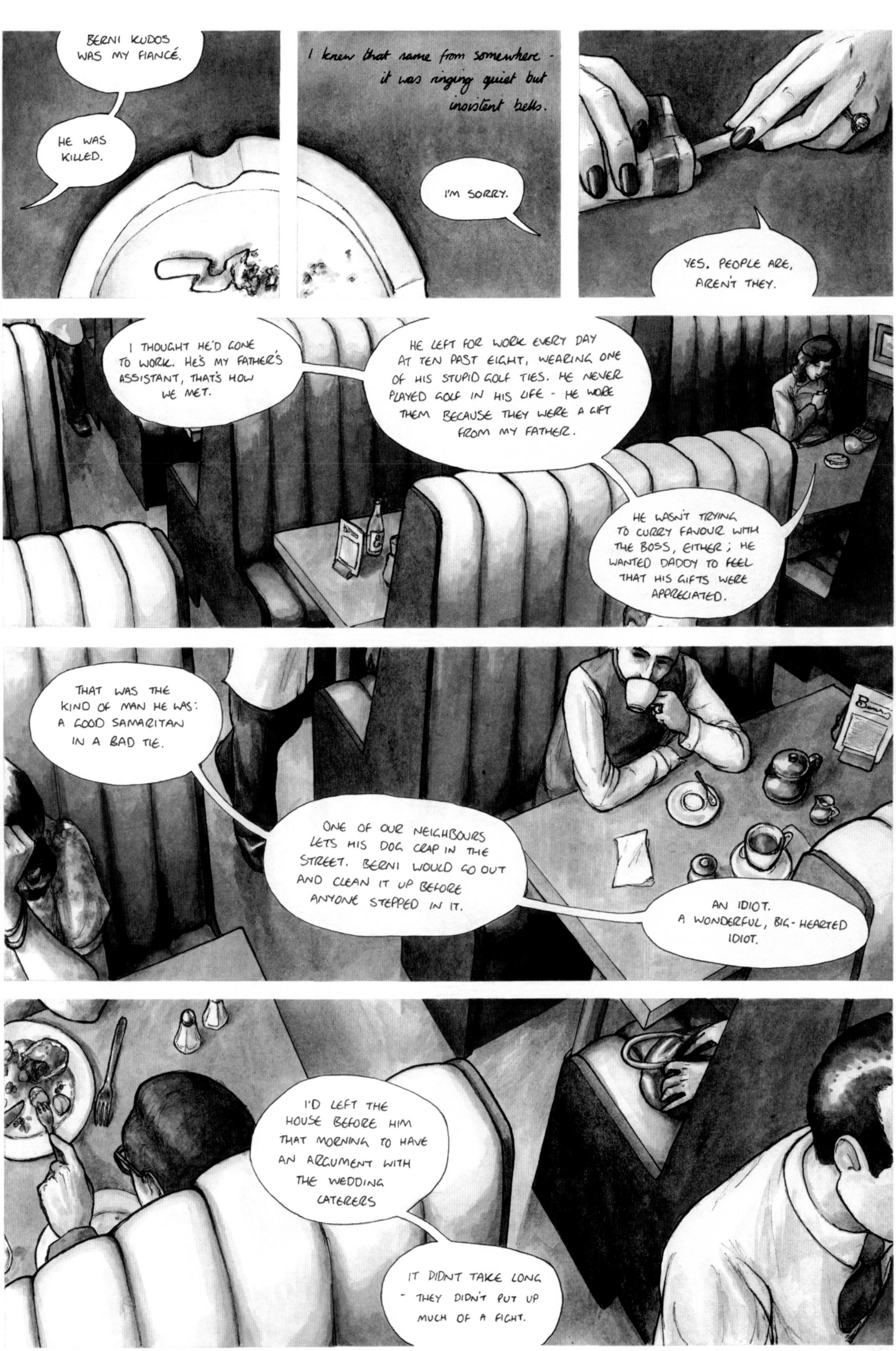

BERNI KUDOS WAS MY FIANCÉ.
HE WAS KILLED.
I knew that name from somewhere - it was ringing quiet but insistent bells.
I'M SORRY.
YES. PEOPLE ARE, AREN'T THEY.
I THOUGHT HE'D GONE TO WORK. HE'S MY FATHER'S ASSISTANT, THAT'S HOW WE MET.
HE LEFT FOR WORK EVERY DAY AT TEN PAST EIGHT, WEARING ONE OF HIS STUPID GOLF TIES. HE NEVER PLAYED GOLF IN HIS LIFE - HE WORE THEM BECAUSE THEY WERE A GIFT FROM MY FATHER.
HE WASN'T TRYING TO CURRY FAVOUR WITH THE BOSS, EITHER; HE WANTED DADDY TO FEEL THAT HIS GIFTS WERE APPRECIATED.
THAT WAS THE KIND OF MAN HE WAS: A GOOD SAMARITAN IN A BAD TIE.
ONE OF OUR NEIGHBOURS LETS HIS DOG CRAP IN THE STREET. BERNI WOULD GO OUT AND CLEAN IT UP BEFORE ANYONE STEPPED IN IT.
AN IDIOT. A WONDERFUL, BIG-HEARTED IDIOT.
I'D LEFT THE HOUSE BEFORE HIM THAT MORNING TO HAVE AN ARGUMENT WITH THE WEDDING CATERERS
IT DIDNT TAKE LONG - THEY DIDN'T PUT UP MUCH OF A FIGHT.

I CAME BACK AT AROUND TEN-THIRTY.

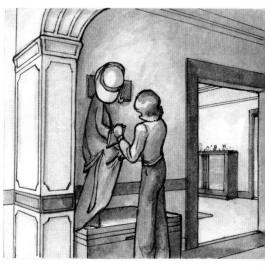

FUCKING GOLF TIE

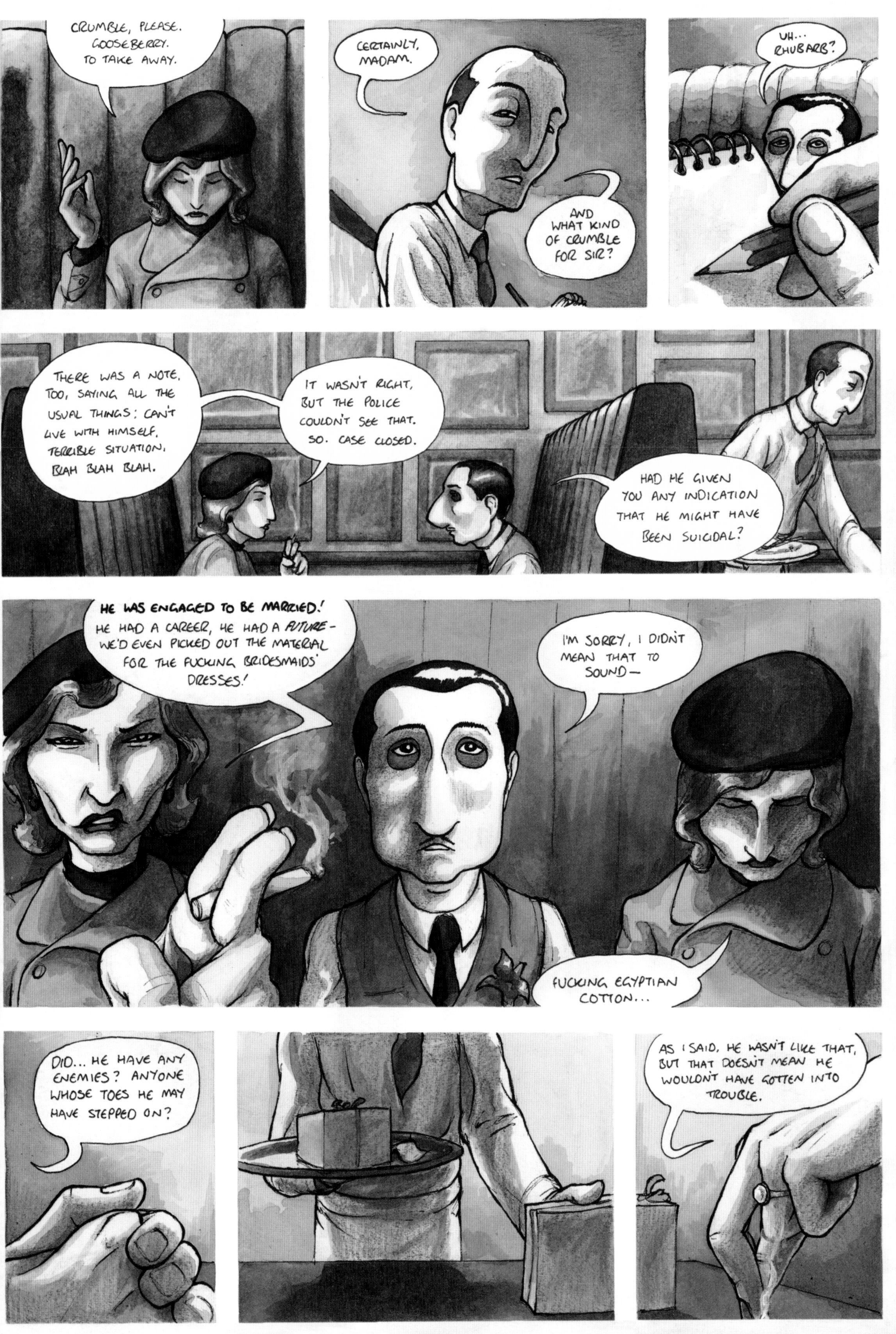

CRUMBLE, PLEASE. GOOSEBERRY. TO TAKE AWAY.
CERTAINLY, MADAM.
AND WHAT KIND OF CRUMBLE FOR SIR?
UH... RHUBARB?
THERE WAS A NOTE, TOO, SAYING ALL THE USUAL THINGS: CAN'T LIVE WITH HIMSELF, TERRIBLE SITUATION, BLAH BLAH BLAH.
IT WASN'T RIGHT, BUT THE POLICE COULDN'T SEE THAT. SO. CASE CLOSED.
HAD HE GIVEN YOU ANY INDICATION THAT HE MIGHT HAVE BEEN SUICIDAL?
HE WAS ENGAGED TO BE MARRIED! HE HAD A CAREER, HE HAD A FUTURE - WE'D EVEN PICKED OUT THE MATERIAL FOR THE FUCKING BRIDESMAIDS' DRESSES!
I'M SORRY, I DIDN'T MEAN THAT TO SOUND—
FUCKING EGYPTIAN COTTON...
DID... HE HAVE ANY ENEMIES? ANYONE WHOSE TOES HE MAY HAVE STEPPED ON?
AS I SAID, HE WASN'T LIKE THAT, BUT THAT DOESN'T MEAN HE WOULDN'T HAVE GOTTEN INTO TROUBLE.

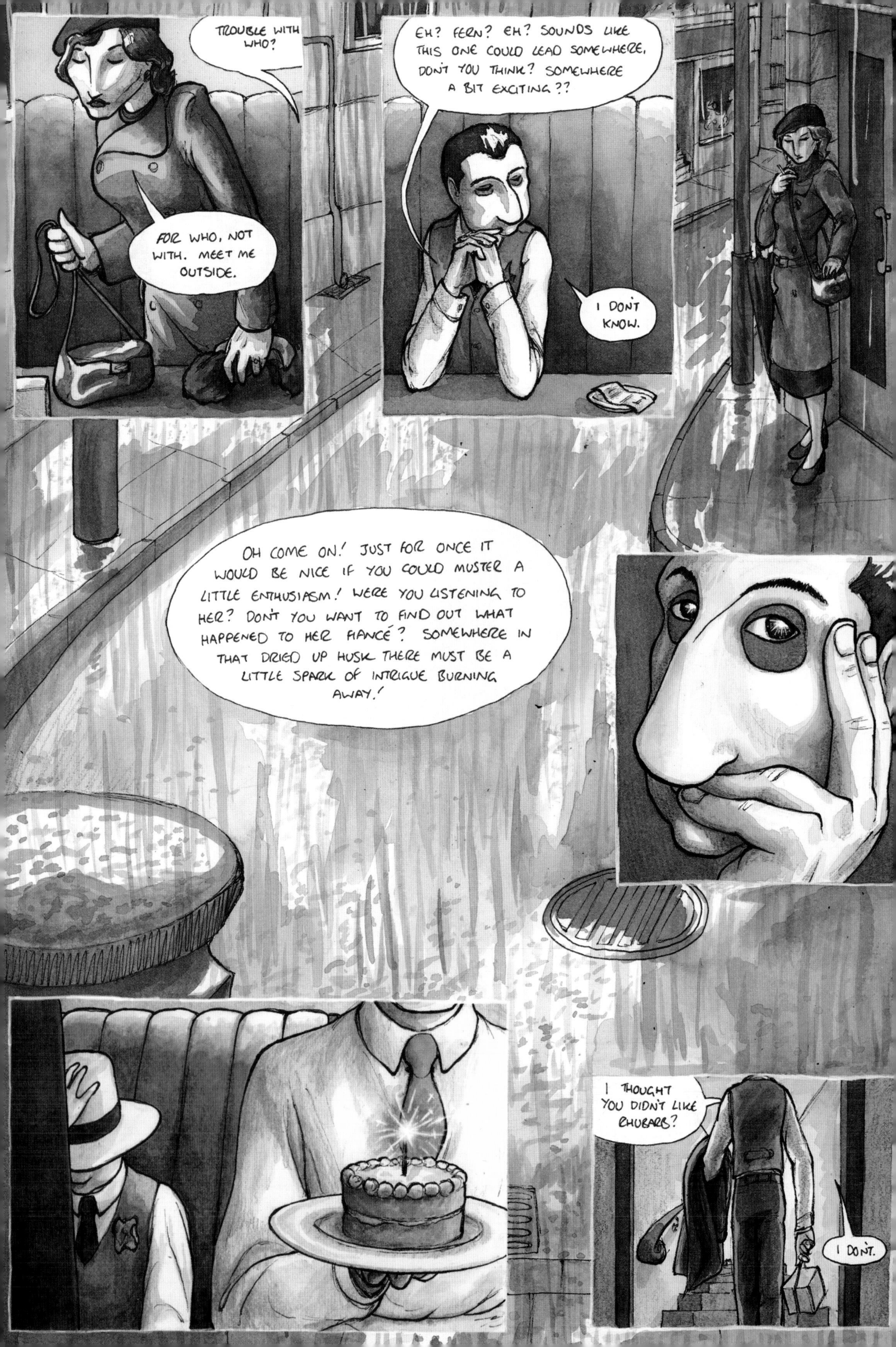
TROUBLE WITH WHO?
FOR WHO, NOT WITH. MEET ME OUTSIDE.
EH? FERN? EH? SOUNDS LIKE THIS ONE COULD LEAD SOMEWHERE, DON'T YOU THINK? SOMEWHERE A BIT EXCITING??
I DON'T KNOW.
OH COME ON! JUST FOR ONCE IT WOULD BE NICE IF YOU COULD MUSTER A LITTLE ENTHUSIASM! WERE YOU LISTENING TO HER? DON'T YOU WANT TO FIND OUT WHAT HAPPENED TO HER FIANCÉ? SOMEWHERE IN THAT DRIED UP HUSK THERE MUST BE A LITTLE SPARK OF INTRIGUE BURNING AWAY!
I THOUGHT YOU DIDN'T LIKE RHUBARB?
I DON'T.

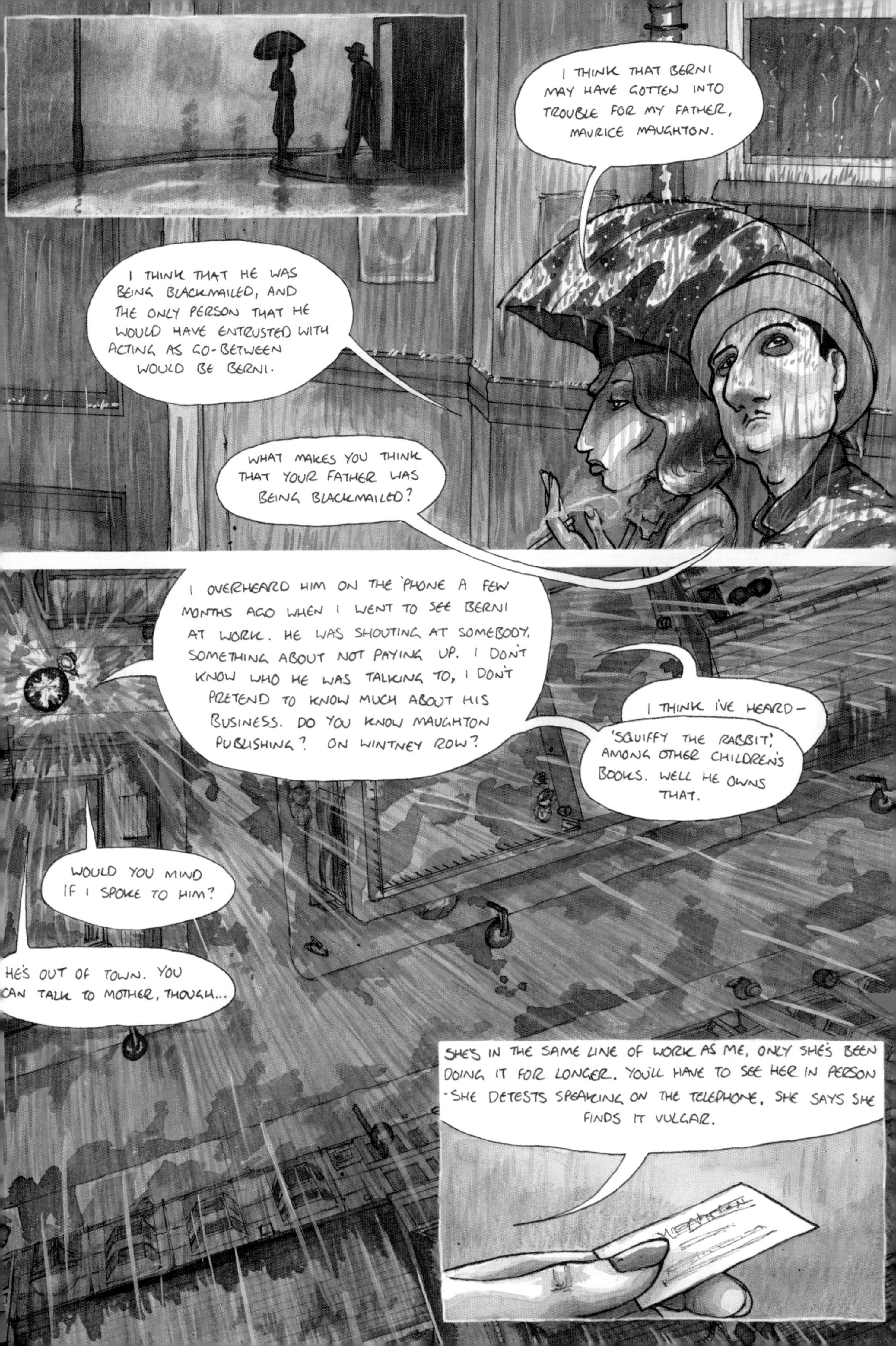
I THINK THAT BERNI MAY HAVE GOTTEN INTO TROUBLE FOR MY FATHER, MAURICE MAUGHTON.
I THINK THAT HE WAS BEING BLACKMAILED, AND THE ONLY PERSON THAT HE WOULD HAVE ENTRUSTED WITH ACTING AS GO-BETWEEN WOULD BE BERNI.
WHAT MAKES YOU THINK THAT YOUR FATHER WAS BEING BLACKMAILED?
I OVERHEARD HIM ON THE 'PHONE A FEW MONTHS AGO WHEN I WENT TO SEE BERNI AT WORK. HE WAS SHOUTING AT SOMEBODY, SOMETHING ABOUT NOT PAYING UP. I DON'T KNOW WHO HE WAS TALKING TO, I DON'T PRETEND TO KNOW MUCH ABOUT HIS BUSINESS. DO YOU KNOW MAUGHTON PUBLISHING? ON WINTNEY ROW?
I THINK I'VE HEARD-
'SQUIFFY THE RABBIT', AMONG OTHER CHILDREN'S BOOKS. WELL HE OWNS THAT.
WOULD YOU MIND IF I SPOKE TO HIM?
HE'S OUT OF TOWN. YOU CAN TALK TO MOTHER, THOUGH...
SHE'S IN THE SAME LINE OF WORK AS ME, ONLY SHE'S BEEN DOING IT FOR LONGER. YOU'LL HAVE TO SEE HER IN PERSON - SHE DETESTS SPEAKING ON THE TELEPHONE. SHE SAYS SHE FINDS IT VULGAR.

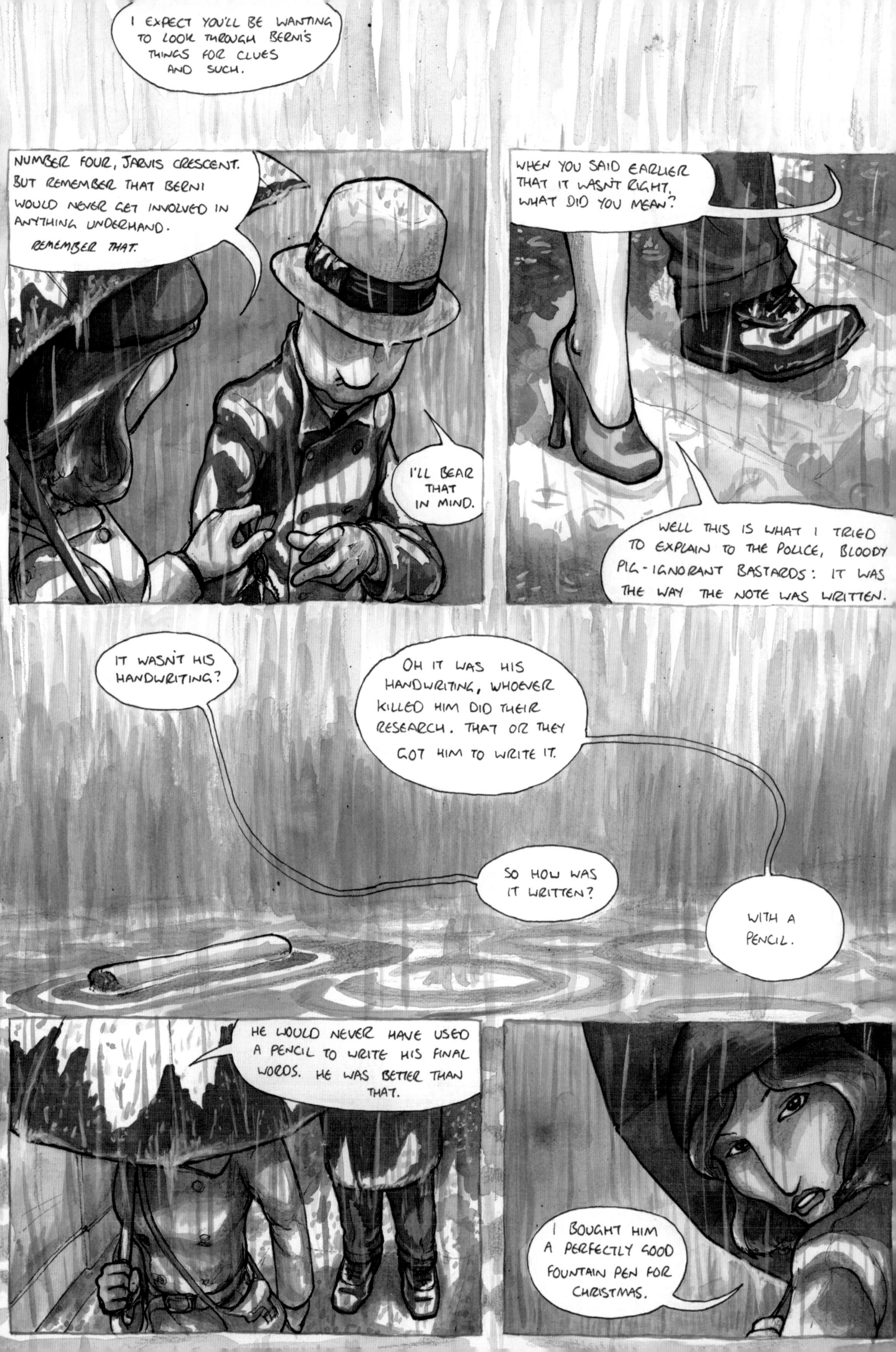
I EXPECT YOU'LL BE WANTING TO LOOK THROUGH BERNI'S THINGS FOR CLUES AND SUCH.
NUMBER FOUR, JARVIS CRESCENT. BUT REMEMBER THAT BERNI WOULD NEVER GET INVOLVED IN ANYTHING UNDERHAND. REMEMBER THAT.
I'LL BEAR THAT IN MIND.
WHEN YOU SAID EARLIER THAT IT WASN'T RIGHT, WHAT DID YOU MEAN?
WELL THIS IS WHAT I TRIED TO EXPLAIN TO THE POLICE, BLOODY PIG-IGNORANT BASTARDS: IT WAS THE WAY THE NOTE WAS WRITTEN.
IT WASN'T HIS HANDWRITING?
OH IT WAS HIS HANDWRITING, WHOEVER KILLED HIM DID THEIR RESEARCH. THAT OR THEY GOT HIM TO WRITE IT.
SO HOW WAS IT WRITTEN?
WITH A PENCIL.
HE WOULD NEVER HAVE USED A PENCIL TO WRITE HIS FINAL WORDS. HE WAS BETTER THAN THAT.
I BOUGHT HIM A PERFECTLY GOOD FOUNTAIN PEN FOR CHRISTMAS.

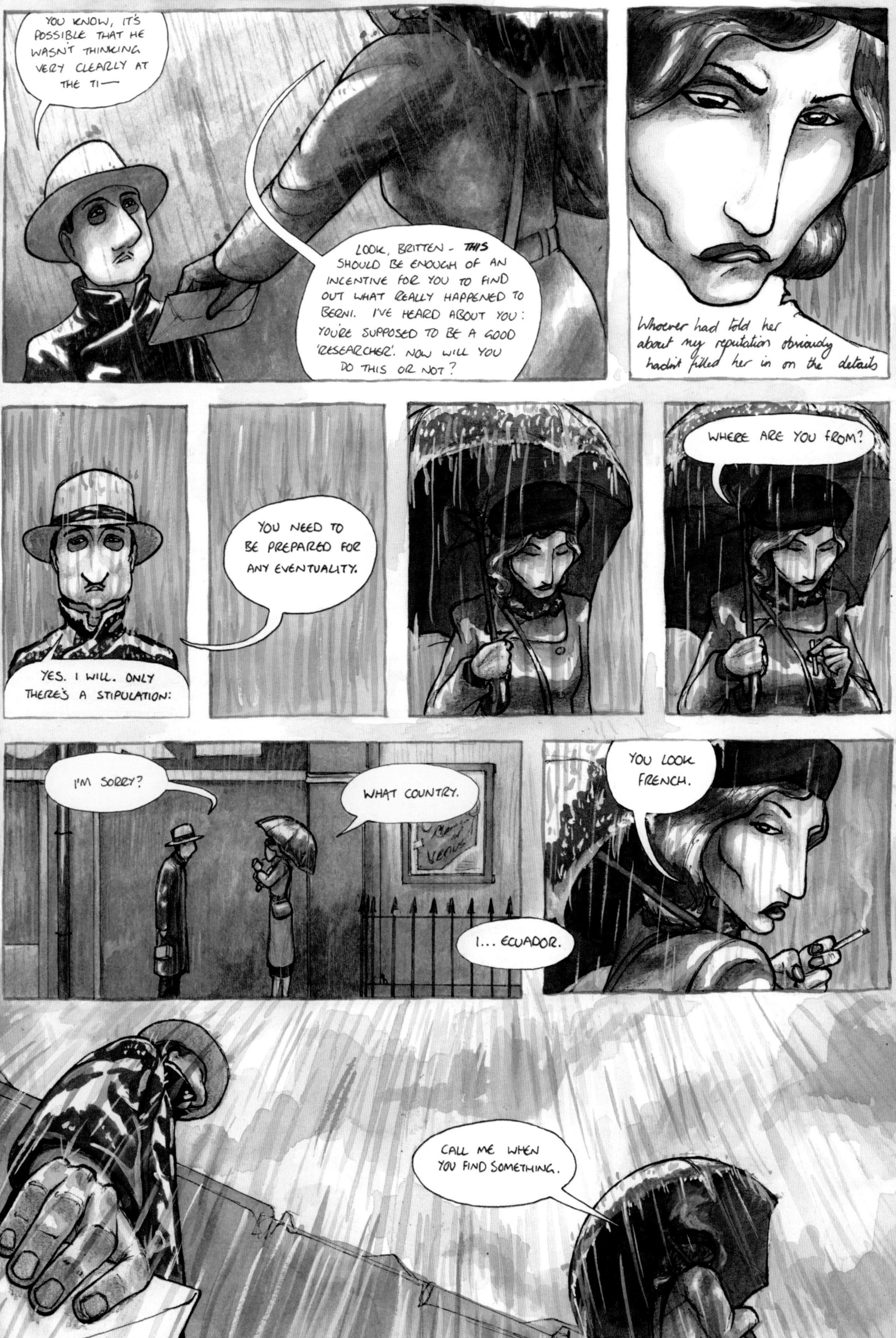
YOU KNOW, IT'S POSSIBLE THAT HE WASN'T THINKING VERY CLEARLY AT THE TI—
LOOK, BRITTEN - THIS SHOULD BE ENOUGH OF AN INCENTIVE FOR YOU TO FIND OUT WHAT REALLY HAPPENED TO BERNI. I'VE HEARD ABOUT YOU: YOU'RE SUPPOSED TO BE A GOOD 'RESEARCHER'. NOW WILL YOU DO THIS OR NOT?
Whoever had told her about my reputation obviously hadn't filled her in on the details
YES. I WILL. ONLY THERE'S A STIPULATION:
YOU NEED TO BE PREPARED FOR ANY EVENTUALITY.
WHERE ARE YOU FROM?
I'M SORRY?
WHAT COUNTRY.
YOU LOOK FRENCH.
I... ECUADOR.
CALL ME WHEN YOU FIND SOMETHING.

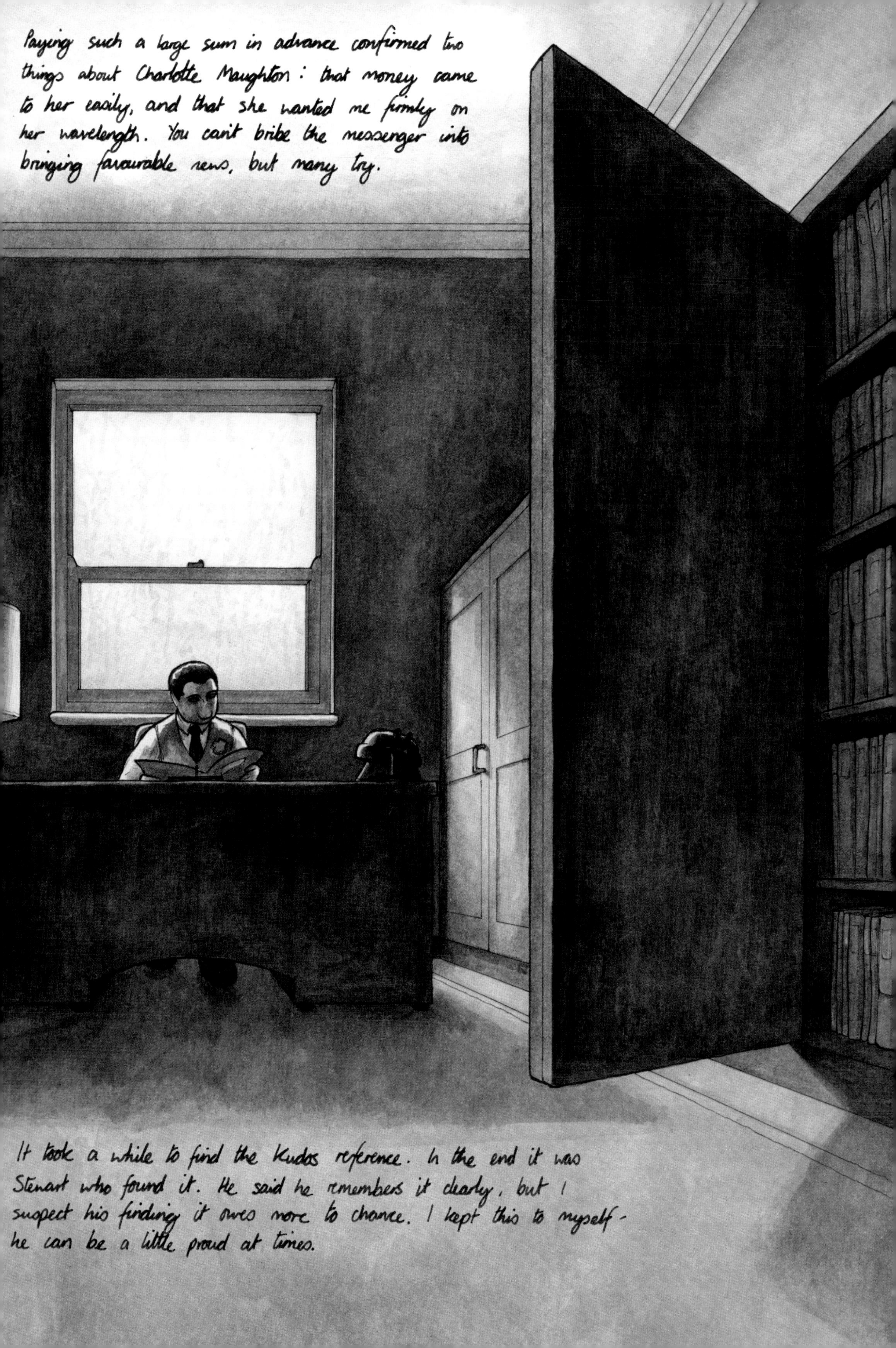
Paying such a large sum in advance confirmed two things about Charlotte Maughton: that money came to her easily, and that she wanted me firmly on her wavelength. You can't bribe the messenger into bringing favourable news, but many try.
It took a while to find the Kudos reference. In the end it was Stewart who found it. He said he remembers it clearly, but I suspect his finding it owes more to chance. I kept this to myself - he can be a little proud at times.

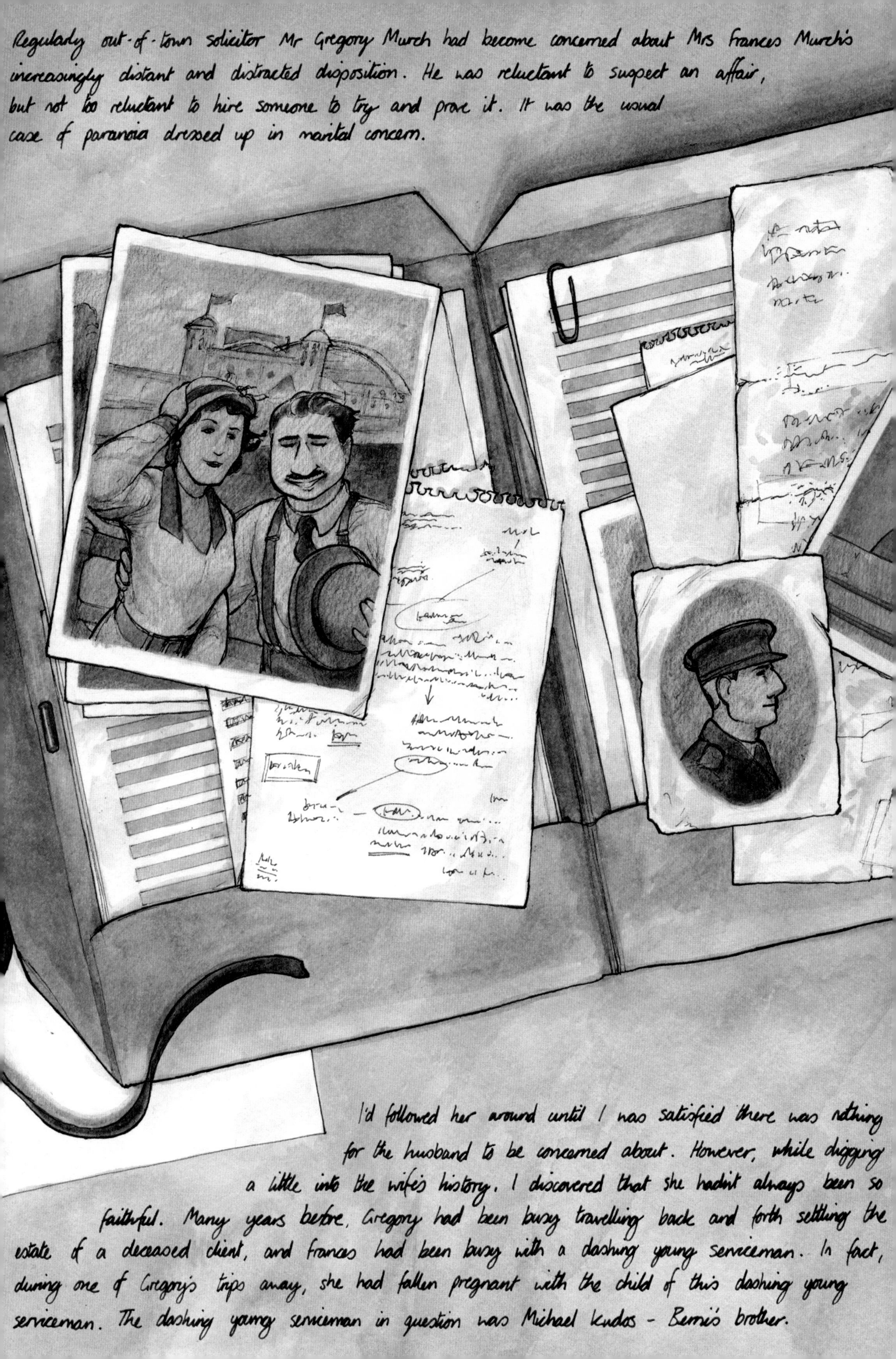
Regularly out-of-town solicitor Mr Gregory Murch had become concerned about Mrs Frances Murch's increasingly distant and distracted disposition. He was reluctant to suspect an affair, but not too reluctant to hire someone to try and prove it. It was the usual case of paranoia dressed up in marital concern.
I'd followed her around until I was satisfied there was nothing for the husband to be concerned about. However, while digging a little into the wife's history, I discovered that she hadn't always been so faithful. Many years before, Gregory had been busy travelling back and forth settling the estate of a deceased client, and Frances had been busy with a dashing young serviceman. In fact, during one of Gregory's trips away, she had fallen pregnant with the child of this dashing young serviceman. The dashing young serviceman in question was Michael Kudos - Bernie's brother.

The relationship ended between Frances and Michael, the last time she tried to contact him was apparently to tell him that he had a daughter, born premature but healthy. She wasn't premature enough, however, to meet her father, whom the army had listed as AWOL some four months earlier. Michael Kudos may never have known that he had a daughter.

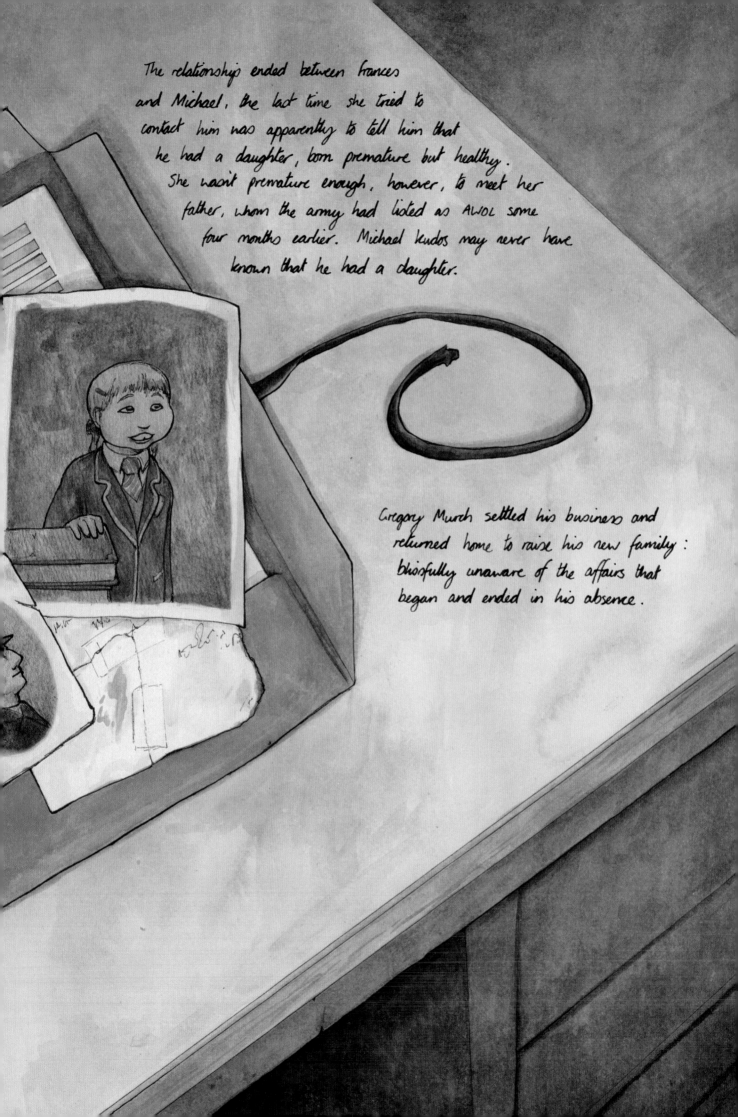

Gregory Murch settled his business and returned home to raise his new family: blissfully unaware of the affairs that began and ended in his absence.

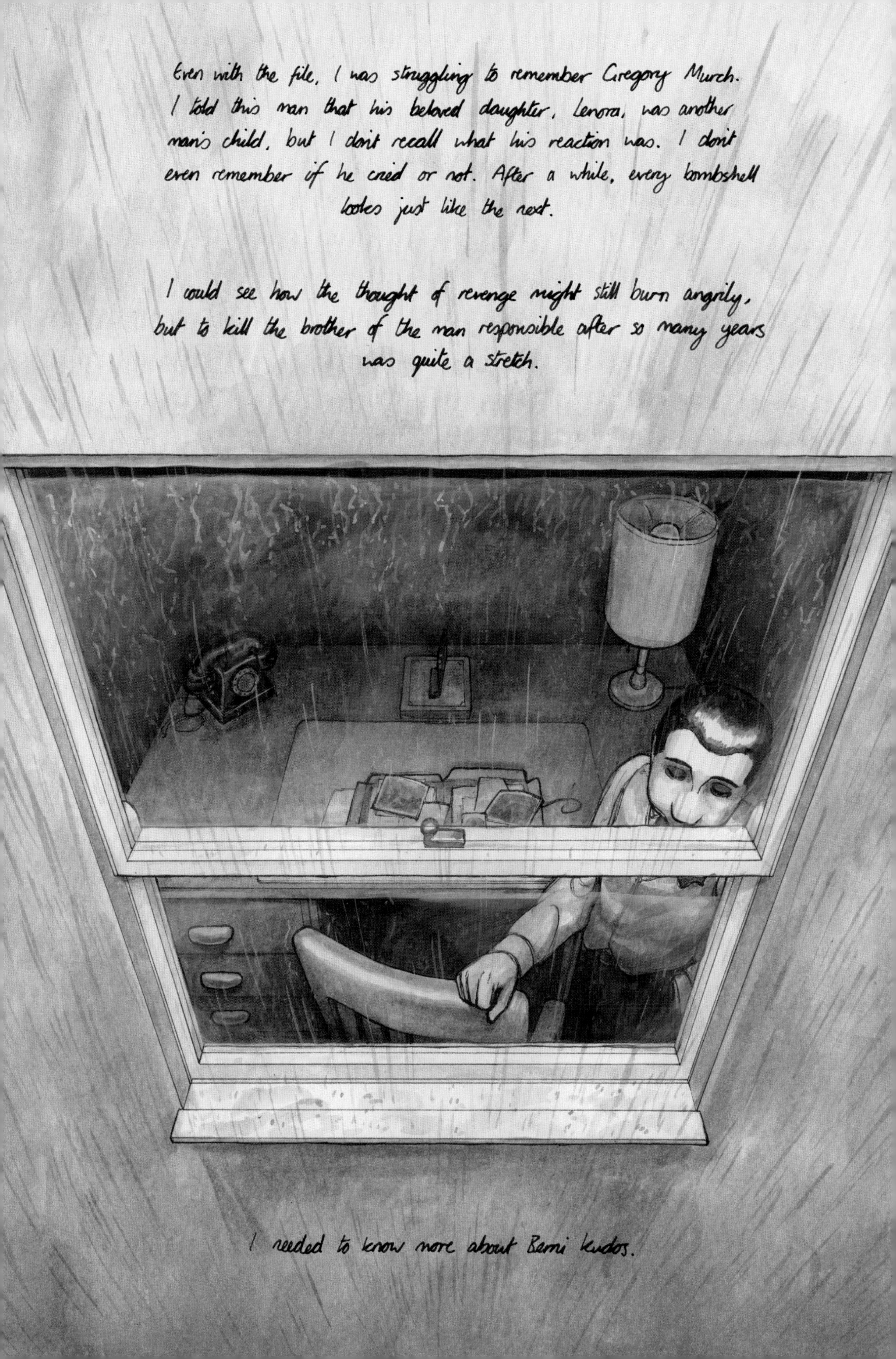
Even with the file, I was struggling to remember Gregory Murch. I told this man that his beloved daughter, Lenora, was another man's child, but I don't recall what his reaction was. I don't even remember if he cried or not. After a while, every bombshell looks just like the next.
I could see how the thought of revenge might still burn angrily, but to kill the brother of the man responsible after so many years was quite a stretch.
I needed to know more about Berni Kudos.

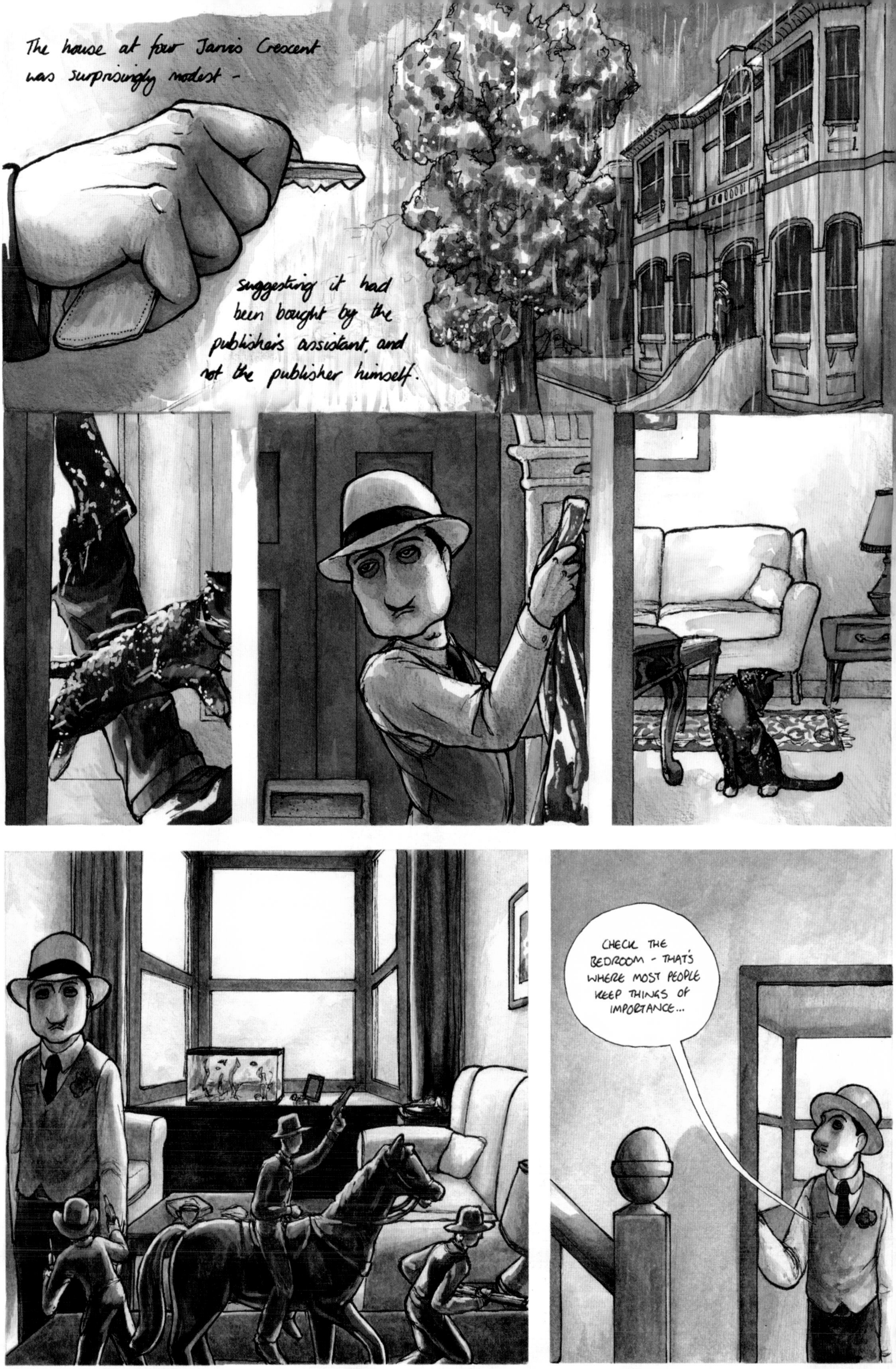
The house at four Jarvis Crescent was surprisingly modest -
suggesting it had been bought by the publisher's assistant, and not the publisher himself.
CHECK THE BEDROOM - THAT'S WHERE MOST PEOPLE KEEP THINGS OF IMPORTANCE...

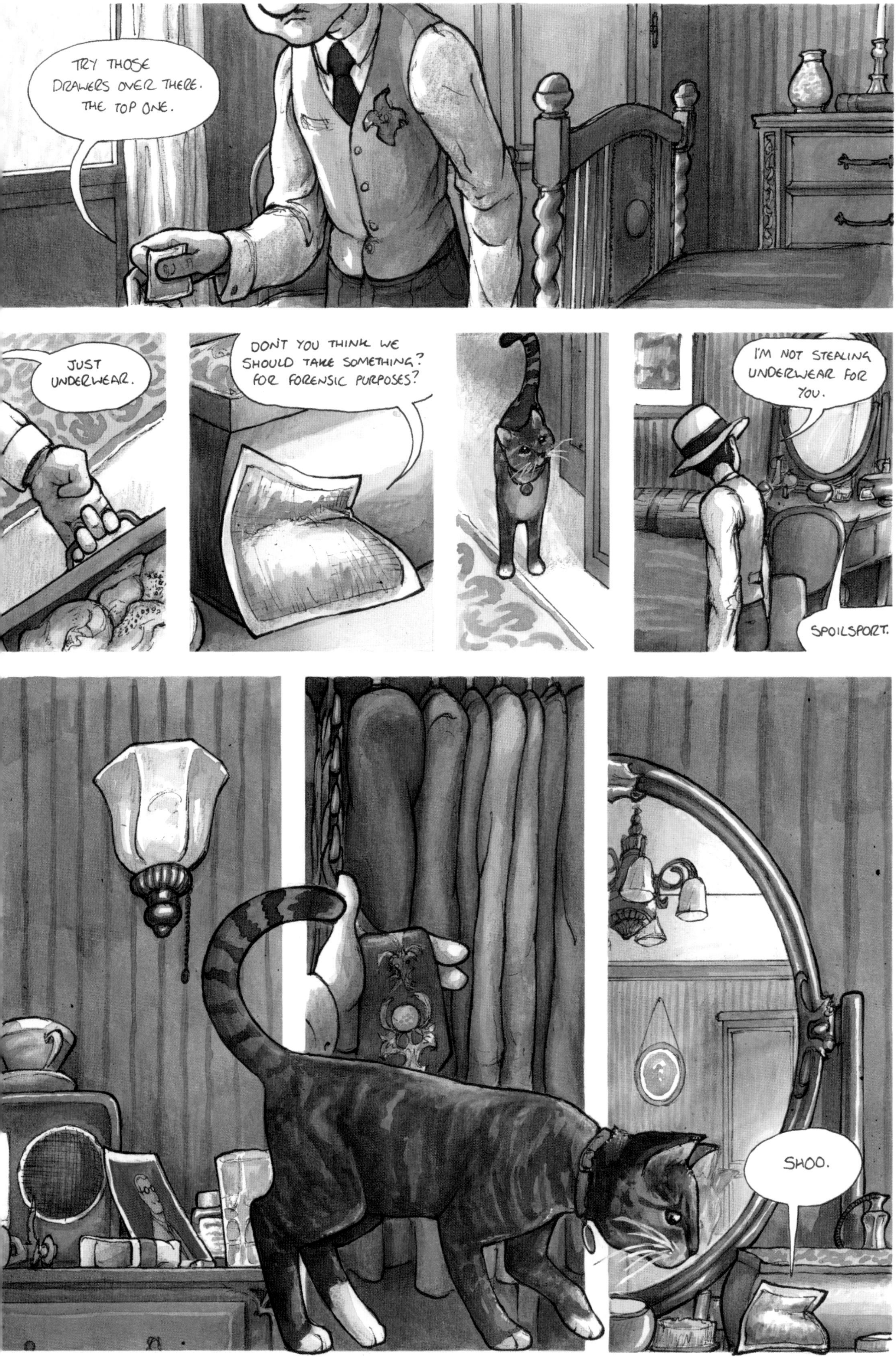
TRY THOSE DRAWERS OVER THERE. THE TOP ONE.
JUST UNDERWEAR.
DON'T YOU THINK WE SHOULD TAKE SOMETHING? FOR FORENSIC PURPOSES?
I'M NOT STEALING UNDERWEAR FOR YOU.
SPOILSPORT.
SHOO.

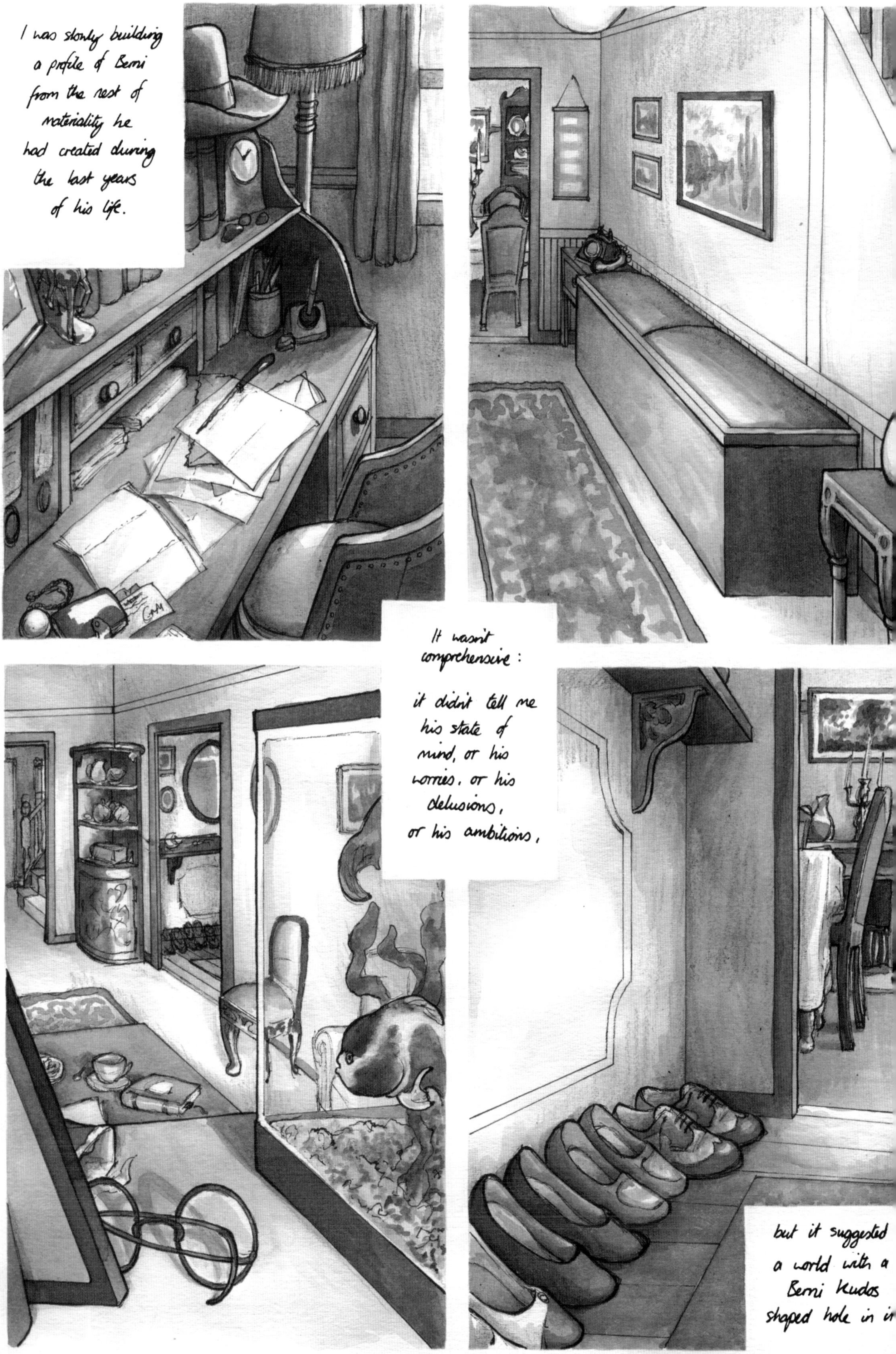
I was slowly building a profile of Berni from the rest of materiality he had created during the last years of his life.
It wasn't comprehensive:
it didn't tell me his state of mind, or his worries, or his delusions, or his ambitions,
but it suggested a world with a Berni Kudos shaped hole in i

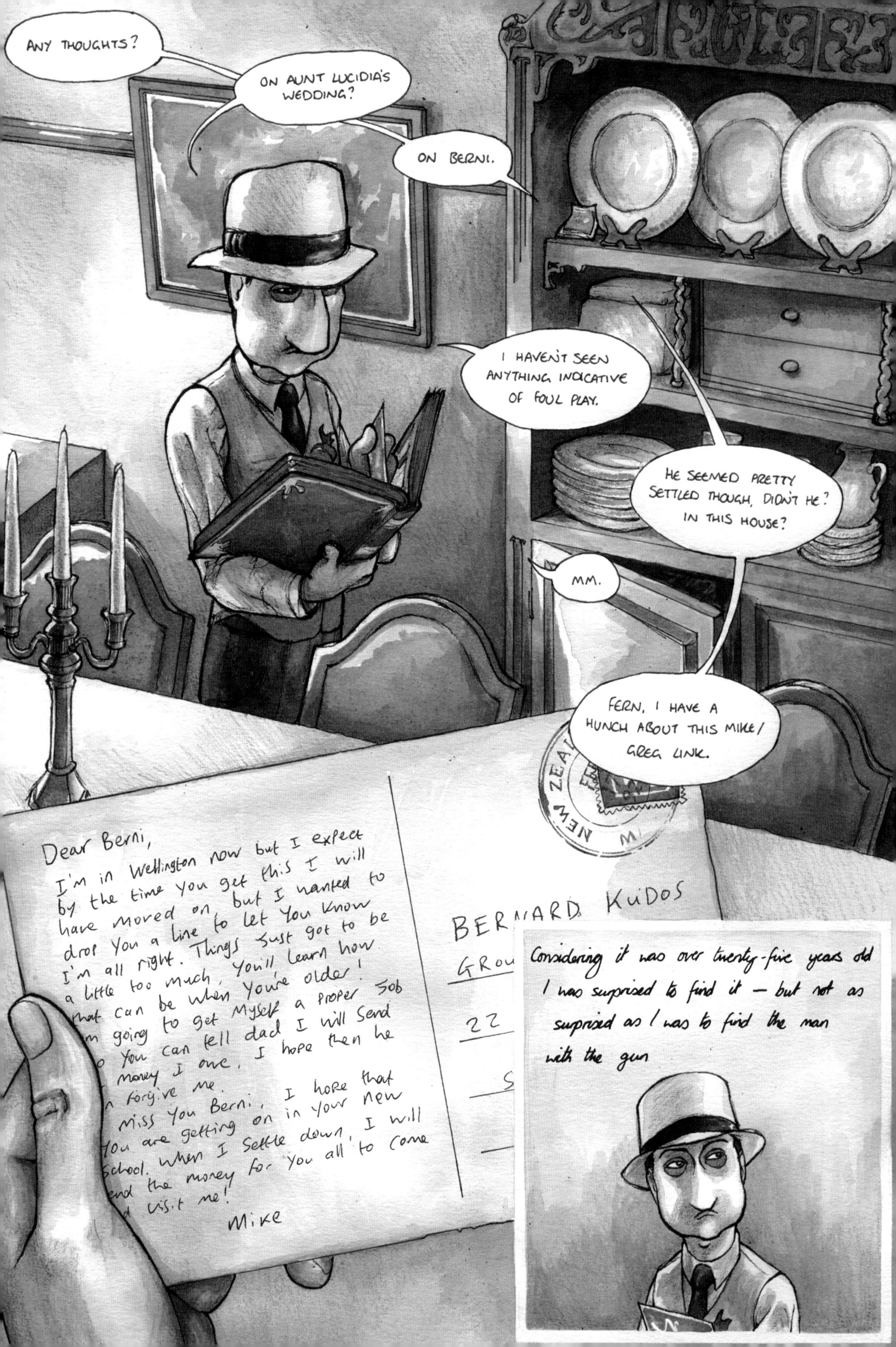
ANY THOUGHTS?
ON AUNT LUCIDIA'S WEDDING?
ON BERNI.
I HAVEN'T SEEN ANYTHING INDICATIVE OF FOUL PLAY.
HE SEEMED PRETTY SETTLED THOUGH, DIDN'T HE? IN THIS HOUSE?
MM.
FERN, I HAVE A HUNCH ABOUT THIS MIKE/GREG LINK.
Dear Berni,
I'm in Wellington now but I expect
by the time you get this I will
have moved on, but I wanted to
drop you a line to let you know
I'm all right. Things just got to be
a little too much, you'll learn how
hat can be when you're older!
m going to get myself a proper job
o you can tell dad I will send
money I owe. I hope then he
n forgive me.
miss you Berni. I hope that
you are getting on in your new
school. When I settle down, I will
end the money for you all to come
d visit me!
Mike
BERNARD KUDOS
GROU
22
S
Considering it was over twenty-five years old I was suprised to find it — but not as suprised as I was to find the man with the gun

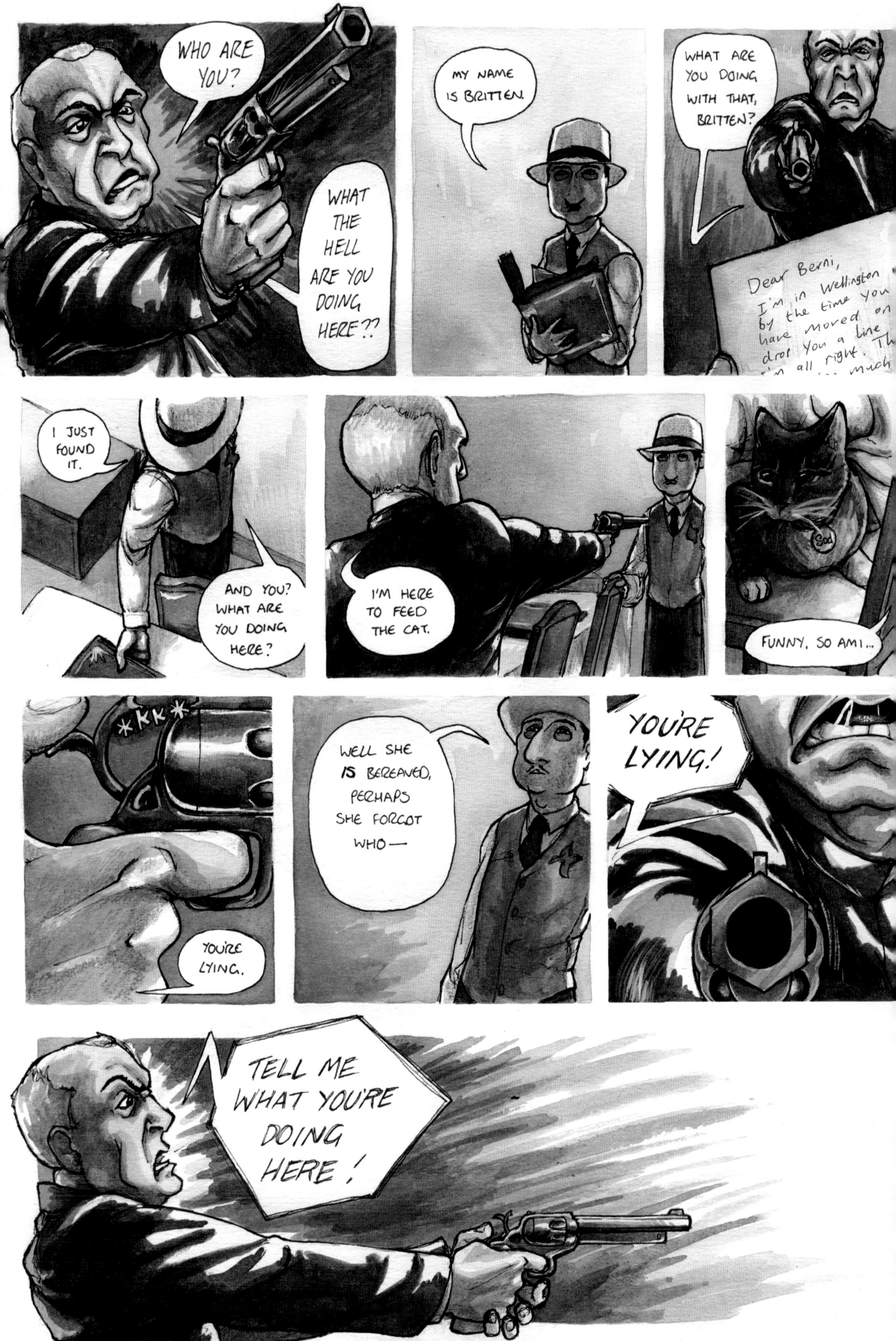
WHO ARE YOU?
WHAT THE HELL ARE YOU DOING HERE??
MY NAME IS BRITTEN.
WHAT ARE YOU DOING WITH THAT, BRITTEN?
Dear Berni,
I'm in Wellington
by the time you
have moved on
drop you a line
all right.
I JUST FOUND IT.
AND YOU? WHAT ARE YOU DOING HERE?
I'M HERE TO FEED THE CAT.
Sod
FUNNY, SO AM I...
KK
YOU'RE LYING.
WELL SHE IS BEREAVED, PERHAPS SHE FORGOT WHO—
YOU'RE LYING!
TELL ME WHAT YOU'RE DOING HERE!

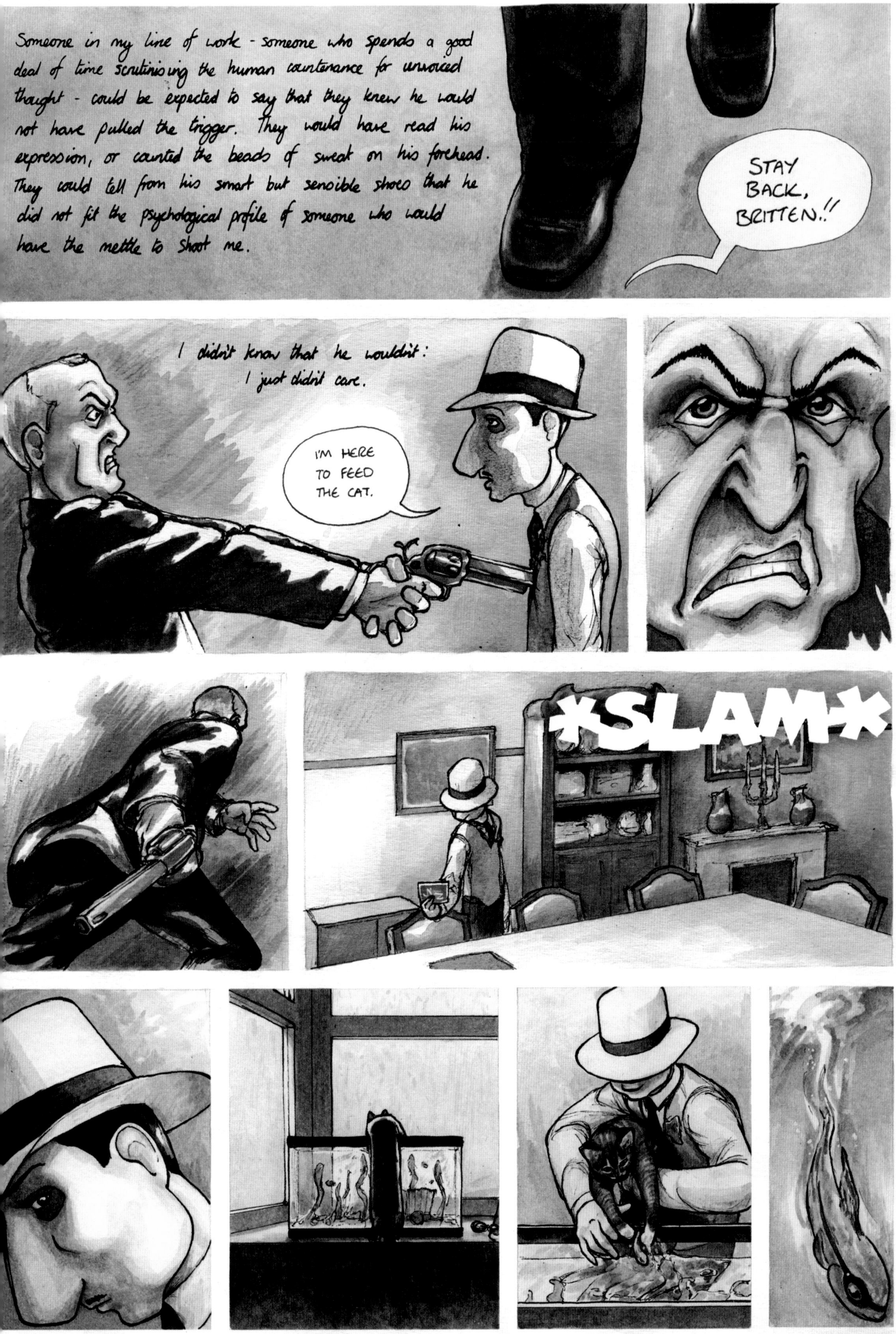
Someone in my line of work - someone who spends a good deal of time scrutinising the human countenance for unvoiced thought - could be expected to say that they knew he would not have pulled the trigger. They would have read his expression, or counted the beads of sweat on his forehead. They could tell from his smart but sensible shoes that he did not fit the psychological profile of someone who would have the mettle to shoot me.
STAY BACK, BRITTEN!!
I didn't know that he wouldn't: I just didn't care.
I'M HERE TO FEED THE CAT.
SLAM

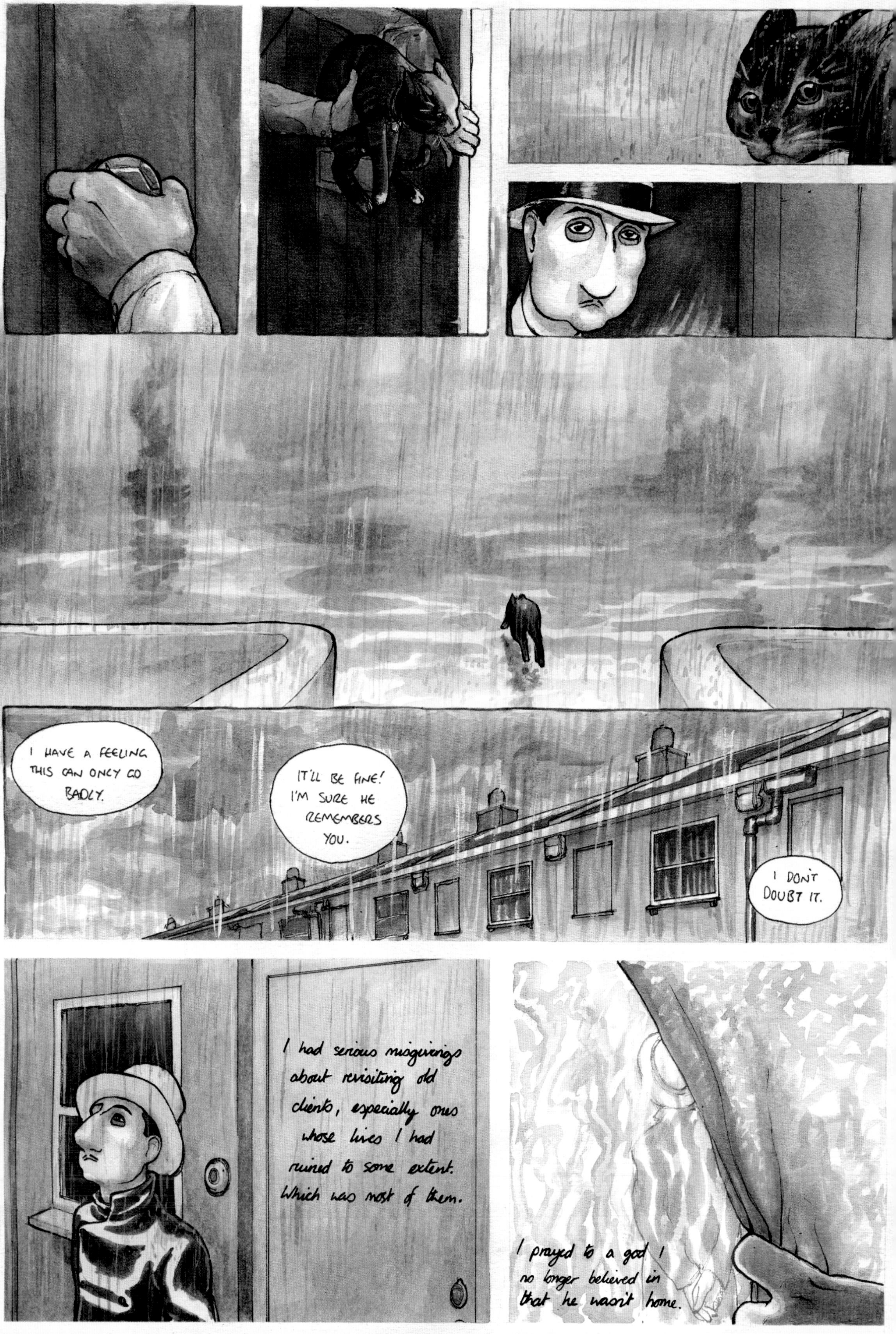
I HAVE A FEELING THIS CAN ONLY GO BADLY.
IT'LL BE FINE! I'M SURE HE REMEMBERS YOU.
I DON'T DOUBT IT.
I had serious misgivings about revisiting old clients, especially ones whose lives I had ruined to some extent. Which was most of them.
I prayed to a god I no longer believed in that he wasn't home.

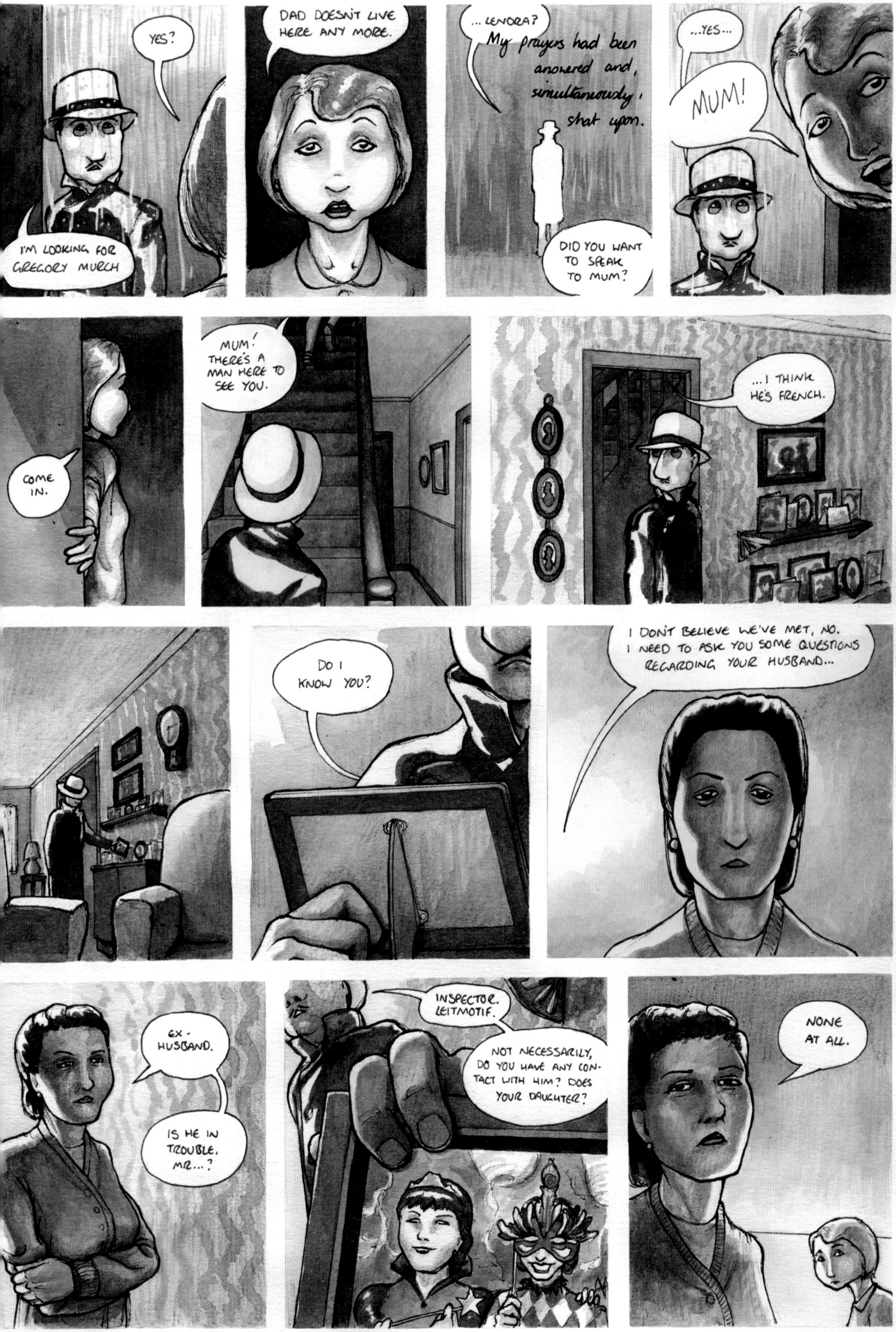
YES?
I'M LOOKING FOR GREGORY MURCH
DAD DOESN'T LIVE HERE ANY MORE.
... LENORA?
My prayers had been answered and, simultaneously, shat upon.
DID YOU WANT TO SPEAK TO MUM?
...YES...
MUM!
COME IN.
MUM! THERE'S A MAN HERE TO SEE YOU.
...I THINK HE'S FRENCH.
DO I KNOW YOU?
I DON'T BELIEVE WE'VE MET, NO. I NEED TO ASK YOU SOME QUESTIONS REGARDING YOUR HUSBAND...
EX-HUSBAND.
IS HE IN TROUBLE, MR...?
INSPECTOR. LEITMOTIF.
NOT NECESSARILY, DO YOU HAVE ANY CONTACT WITH HIM? DOES YOUR DAUGHTER?
NONE AT ALL.

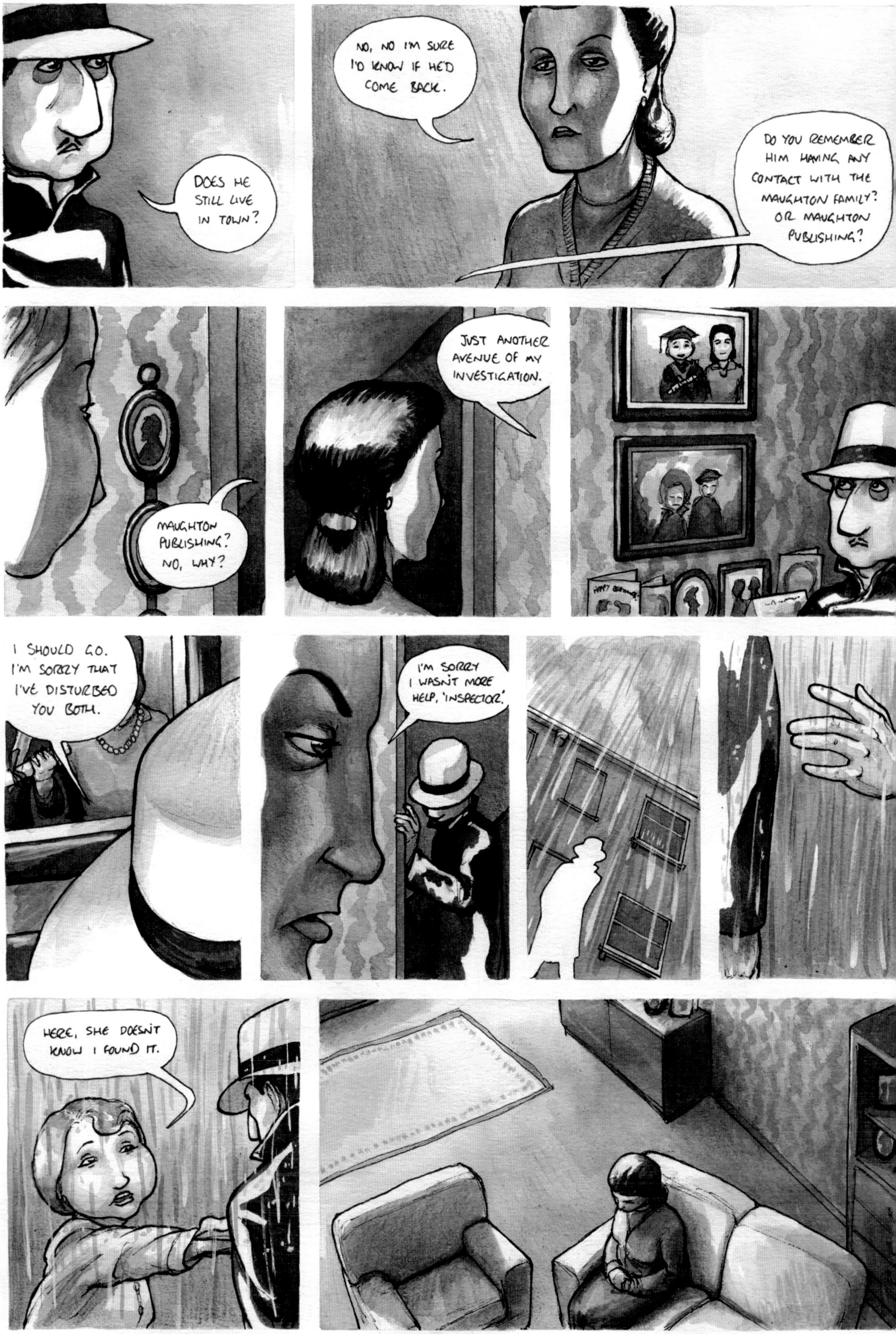
DOES HE STILL LIVE IN TOWN?
NO, NO I'M SURE I'D KNOW IF HE'D COME BACK.
DO YOU REMEMBER HIM HAVING ANY CONTACT WITH THE MAUGHTON FAMILY? OR MAUGHTON PUBLISHING?
MAUGHTON PUBLISHING? NO, WHY?
JUST ANOTHER AVENUE OF MY INVESTIGATION.
I SHOULD GO. I'M SORRY THAT I'VE DISTURBED YOU BOTH.
I'M SORRY I WASN'T MORE HELP, 'INSPECTOR.'
HERE, SHE DOESN'T KNOW I FOUND IT.

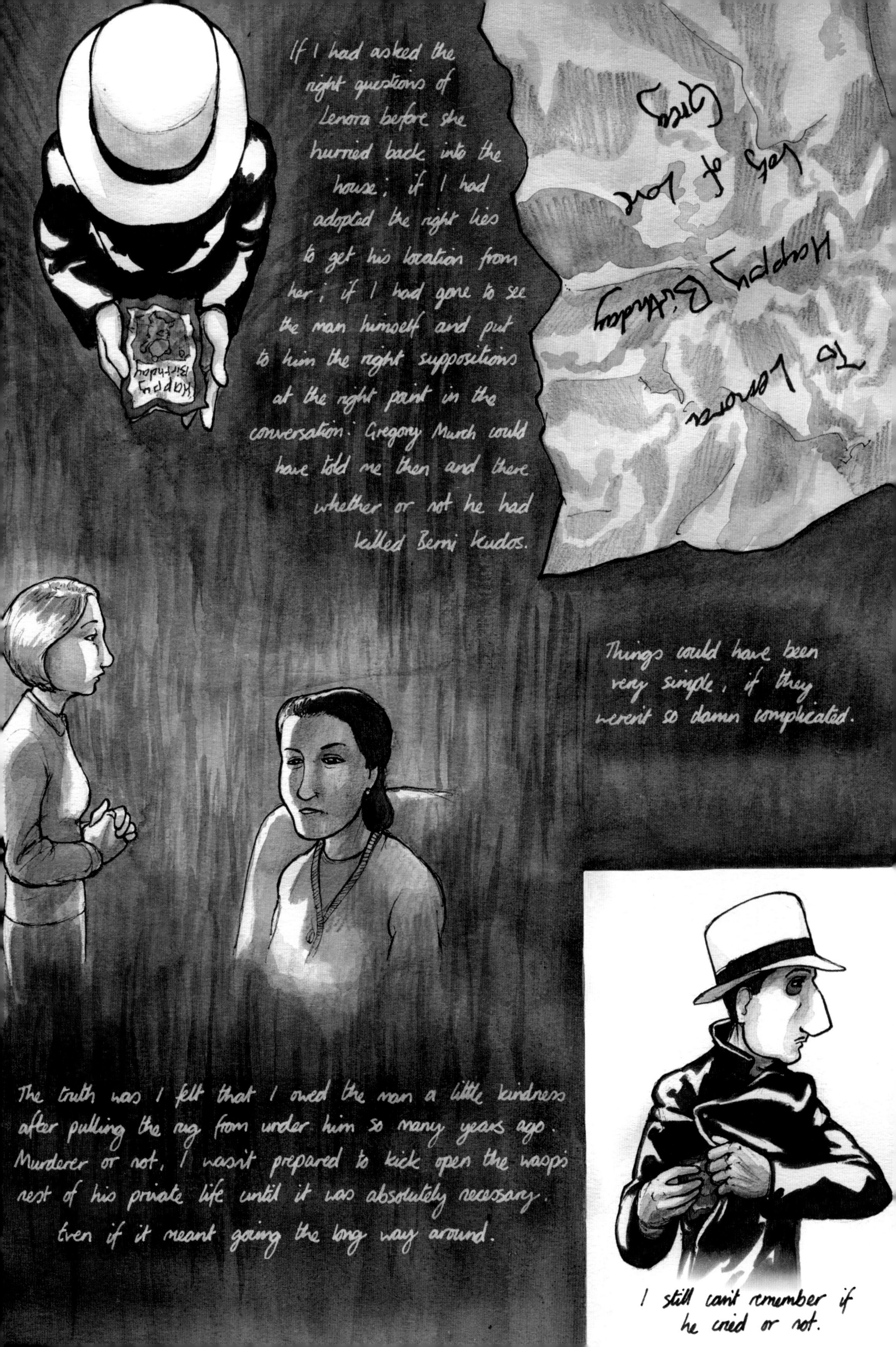
If I had asked the right questions of Lenora before she hurried back into the house; if I had adopted the right lies to get his location from her; if I had gone to see the man himself and put to him the right suppositions at the right point in the conversation: Gregory March could have told me then and there whether or not he had killed Berni Kudos.
To Lenora
Happy Birthday
Lots of Love
Greg
Things could have been very simple, if they weren't so damn complicated.
The truth was I felt that I owed the man a little kindness after pulling the rug from under him so many years ago. Murderer or not, I wasn't prepared to kick open the wasps' nest of his private life until it was absolutely necessary. Even if it meant going the long way around.
I still can't remember if he cried or not.

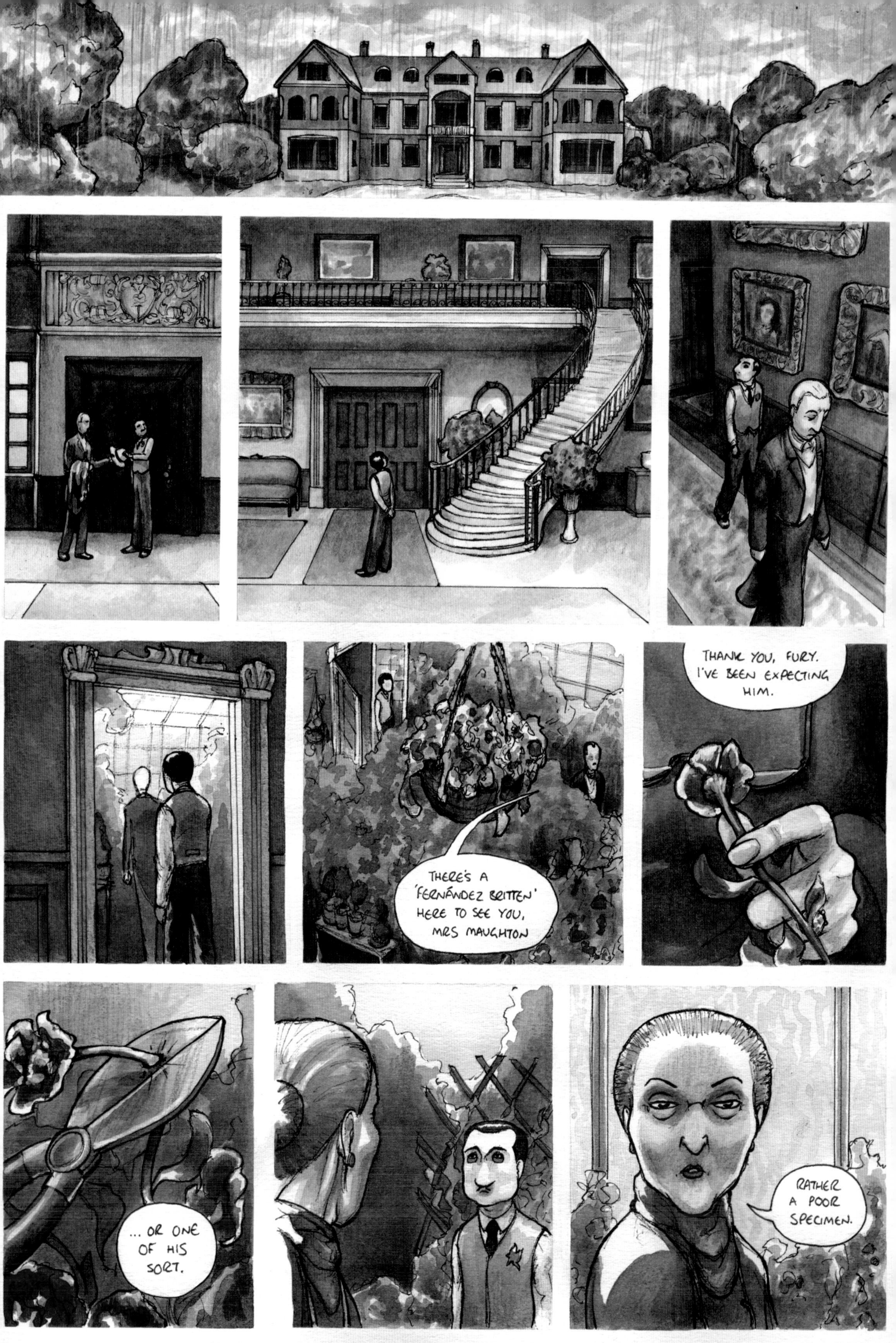
THERE'S A 'FERNÁNDEZ BRITTEN' HERE TO SEE YOU, MRS MAUGHTON
THANK YOU, FURY. I'VE BEEN EXPECTING HIM.
... OR ONE OF HIS SORT.
RATHER A POOR SPECIMEN.

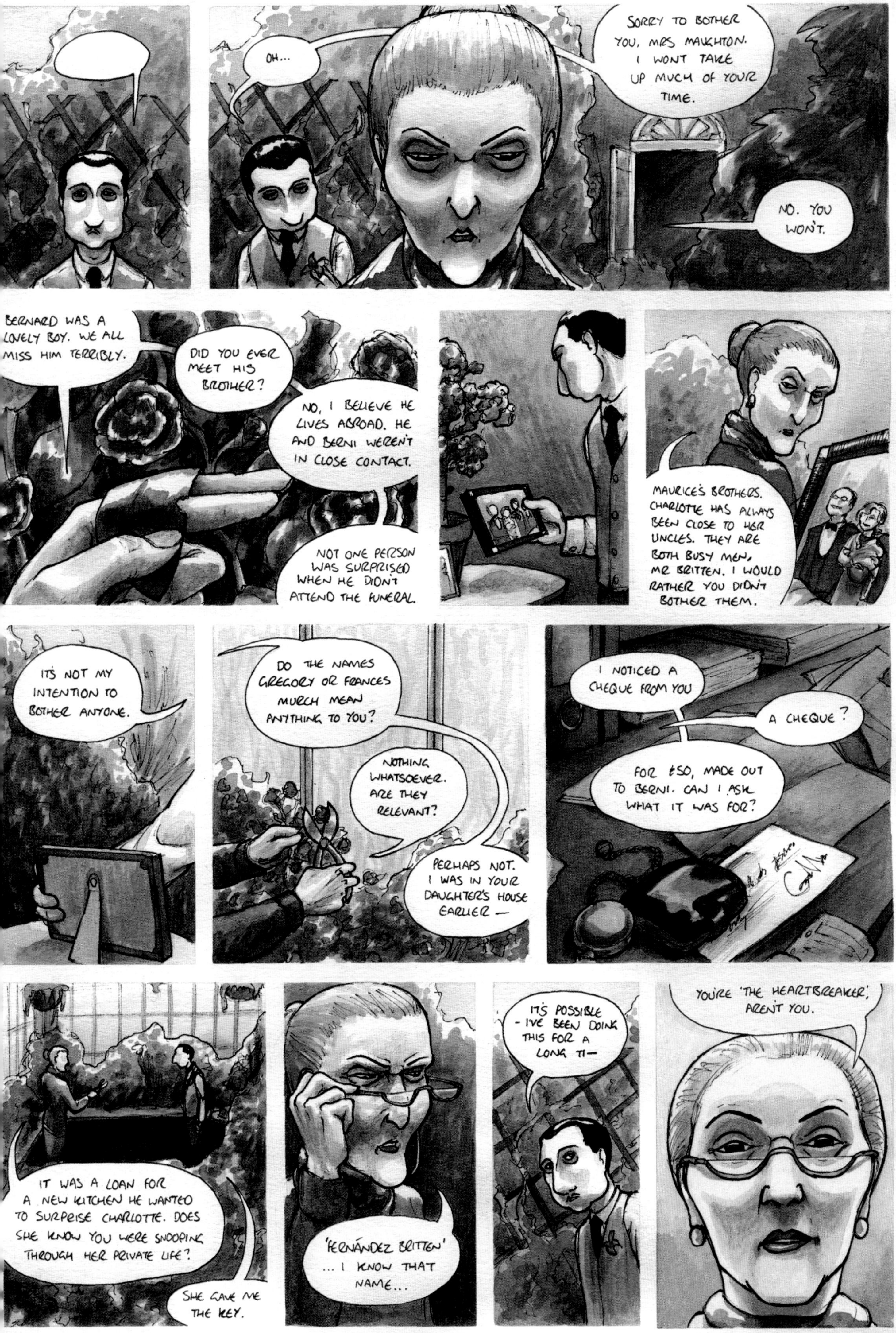
OH...
SORRY TO BOTHER YOU, MRS MAUGHTON. I WONT TAKE UP MUCH OF YOUR TIME.
NO. YOU WON'T.
BERNARD WAS A LOVELY BOY. WE ALL MISS HIM TERRIBLY.
DID YOU EVER MEET HIS BROTHER?
NO, I BELIEVE HE LIVES ABROAD. HE AND BERNI WEREN'T IN CLOSE CONTACT.
NOT ONE PERSON WAS SURPRISED WHEN HE DIDN'T ATTEND THE FUNERAL.
MAURICE'S BROTHERS. CHARLOTTE HAS ALWAYS BEEN CLOSE TO HER UNCLES. THEY ARE BOTH BUSY MEN, MR BRITTEN. I WOULD RATHER YOU DIDN'T BOTHER THEM.
IT'S NOT MY INTENTION TO BOTHER ANYONE.
DO THE NAMES GREGORY OR FRANCES MURCH MEAN ANYTHING TO YOU?
NOTHING WHATSOEVER. ARE THEY RELEVANT?
PERHAPS NOT. I WAS IN YOUR DAUGHTER'S HOUSE EARLIER —
I NOTICED A CHEQUE FROM YOU
A CHEQUE?
FOR £50, MADE OUT TO BERNI. CAN I ASK WHAT IT WAS FOR?
IT WAS A LOAN FOR A NEW KITCHEN HE WANTED TO SURPRISE CHARLOTTE. DOES SHE KNOW YOU WERE SNOOPING THROUGH HER PRIVATE LIFE?
SHE GAVE ME THE KEY.
'FERNÁNDEZ BRITTEN' ... I KNOW THAT NAME...
IT'S POSSIBLE - I'VE BEEN DOING THIS FOR A LONG TI—
YOU'RE 'THE HEARTBREAKER', AREN'T YOU.

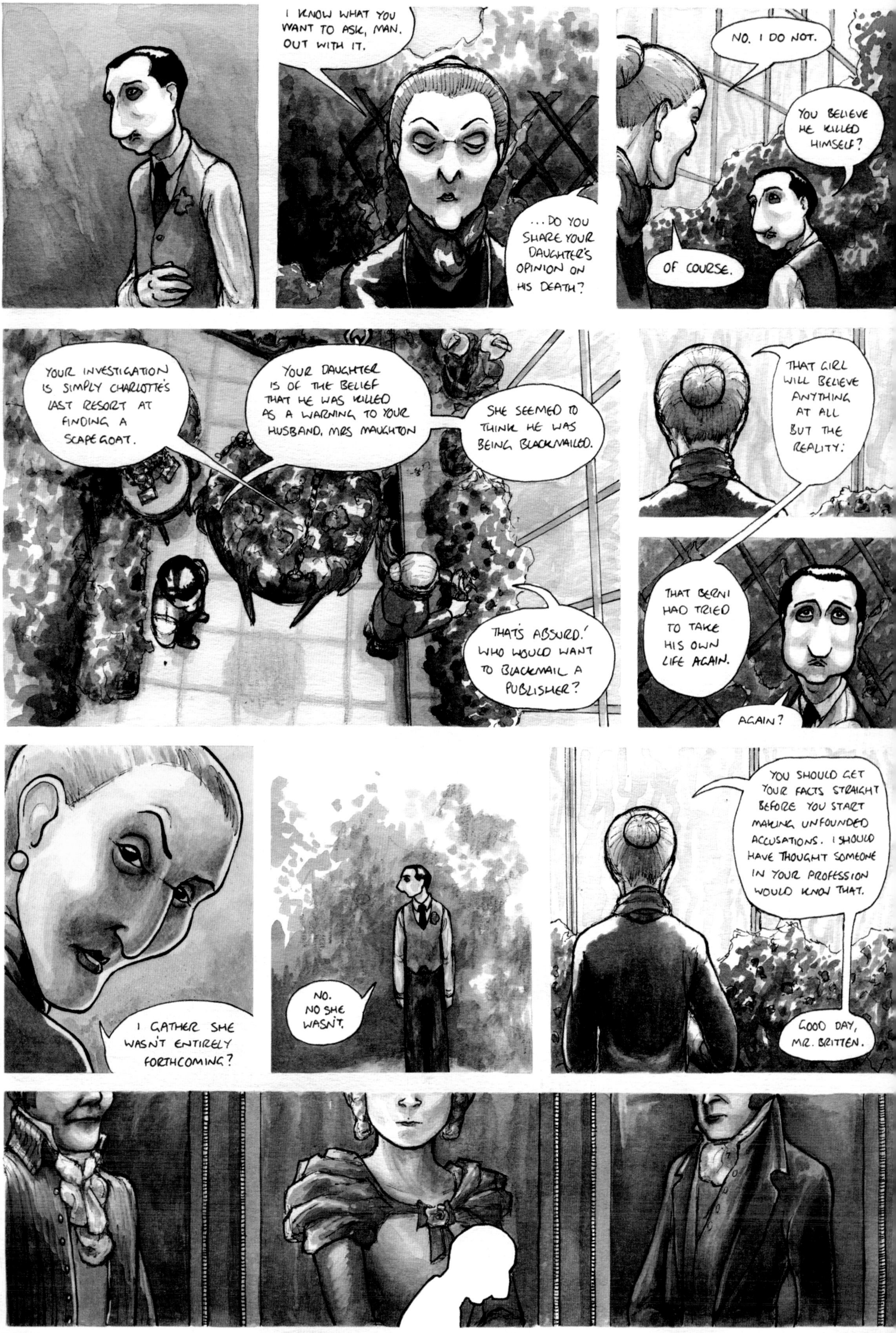
I KNOW WHAT YOU WANT TO ASK, MAN. OUT WITH IT.
...DO YOU SHARE YOUR DAUGHTER'S OPINION ON HIS DEATH?
NO. I DO NOT.
YOU BELIEVE HE KILLED HIMSELF?
OF COURSE.
YOUR INVESTIGATION IS SIMPLY CHARLOTTE'S LAST RESORT AT FINDING A SCAPEGOAT.
YOUR DAUGHTER IS OF THE BELIEF THAT HE WAS KILLED AS A WARNING TO YOUR HUSBAND, MRS MAUGHTON
SHE SEEMED TO THINK HE WAS BEING BLACKMAILED.
THAT'S ABSURD! WHO WOULD WANT TO BLACKMAIL A PUBLISHER?
THAT GIRL WILL BELIEVE ANYTHING AT ALL BUT THE REALITY:
THAT BERNI HAD TRIED TO TAKE HIS OWN LIFE AGAIN.
AGAIN?
I GATHER SHE WASN'T ENTIRELY FORTHCOMING?
NO. NO SHE WASN'T.
YOU SHOULD GET YOUR FACTS STRAIGHT BEFORE YOU START MAKING UNFOUNDED ACCUSATIONS. I SHOULD HAVE THOUGHT SOMEONE IN YOUR PROFESSION WOULD KNOW THAT.
GOOD DAY, MR. BRITTEN.

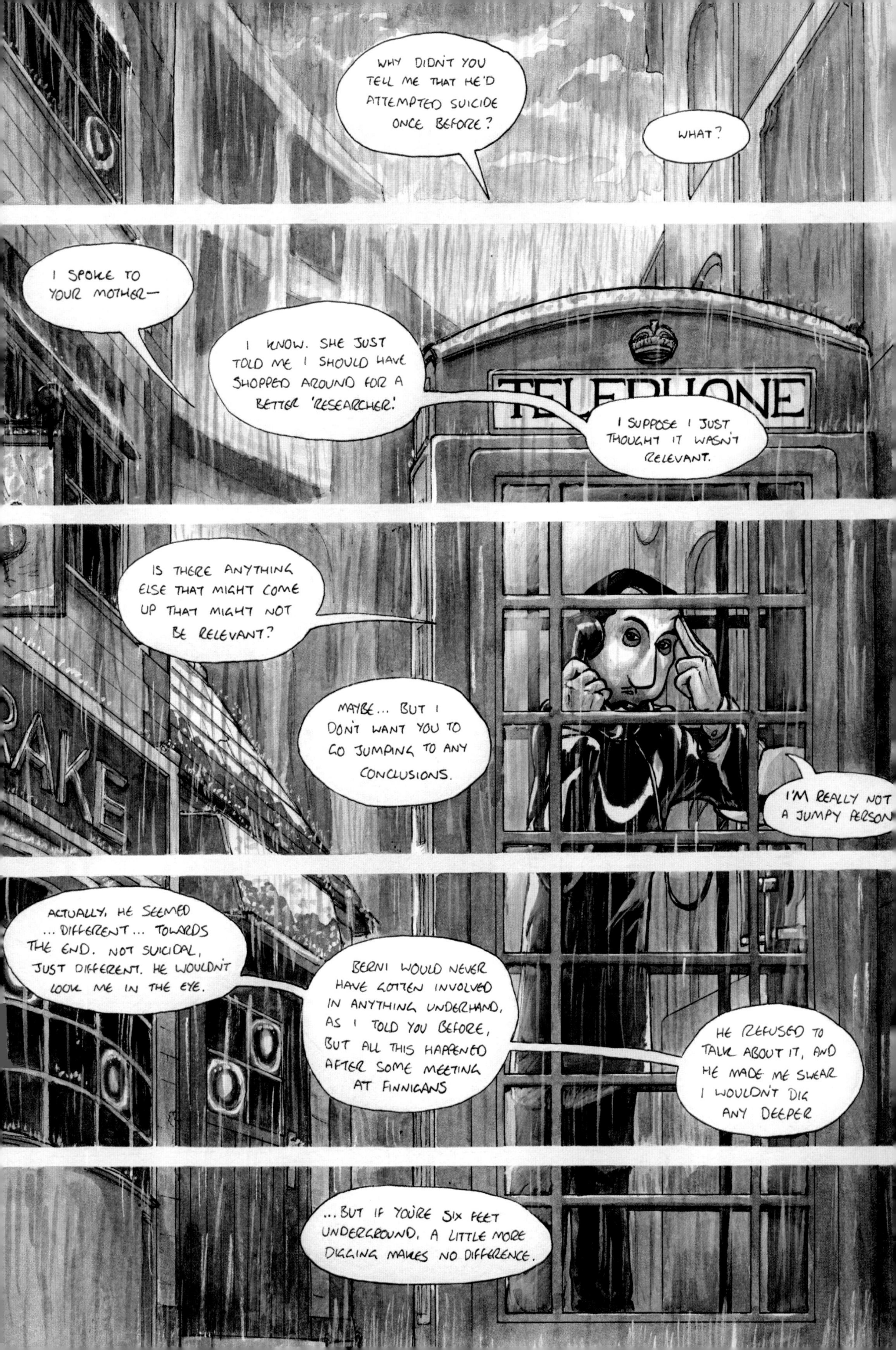
WHY DIDN'T YOU TELL ME THAT HE'D ATTEMPTED SUICIDE ONCE BEFORE?
WHAT?
I SPOKE TO YOUR MOTHER—
I KNOW. SHE JUST TOLD ME I SHOULD HAVE SHOPPED AROUND FOR A BETTER 'RESEARCHER.'
TELEPHONE
I SUPPOSE I JUST THOUGHT IT WASN'T RELEVANT.
IS THERE ANYTHING ELSE THAT MIGHT COME UP THAT MIGHT NOT BE RELEVANT?
MAYBE... BUT I DON'T WANT YOU TO GO JUMPING TO ANY CONCLUSIONS.
I'M REALLY NOT A JUMPY PERSON
AKE
ACTUALLY, HE SEEMED ...DIFFERENT... TOWARDS THE END. NOT SUICIDAL, JUST DIFFERENT. HE WOULDN'T LOOK ME IN THE EYE.
BERNI WOULD NEVER HAVE GOTTEN INVOLVED IN ANYTHING UNDERHAND, AS I TOLD YOU BEFORE, BUT ALL THIS HAPPENED AFTER SOME MEETING AT FINNIGANS
HE REFUSED TO TALK ABOUT IT, AND HE MADE ME SWEAR I WOULDN'T DIG ANY DEEPER
...BUT IF YOU'RE SIX FEET UNDERGROUND, A LITTLE MORE DIGGING MAKES NO DIFFERENCE.

IF YOU NEED A LEAD, YOU CAN LOOK INTO THAT.

CLICK

WE SHOULD HAVE A LOOK AT THIS BLACKMAIL ALLEGATION, DON'T YOU THINK?

FERN? DON'T YOU THINK?

I was prepared to forget the whole investigation and stay in that telephone-box, but for two loose ends. One was the blackmail.

The other belonged to whoever had urinated behind the door.

IS THERE SOMEONE WHO DEALS WITH MR. MAUGHTON'S AFFAIRS IN HIS ABSENCE?

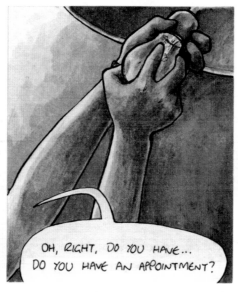

OH, RIGHT, DO YOU HAVE... DO YOU HAVE AN APPOINTMENT?

NO, BUT I'M ... A FRIEND OF MR. MAUGHTON'S.

DO YOU WANT ME TO TAKE A MESSAGE?

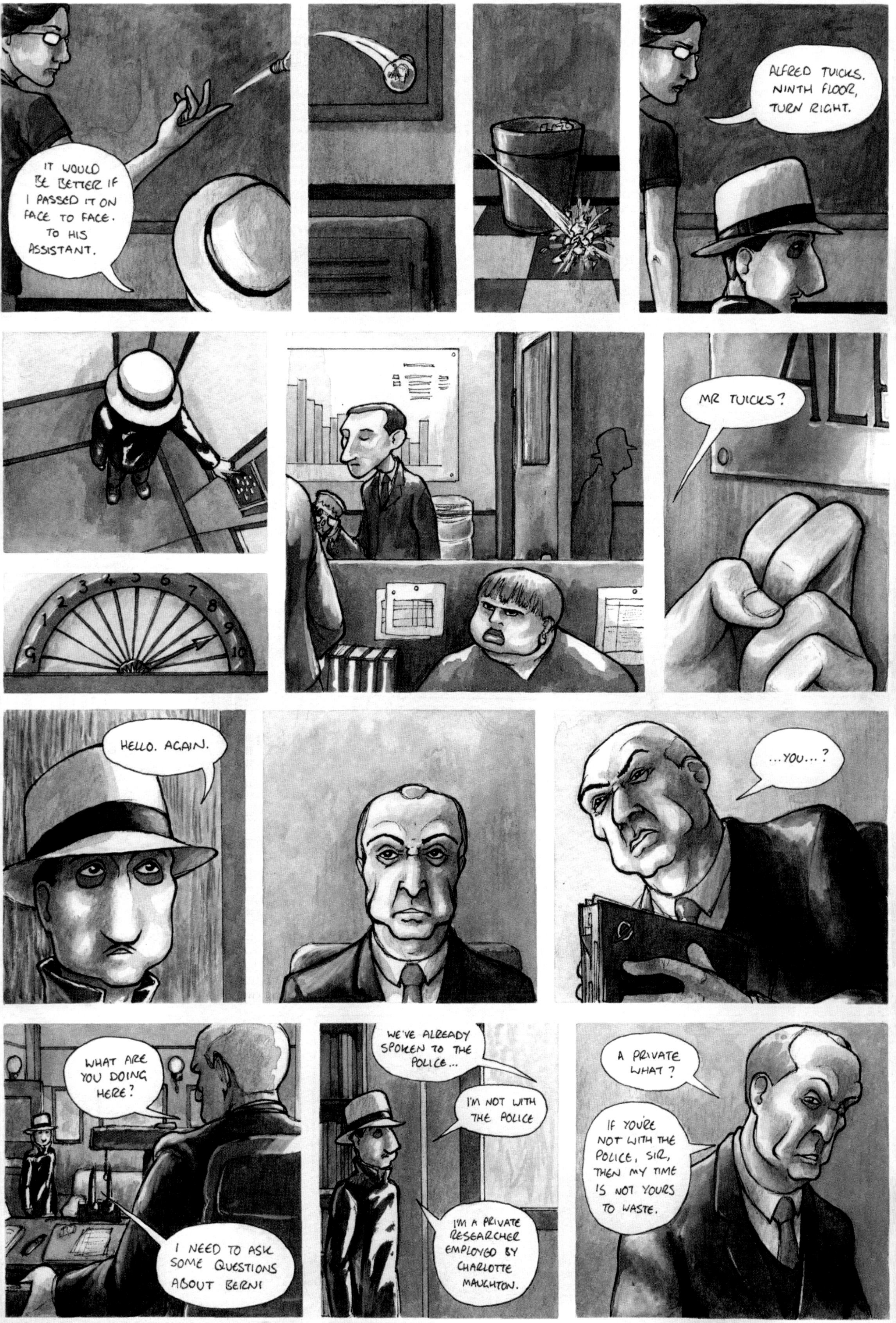
IT WOULD BE BETTER IF I PASSED IT ON FACE TO FACE. TO HIS ASSISTANT.
ALFRED TUICKS. NINTH FLOOR, TURN RIGHT.
G 1 2 3 4 5 6 7 8 9 10
MR TUICKS?
HELLO. AGAIN.
...YOU...?
WHAT ARE YOU DOING HERE?
I NEED TO ASK SOME QUESTIONS ABOUT BERNI
WE'VE ALREADY SPOKEN TO THE POLICE...
I'M NOT WITH THE POLICE
I'M A PRIVATE RESEARCHER EMPLOYED BY CHARLOTTE MAUGHTON.
A PRIVATE WHAT?
IF YOU'RE NOT WITH THE POLICE, SIR, THEN MY TIME IS NOT YOURS TO WASTE.

I'M SURE MR MAUGHTON WOULD BE PROUD TO KNOW YOU HAVE HIS FAMILY'S BEST INTERESTS AT HEART...

I'VE NO DOUBT. NOW PLEASE—

...BUT DOES HIS DAUGHTER KNOW YOU WERE SNOOPING AROUND HER HOME?

I WAS THERE TO FEED THE CAT—

AS YOU SAID. BUT OF COURSE, CHARLOTTE DOESN'T HAVE A CAT.

WHAT GAME IS THIS? I SAW IT SITTING THERE!

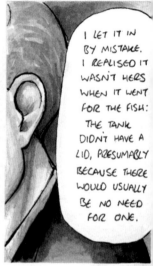

I LET IT IN BY MISTAKE. I REALISED IT WASN'T HERS WHEN IT WENT FOR THE FISH: THE TANK DIDN'T HAVE A LID, PRESUMABLY BECAUSE THERE WOULD USUALLY BE NO NEED FOR ONE.

IS CREEPING AROUND PART OF YOUR JOB DESCRIPTION, MR TUICKS?

SQUIFFY DOES D... SQUIFFY AND THE R... SQUIFFY GOES TO... SQUIFFY MAKES TE... SQUIFFY FINDS A FRIE... SQUIFFY AND THE SURP... SQUIFFY BUILDS A HOU...

IT WAS JUST A CHEQUE— I WAS ASKED TO RECOVER IT BY MRS MAUGHTON

IT WAS FOR BERNI - SHE DIDN'T WANT CHARLOTTE TO FIND IT.

CHARLOTTE HAS BEEN A BIT... PARANOID...

AND BERNI? WAS CREEPING PART OF HIS JOB DESCRIPTION AS WELL?

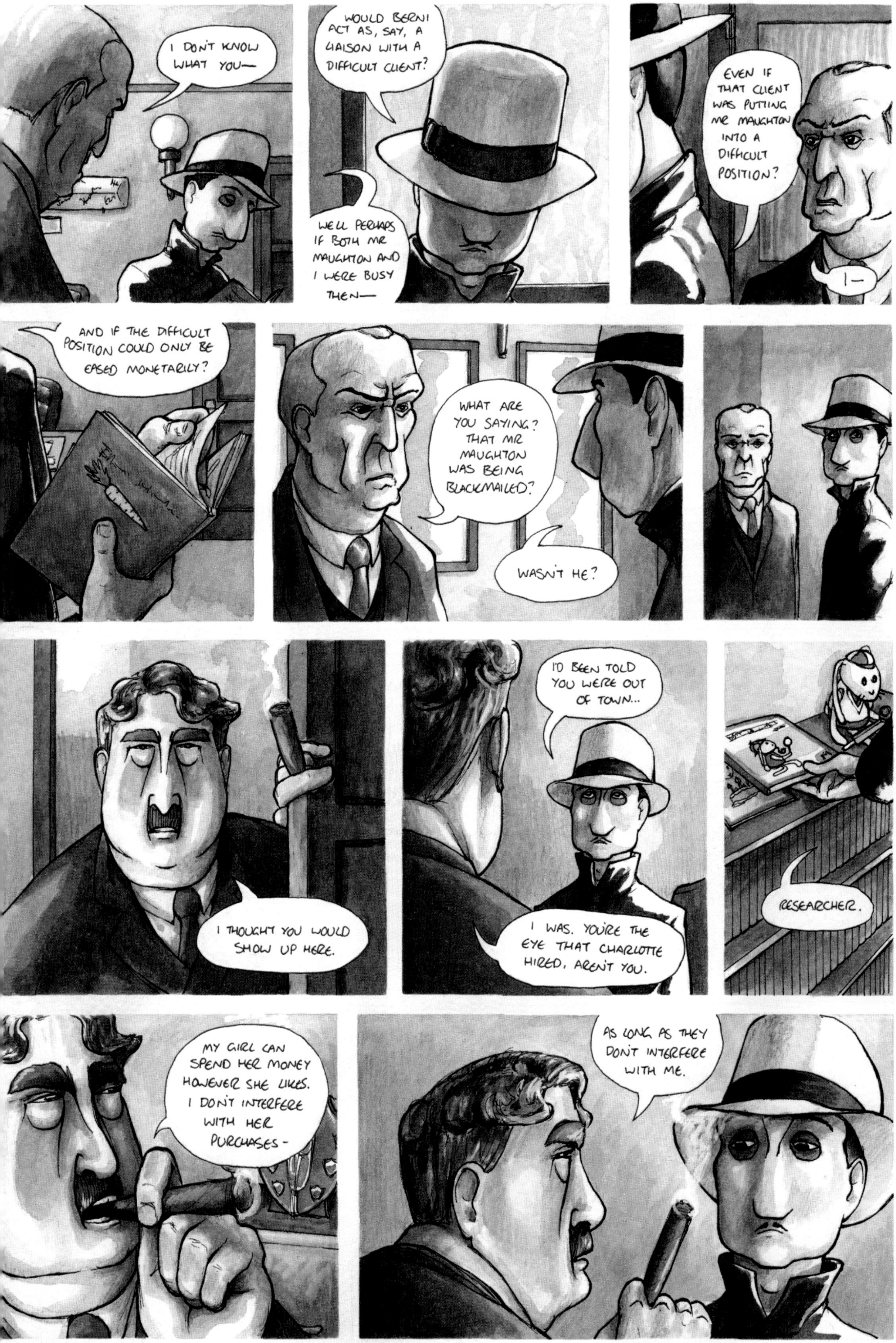
I DON'T KNOW WHAT YOU—
WOULD BERNI ACT AS, SAY, A LIAISON WITH A DIFFICULT CLIENT?
WELL PERHAPS IF BOTH MR MAUGHTON AND I WERE BUSY THEN—
EVEN IF THAT CLIENT WAS PUTTING MR MAUGHTON INTO A DIFFICULT POSITION?
I—
AND IF THE DIFFICULT POSITION COULD ONLY BE EASED MONETARILY?
WHAT ARE YOU SAYING? THAT MR MAUGHTON WAS BEING BLACKMAILED?
WASN'T HE?
I THOUGHT YOU WOULD SHOW UP HERE.
I'D BEEN TOLD YOU WERE OUT OF TOWN...
I WAS. YOU'RE THE EYE THAT CHARLOTTE HIRED, AREN'T YOU.
RESEARCHER.
MY GIRL CAN SPEND HER MONEY HOWEVER SHE LIKES. I DON'T INTERFERE WITH HER PURCHASES-
AS LONG AS THEY DON'T INTERFERE WITH ME.

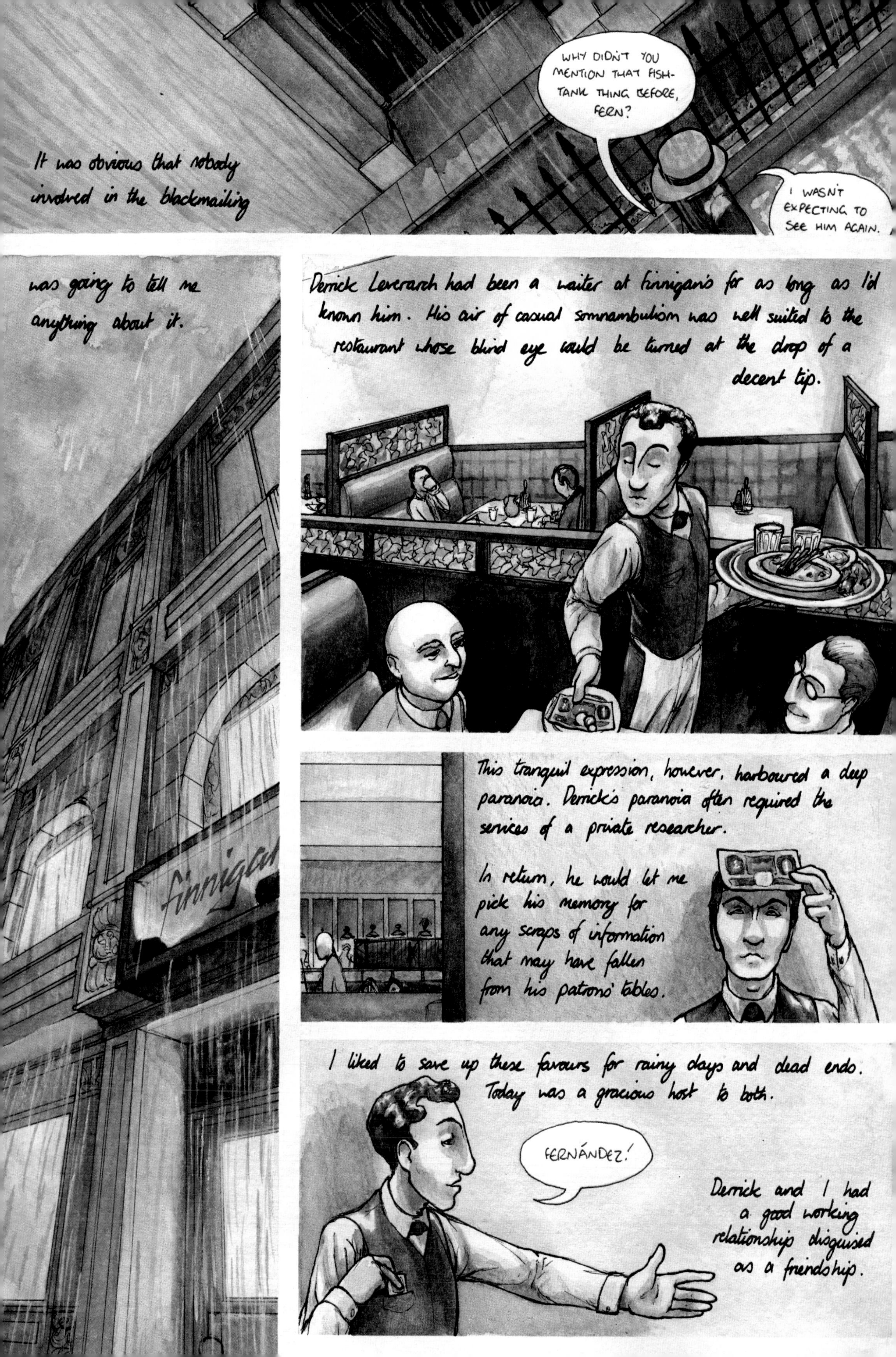
It was obvious that nobody involved in the blackmailing
WHY DIDN'T YOU MENTION THAT FISH-TANK THING BEFORE, FERN?
I WASN'T EXPECTING TO SEE HIM AGAIN.
was going to tell me anything about it.
finnigan
Derrick Leverarch had been a waiter at Finnigan's for as long as I'd known him. His air of casual somnambulism was well suited to the restaurant whose blind eye could be turned at the drop of a decent tip.
This tranquil expression, however, harboured a deep paranoia. Derrick's paranoia often required the services of a private researcher.
In return, he would let me pick his memory for any scraps of information that may have fallen from his patrons' tables.
I liked to save up these favours for rainy days and dead ends. Today was a gracious host to both.
FERNÁNDEZ!
Derrick and I had a good working relationship disguised as a friendship.

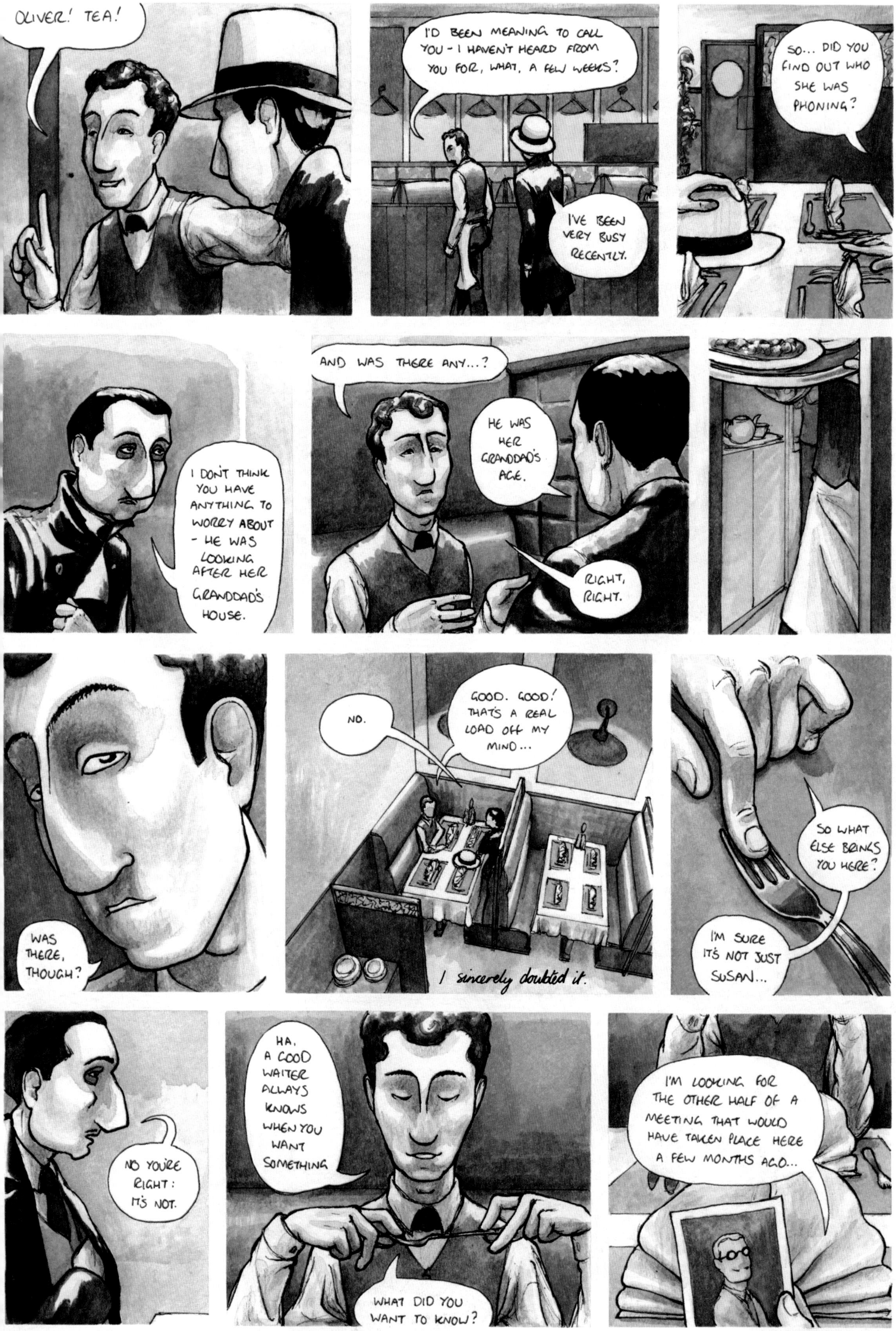
OLIVER! TEA!
I'D BEEN MEANING TO CALL YOU - I HAVEN'T HEARD FROM YOU FOR, WHAT, A FEW WEEKS?
I'VE BEEN VERY BUSY RECENTLY.
SO... DID YOU FIND OUT WHO SHE WAS PHONING?
I DON'T THINK YOU HAVE ANYTHING TO WORRY ABOUT - HE WAS LOOKING AFTER HER GRANDDAD'S HOUSE.
AND WAS THERE ANY...?
HE WAS HER GRANDDAD'S AGE.
RIGHT, RIGHT.
WAS THERE, THOUGH?
NO.
GOOD. GOOD! THAT'S A REAL LOAD OFF MY MIND...
I sincerely doubted it.
SO WHAT ELSE BRINGS YOU HERE?
I'M SURE IT'S NOT JUST SUSAN...
NO YOU'RE RIGHT: IT'S NOT.
HA. A GOOD WAITER ALWAYS KNOWS WHEN YOU WANT SOMETHING
WHAT DID YOU WANT TO KNOW?
I'M LOOKING FOR THE OTHER HALF OF A MEETING THAT WOULD HAVE TAKEN PLACE HERE A FEW MONTHS AGO...

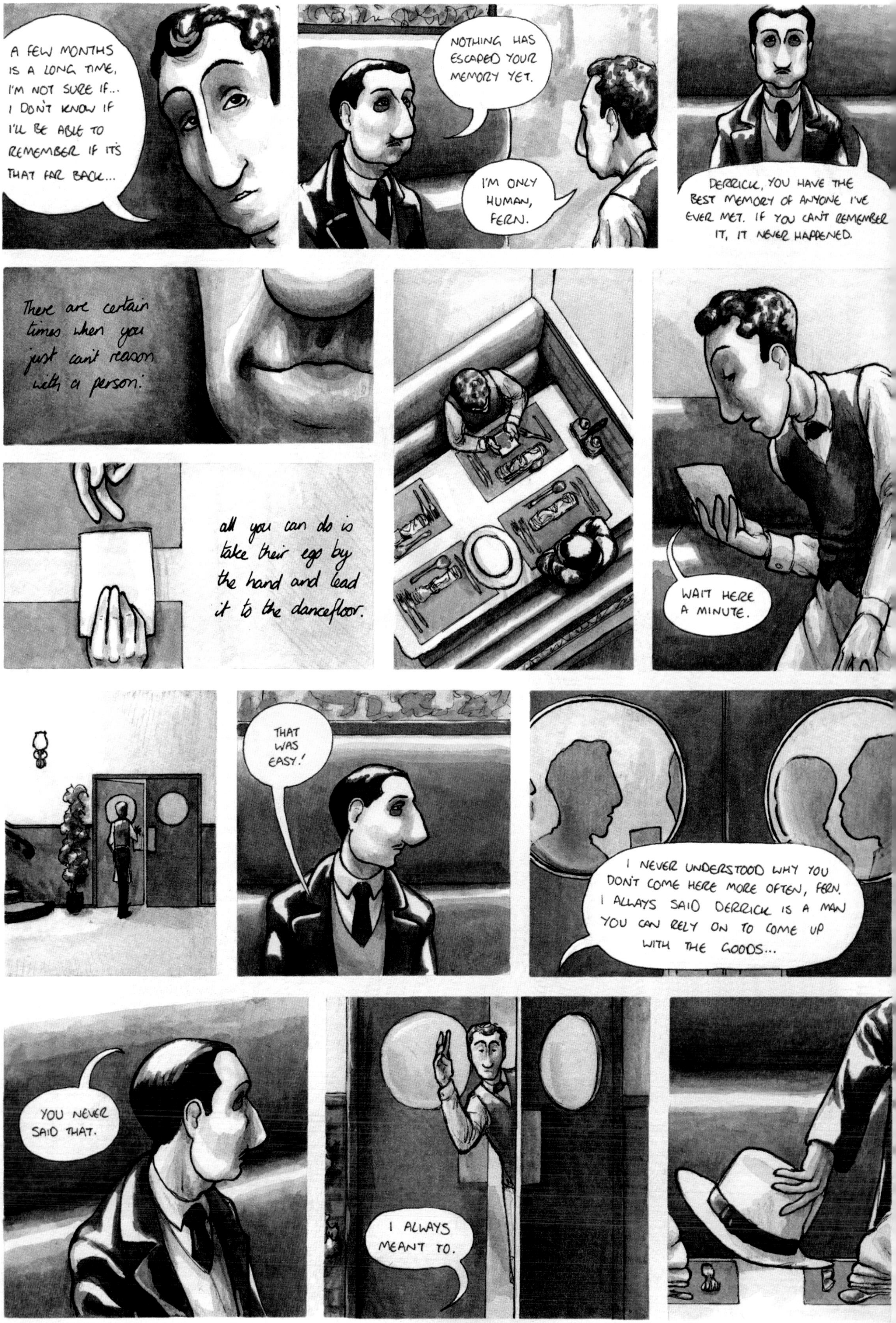
A FEW MONTHS IS A LONG TIME, I'M NOT SURE IF... I DON'T KNOW IF I'LL BE ABLE TO REMEMBER IF IT'S THAT FAR BACK...
NOTHING HAS ESCAPED YOUR MEMORY YET.
I'M ONLY HUMAN, FERN.
DERRICK, YOU HAVE THE BEST MEMORY OF ANYONE I'VE EVER MET. IF YOU CAN'T REMEMBER IT, IT NEVER HAPPENED.
There are certain times when you just can't reason with a person:
all you can do is take their ego by the hand and lead it to the dancefloor.
WAIT HERE A MINUTE.
THAT WAS EASY!
I NEVER UNDERSTOOD WHY YOU DON'T COME HERE MORE OFTEN, FERN. I ALWAYS SAID DERRICK IS A MAN YOU CAN RELY ON TO COME UP WITH THE GOODS...
YOU NEVER SAID THAT.
I ALWAYS MEANT TO.

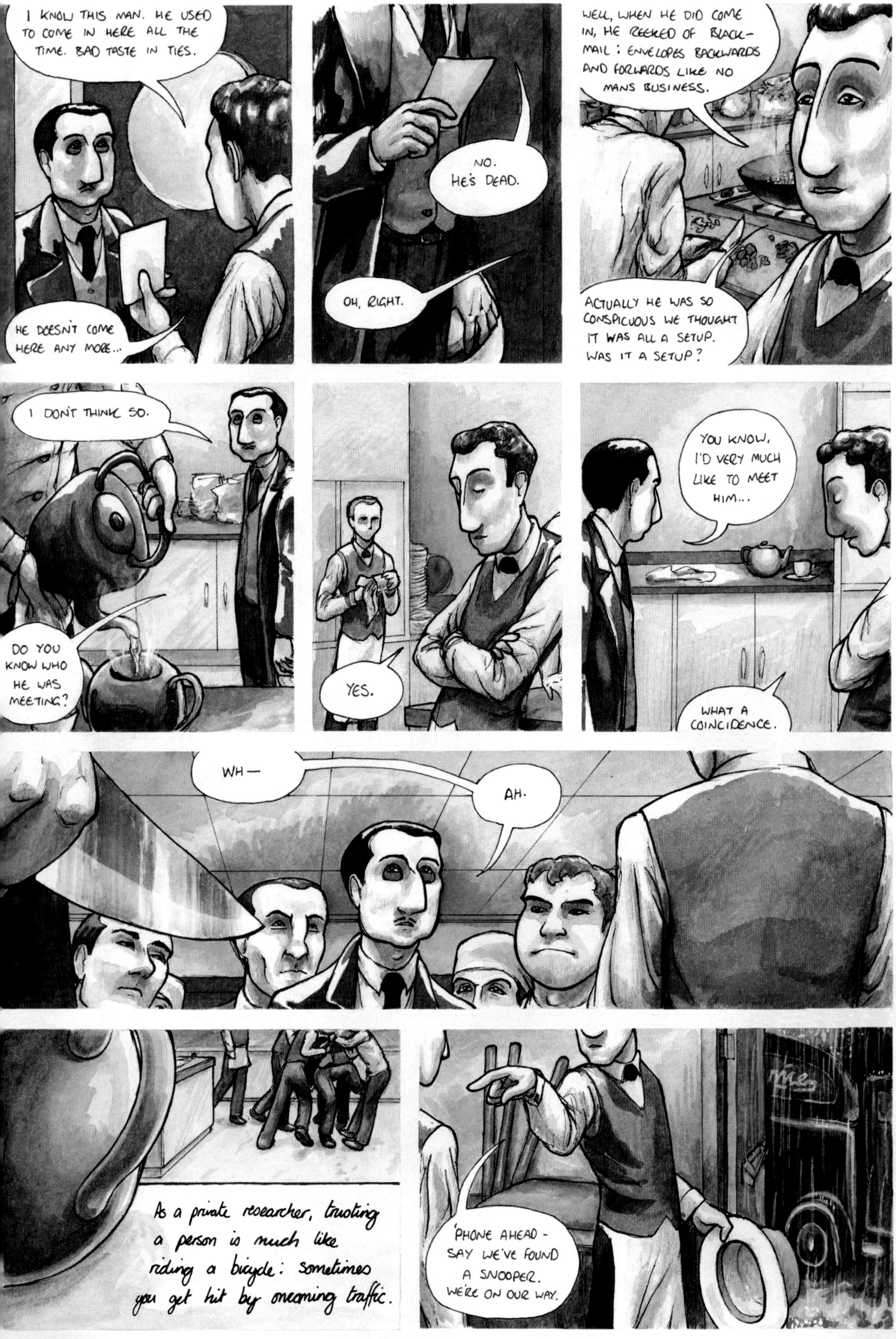
I KNOW THIS MAN. HE USED TO COME IN HERE ALL THE TIME. BAD TASTE IN TIES.
HE DOESN'T COME HERE ANY MORE...
NO. HE'S DEAD.
OH, RIGHT.
WELL, WHEN HE DID COME IN, HE REEKED OF BLACK-MAIL: ENVELOPES BACKWARDS AND FORWARDS LIKE NO MANS BUSINESS.
ACTUALLY HE WAS SO CONSPICUOUS WE THOUGHT IT WAS ALL A SETUP. WAS IT A SETUP?
I DON'T THINK SO.
DO YOU KNOW WHO HE WAS MEETING?
YES.
YOU KNOW, I'D VERY MUCH LIKE TO MEET HIM...
WHAT A COINCIDENCE.
WH—
AH.
As a private researcher, trusting a person is much like riding a bicycle: sometimes you get hit by oncoming traffic.
'PHONE AHEAD - SAY WE'VE FOUND A SNOOPER. WE'RE ON OUR WAY.

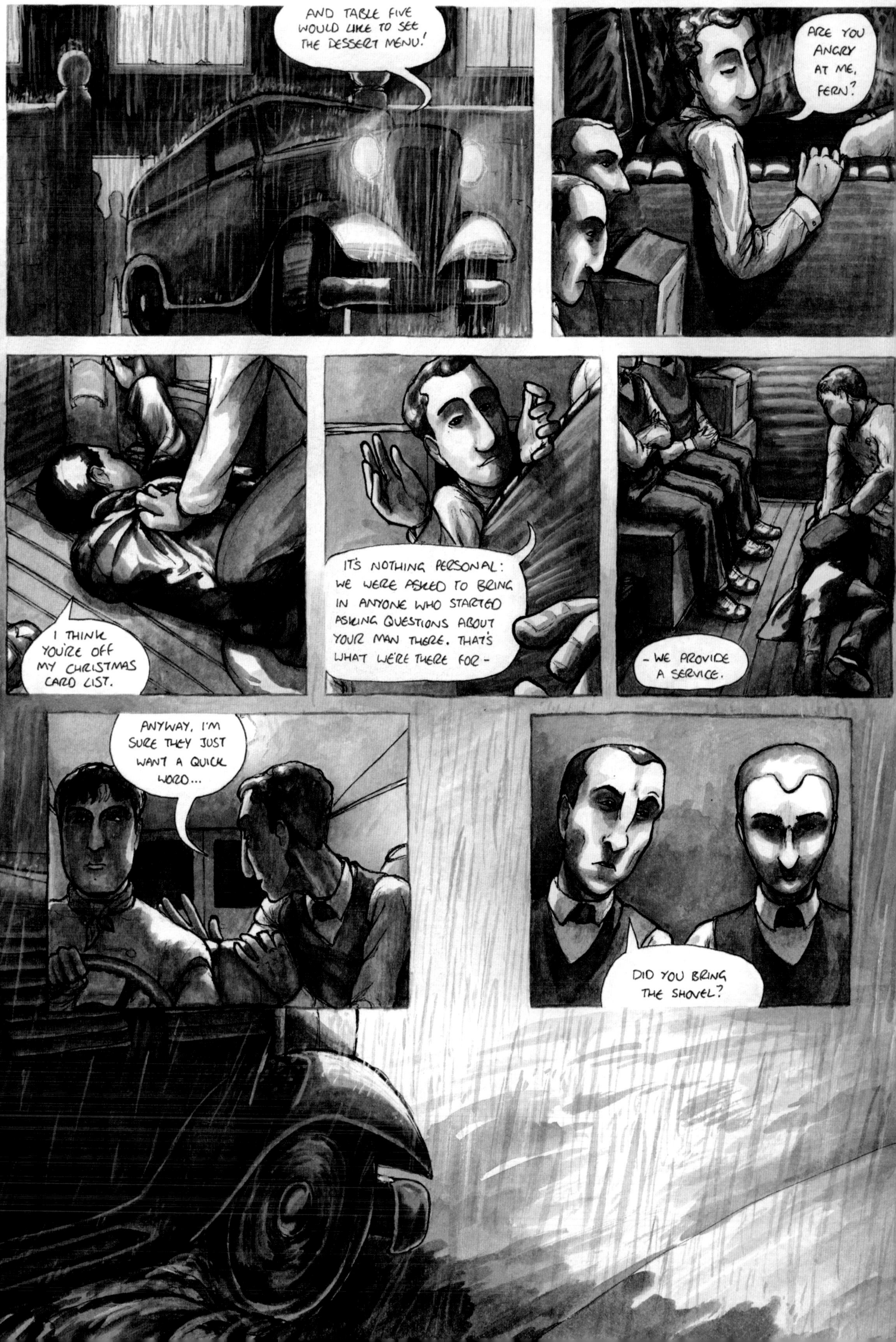
AND TABLE FIVE WOULD LIKE TO SEE THE DESSERT MENU!
ARE YOU ANGRY AT ME, FERN?
I THINK YOU'RE OFF MY CHRISTMAS CARD LIST.
IT'S NOTHING PERSONAL: WE WERE ASKED TO BRING IN ANYONE WHO STARTED ASKING QUESTIONS ABOUT YOUR MAN THERE. THAT'S WHAT WE'RE THERE FOR -
- WE PROVIDE A SERVICE.
ANYWAY, I'M SURE THEY JUST WANT A QUICK WORD...
DID YOU BRING THE SHOVEL?

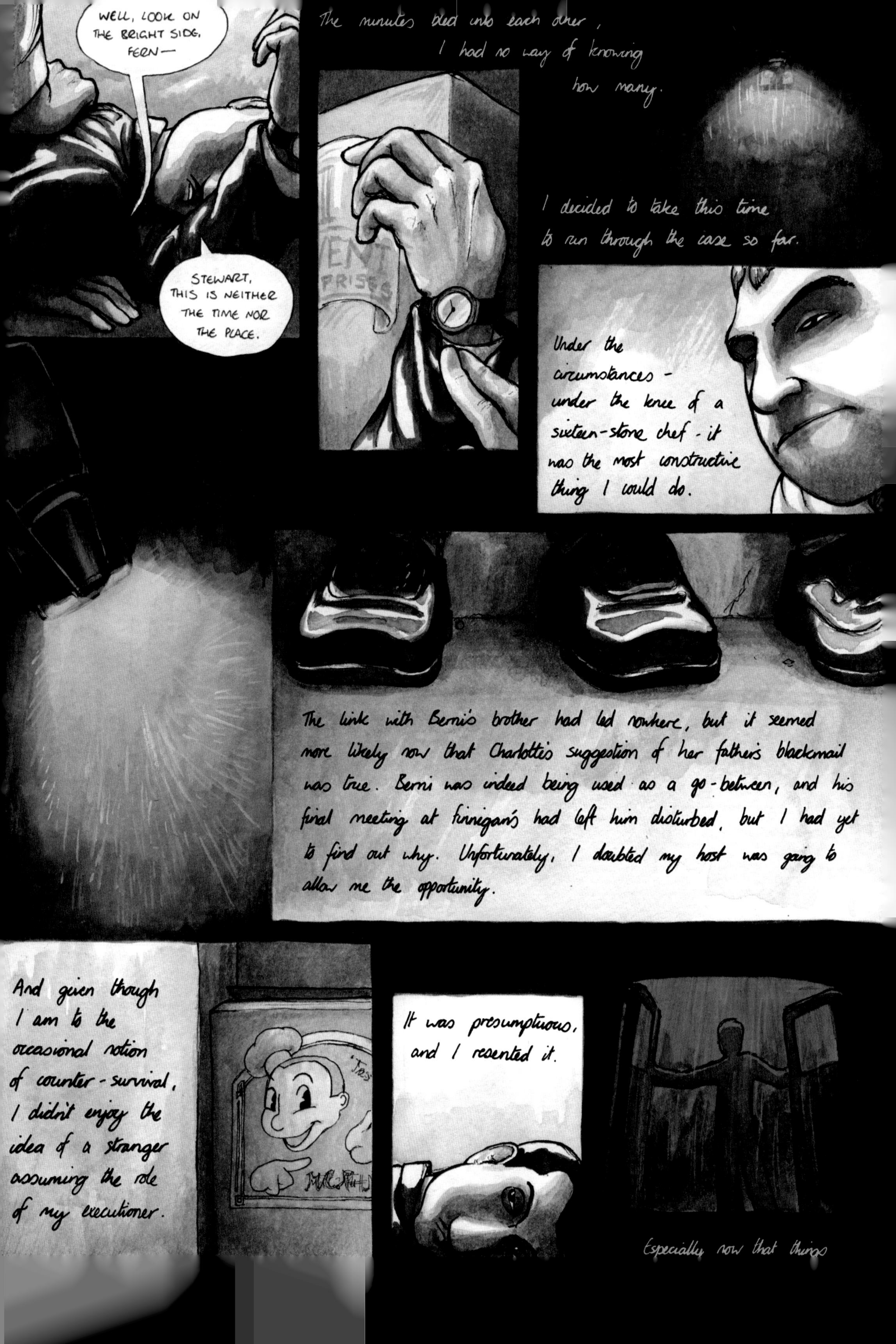
WELL, LOOK ON THE BRIGHT SIDE, FERN—
STEWART, THIS IS NEITHER THE TIME NOR THE PLACE.
The minutes bled into each other, I had no way of knowing how many.
I decided to take this time to run through the case so far.
Under the circumstances - under the knee of a sixteen-stone chef - it was the most constructive thing I could do.
The link with Berni's brother had led nowhere, but it seemed more likely now that Charlotte's suggestion of her father's blackmail was true. Berni was indeed being used as a go-between, and his final meeting at Finnigan's had left him disturbed, but I had yet to find out why. Unfortunately, I doubted my host was going to allow me the opportunity.
And given though I am to the occasional notion of counter-survival, I didn't enjoy the idea of a stranger assuming the role of my executioner.
It was presumptuous, and I resented it.
Especially now that things

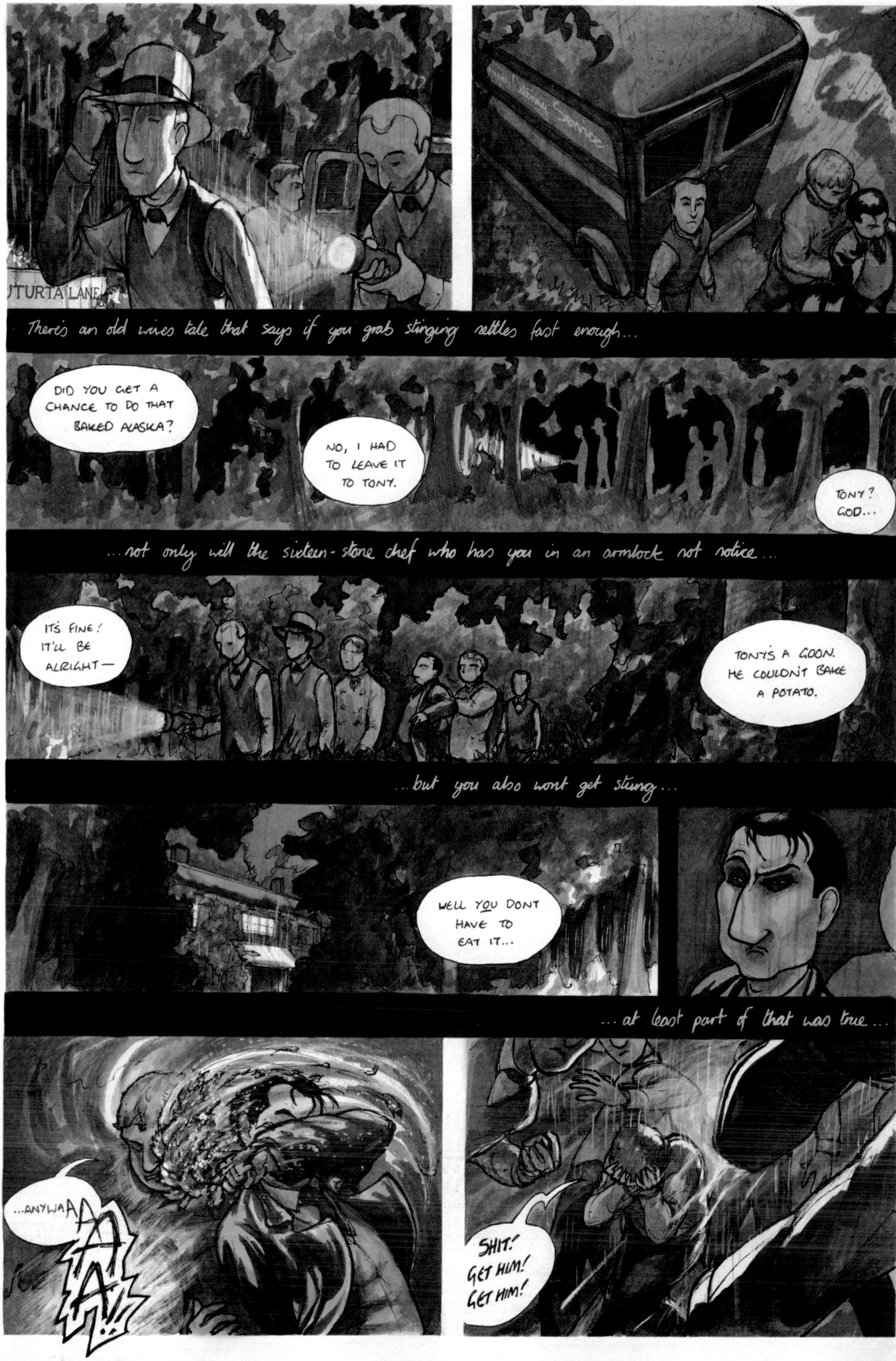
UTURTA LANE
Catering Service
There's an old wives tale that says if you grab stinging nettles fast enough...
DID YOU GET A CHANCE TO DO THAT BAKED ALASKA?
NO, I HAD TO LEAVE IT TO TONY.
TONY? GOD...
...not only will the sixteen-stone chef who has you in an armlock not notice...
IT'S FINE! IT'LL BE ALRIGHT—
TONY'S A GOON. HE COULDN'T BAKE A POTATO.
...but you also wont get stung...
WELL YOU DONT HAVE TO EAT IT...
...at least part of that was true...
...ANYWAAAAA!!
SHIT! GET HIM! GET HIM!

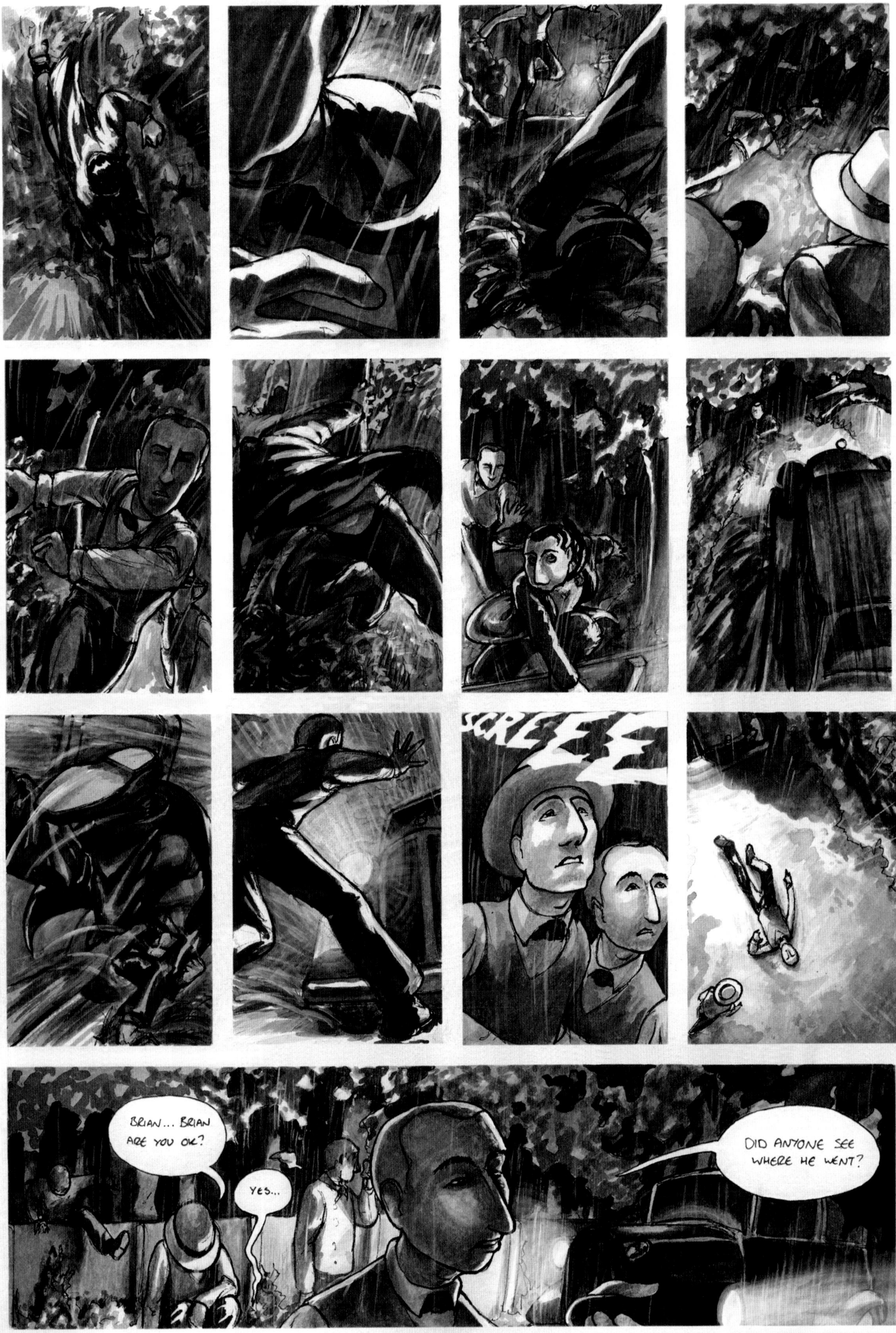
SCREEE
BRIAN... BRIAN
ARE YOU OK?
YES...
DID ANYONE SEE
WHERE HE WENT?

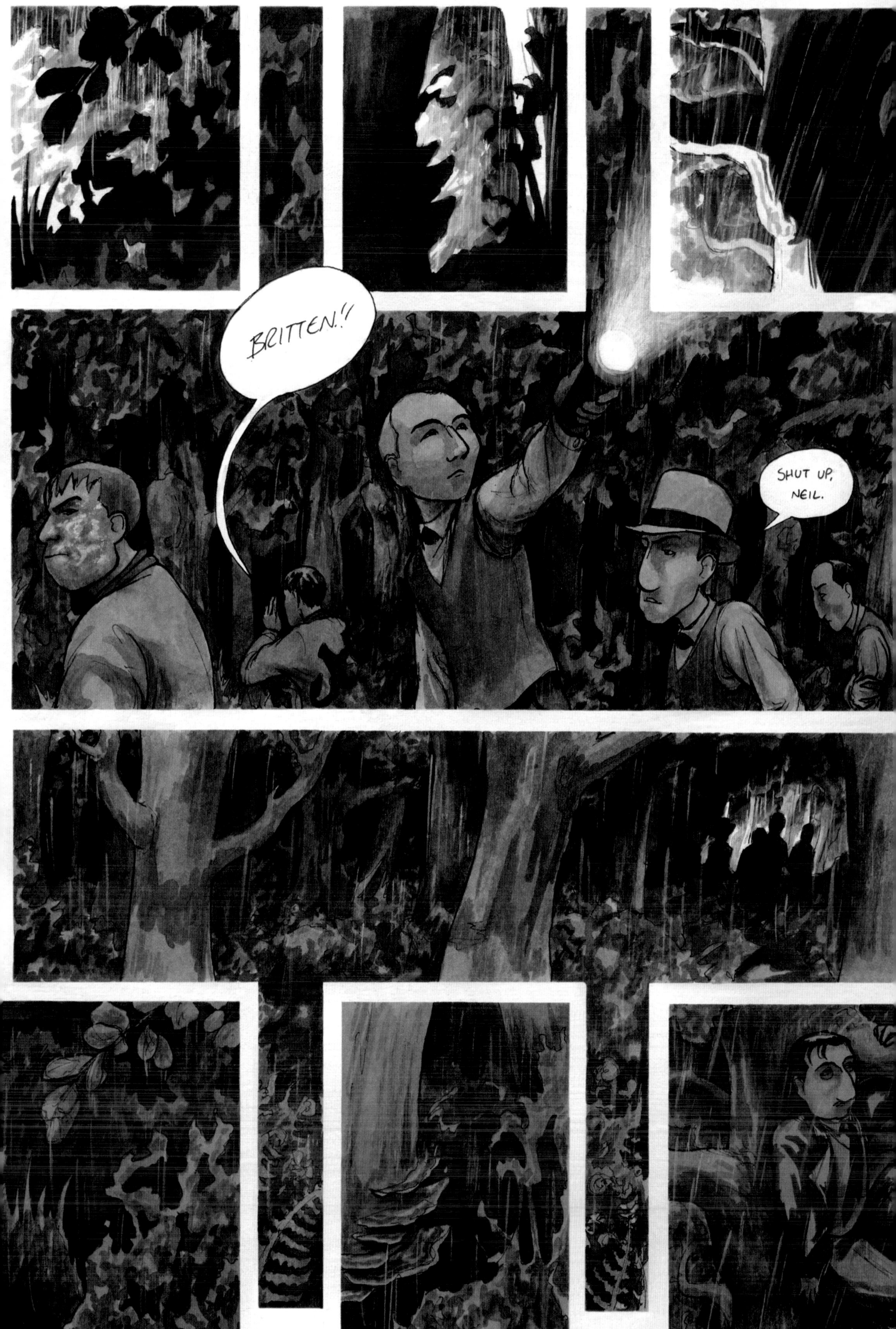
BRITTEN!!
SHUT UP, NEIL.

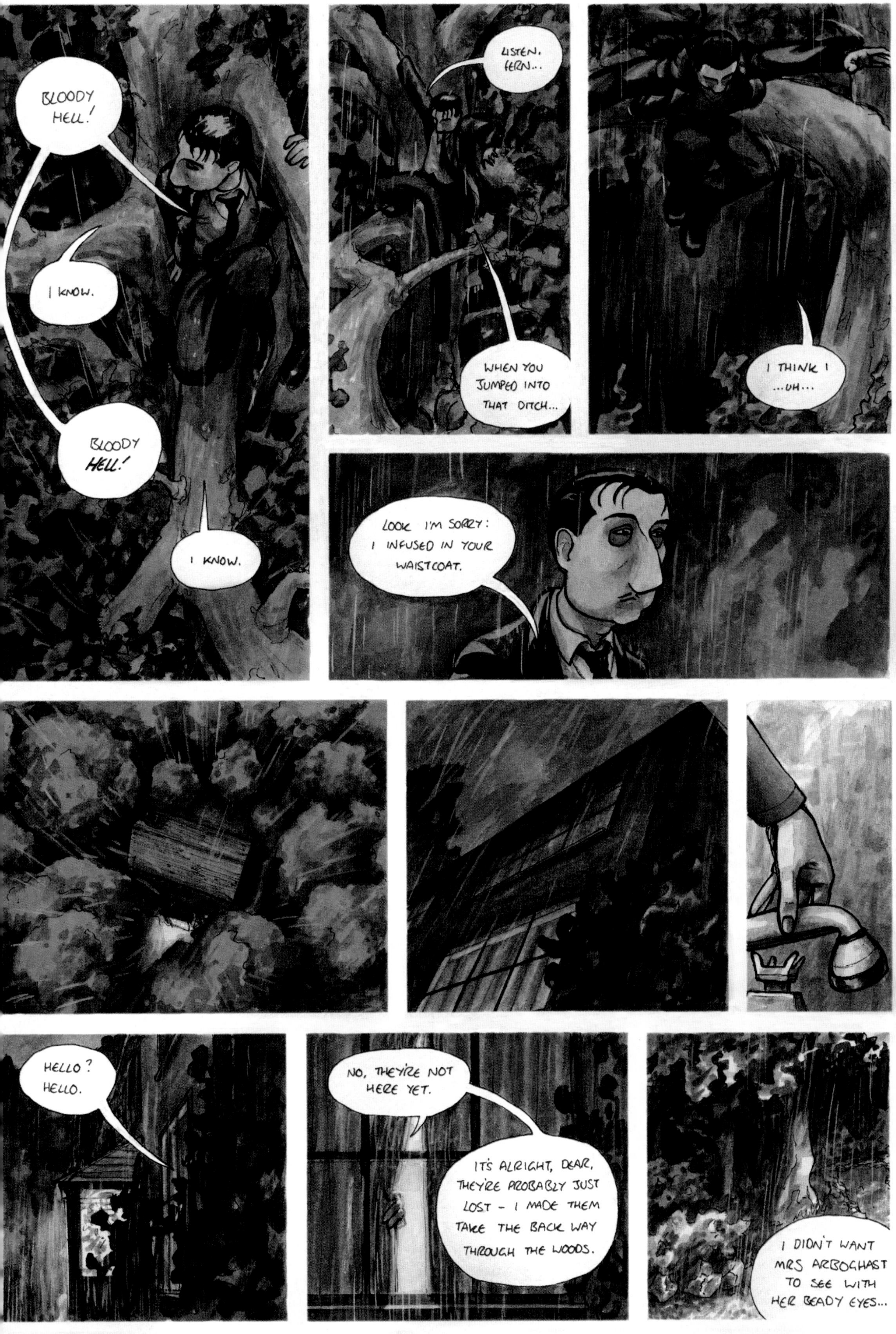
BLOODY HELL!
I KNOW.
BLOODY HELL!
I KNOW.
LISTEN, FERN...
WHEN YOU JUMPED INTO THAT DITCH...
I THINK I ...UH...
LOOK I'M SORRY: I INFUSED IN YOUR WAISTCOAT.
HELLO? HELLO.
NO, THEY'RE NOT HERE YET.
IT'S ALRIGHT, DEAR, THEY'RE PROBABLY JUST LOST - I MADE THEM TAKE THE BACK WAY THROUGH THE WOODS.
I DIDN'T WANT MRS ARBOGHAST TO SEE WITH HER BEADY EYES...

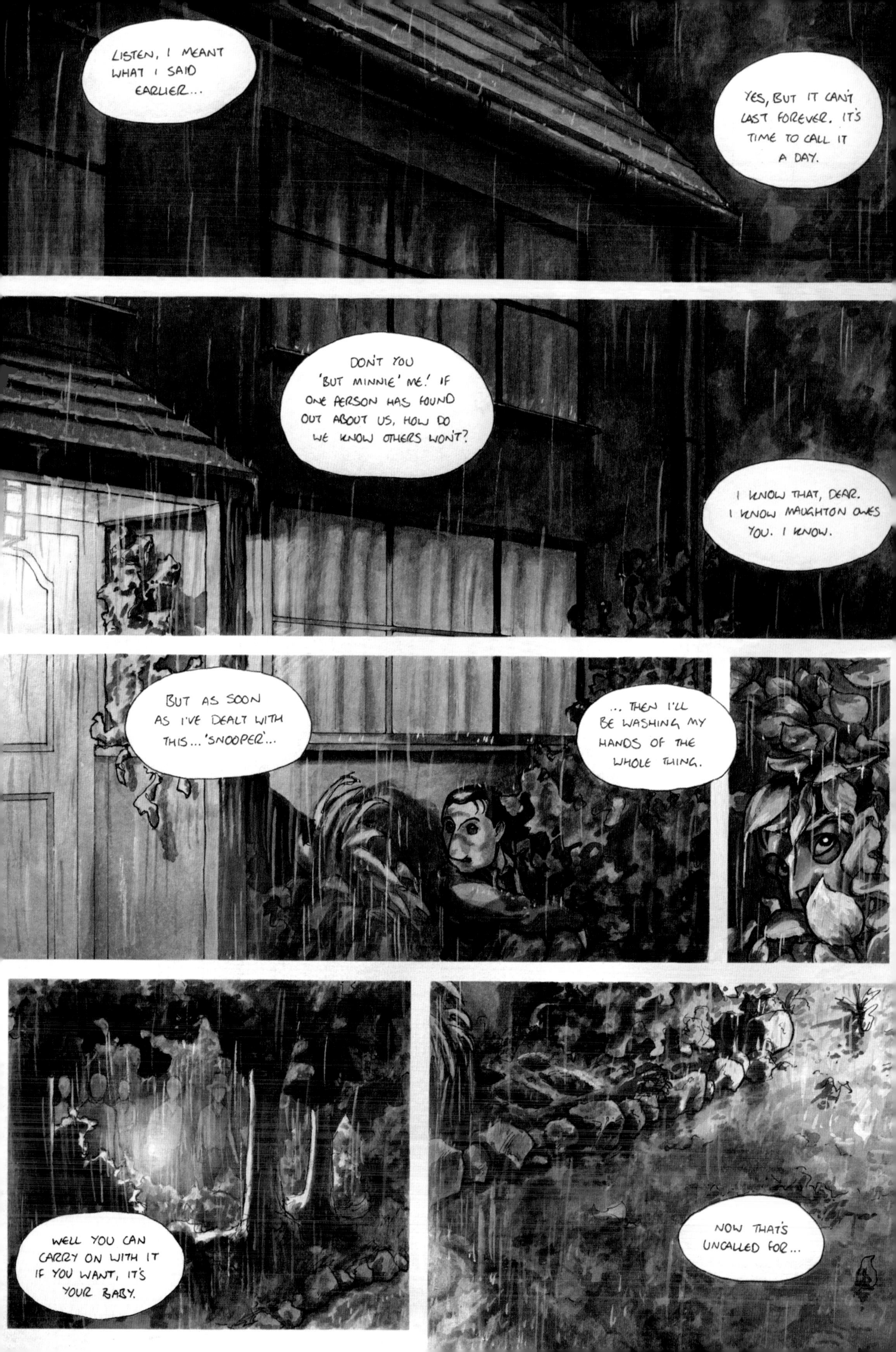
LISTEN, I MEANT WHAT I SAID EARLIER...
YES, BUT IT CAN'T LAST FOREVER. IT'S TIME TO CALL IT A DAY.
DON'T YOU 'BUT MINNIE' ME! IF ONE PERSON HAS FOUND OUT ABOUT US, HOW DO WE KNOW OTHERS WON'T?
I KNOW THAT, DEAR. I KNOW MAUGHTON OWES YOU. I KNOW.
BUT AS SOON AS I'VE DEALT WITH THIS... 'SNOOPER'...
... THEN I'LL BE WASHING MY HANDS OF THE WHOLE THING.
WELL YOU CAN CARRY ON WITH IT IF YOU WANT, IT'S YOUR BABY.
NOW THAT'S UNCALLED FOR...

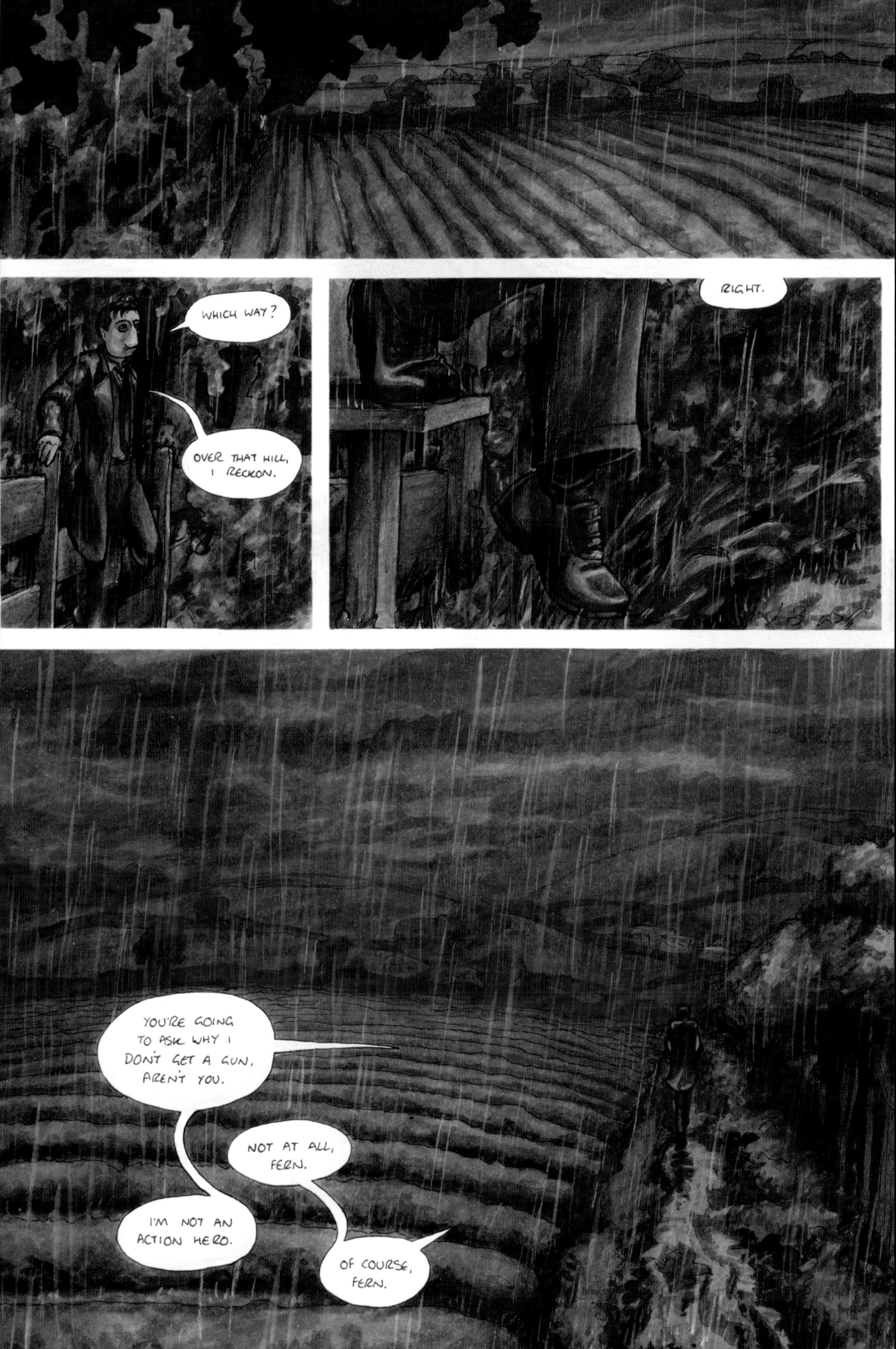
WHICH WAY?
OVER THAT HILL, I RECKON.
RIGHT.
YOU'RE GOING TO ASK WHY I DON'T GET A GUN, AREN'T YOU.
NOT AT ALL, FERN.
I'M NOT AN ACTION HERO.
OF COURSE, FERN.

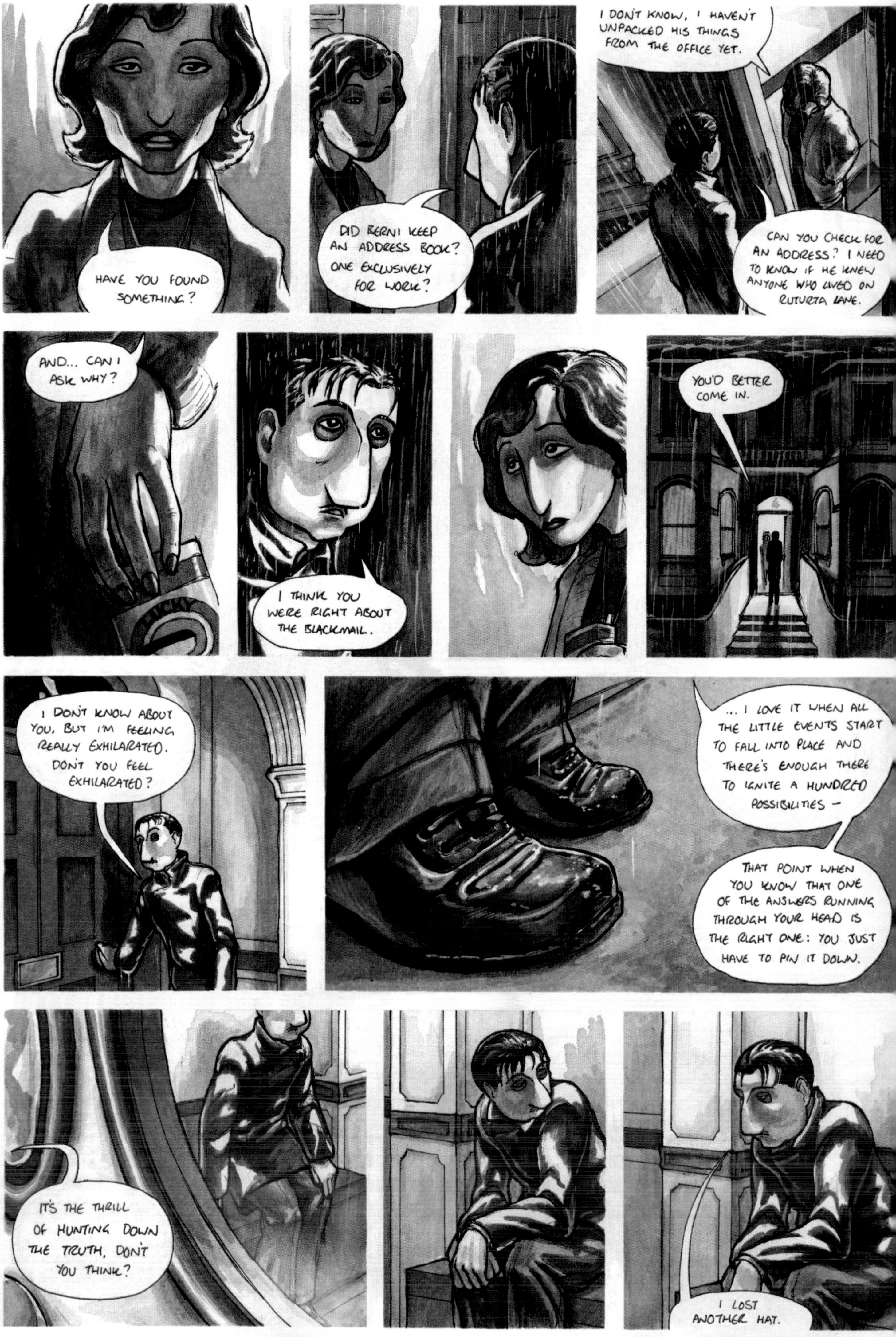
HAVE YOU FOUND SOMETHING?
DID BERNI KEEP AN ADDRESS BOOK? ONE EXCLUSIVELY FOR WORK?
I DON'T KNOW, I HAVEN'T UNPACKED HIS THINGS FROM THE OFFICE YET.
CAN YOU CHECK FOR AN ADDRESS? I NEED TO KNOW IF HE KNEW ANYONE WHO LIVED ON RUTURTA LANE.
AND... CAN I ASK WHY?
I THINK YOU WERE RIGHT ABOUT THE BLACKMAIL.
YOU'D BETTER COME IN.
I DON'T KNOW ABOUT YOU, BUT I'M FEELING REALLY EXHILARATED. DON'T YOU FEEL EXHILARATED?
... I LOVE IT WHEN ALL THE LITTLE EVENTS START TO FALL INTO PLACE AND THERE'S ENOUGH THERE TO IGNITE A HUNDRED POSSIBILITIES –
THAT POINT WHEN YOU KNOW THAT ONE OF THE ANSWERS RUNNING THROUGH YOUR HEAD IS THE RIGHT ONE: YOU JUST HAVE TO PIN IT DOWN.
IT'S THE THRILL OF HUNTING DOWN THE TRUTH, DON'T YOU THINK?
I LOST ANOTHER HAT.

I COULDN'T FIND ANYONE WHO LIVES ON RUTURTA LANE...

DO YOU THINK THIS PERSON COULD HAVE MURDERED BERNI?

PEOPLE. THERE ARE TWO OF THEM.

I KNOW THAT ONE OF THEM MET WITH HIM SEVERAL TIMES AT FINNIGAN'S, MAYBE EVEN ON THE NIGHT YOU SAID HE SEEMED DIFFERENT.

HE WAS DIFFERENT, BRITTEN. IT WAS AS IF HE'D SUDDENLY CLOUDED OVER.

BERNI REALLY WAS TERRIBLE AT KEEPING SECRETS:

THE ONLY SECRET HE HAD WAS THE HOUSE HE WAS PLANNING TO BUY US ON WATTERSON HILL

AND EVEN THAT HE TOLD ME ABOUT, THE SILLY GIT.

BUT HE NEVER SPOKE ABOUT THAT MEETING.

ERIC BLICESTER. LIVES ON STRONGROCK VIEW — JUST OFF RUTURTA LANE.

Strongrock View, Upper Croesey

14 Brock, Forthinde Road

134

Lip

I DON'T KNOW HIM, BUT I KNOW HE WORKS OVER AT THE PUBLISHERS...

BERNI WAS FOND OF COLOUR-CODING. ALL THE EMPLOYEES ARE IN BLUE.

DID YOU NOTICE ANYONE IN THERE CALLED 'MINNIE'?

NO.

THANK YOU. I'LL BE IN TOUCH IF I FIND ANYTHING ELSE —

DID HE KILL BERNI?

I DON'T KNOW.

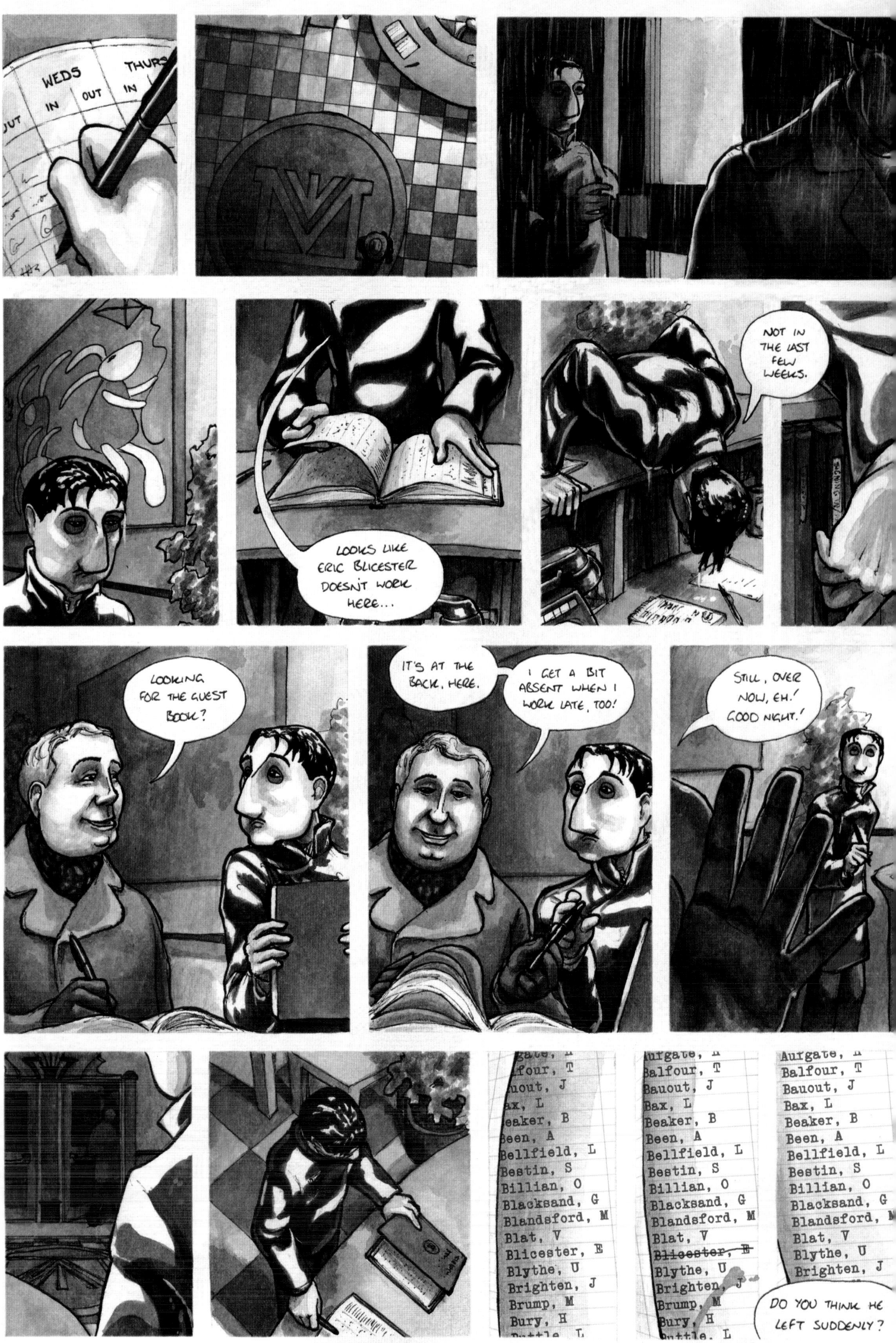
WEDS
THURS
OUT
IN
OUT
IN
LOOKS LIKE ERIC BLICESTER DOESN'T WORK HERE...
NOT IN THE LAST FEW WEEKS.
LOOKING FOR THE GUEST BOOK?
IT'S AT THE BACK, HERE.
I GET A BIT ABSENT WHEN I WORK LATE, TOO!
STILL, OVER NOW, EH! GOOD NIGHT!
Balfour, T
Bax, L
Been, A
Bellfield, L
Bestin, S
Billian, O
Blacksand, G
Blandsford, M
Blat, V
Blicester, E
Blythe, U
Brighten, J
Brump, M
Bury, H
Aurgate, H
Balfour, T
Bauout, J
Bax, L
Beaker, B
Been, A
Bellfield, L
Bestin, S
Billian, O
Blacksand, G
Blandsford, M
Blat, V
~~Blicester, E~~
Blythe, U
Brighten, J
Brump, M
Bury, H
Aurgate, H
Balfour, T
Bauout, J
Bax, L
Beaker, B
Been, A
Bellfield, L
Bestin, S
Billian, O
Blacksand, G
Blat, V
Blythe, U
Brighten, J
DO YOU THINK HE LEFT SUDDENLY?

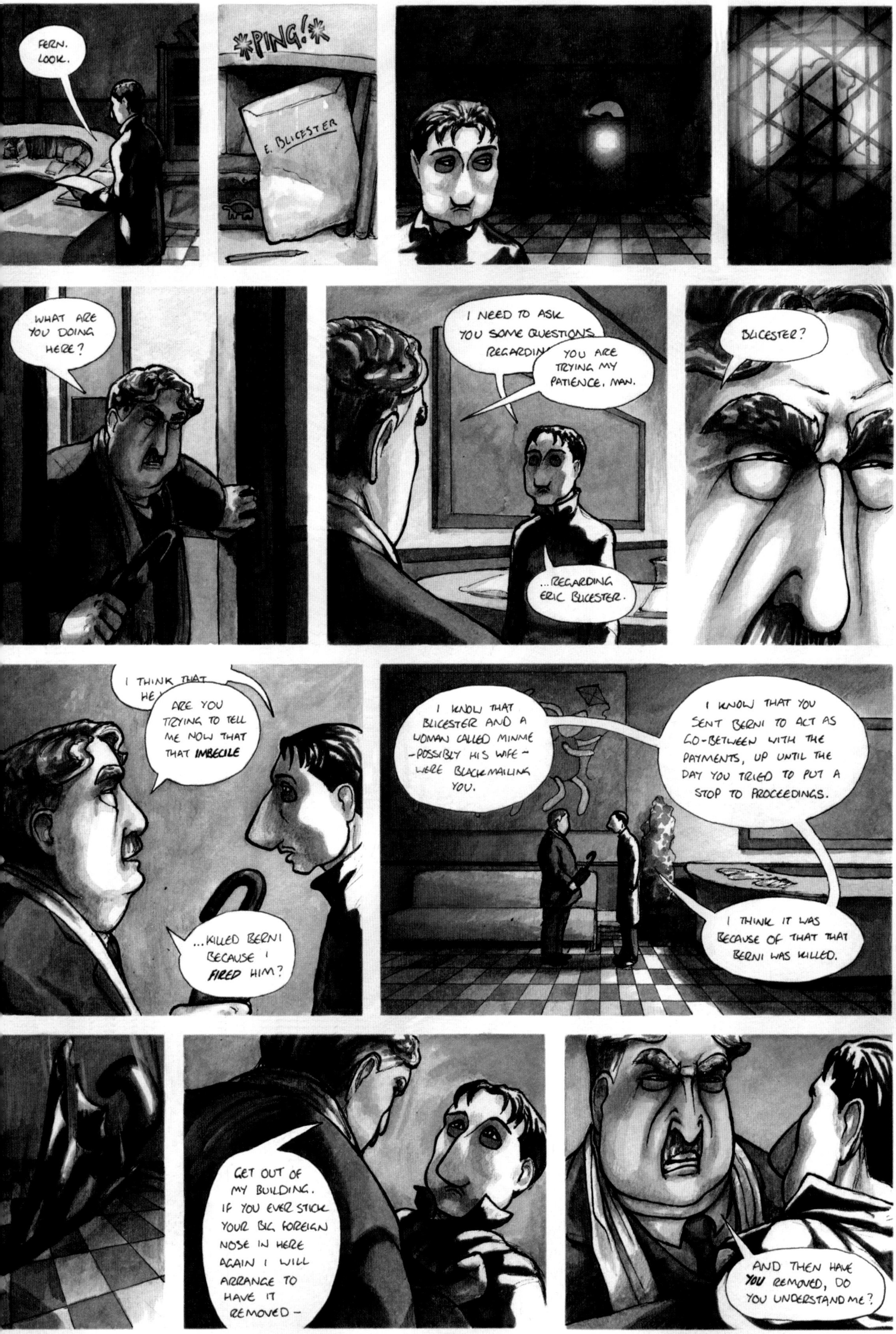
FERN. LOOK.
PING!
E. BLICESTER
WHAT ARE YOU DOING HERE?
I NEED TO ASK YOU SOME QUESTIONS REGARDIN
YOU ARE TRYING MY PATIENCE, MAN.
...REGARDING ERIC BLICESTER.
BLICESTER?
I THINK THAT HE
ARE YOU TRYING TO TELL ME NOW THAT THAT **IMBECILE**
...KILLED BERNI BECAUSE I ***FIRED*** HIM?
I KNOW THAT BLICESTER AND A WOMAN CALLED MINNIE —POSSIBLY HIS WIFE— WERE BLACKMAILING YOU.
I KNOW THAT YOU SENT BERNI TO ACT AS GO-BETWEEN WITH THE PAYMENTS, UP UNTIL THE DAY YOU TRIED TO PUT A STOP TO PROCEEDINGS.
I THINK IT WAS BECAUSE OF THAT THAT BERNI WAS KILLED.
GET OUT OF MY BUILDING. IF YOU EVER STICK YOUR BIG FOREIGN NOSE IN HERE AGAIN I WILL ARRANGE TO HAVE IT REMOVED—
AND THEN HAVE ***YOU*** REMOVED, DO YOU UNDERSTAND ME?

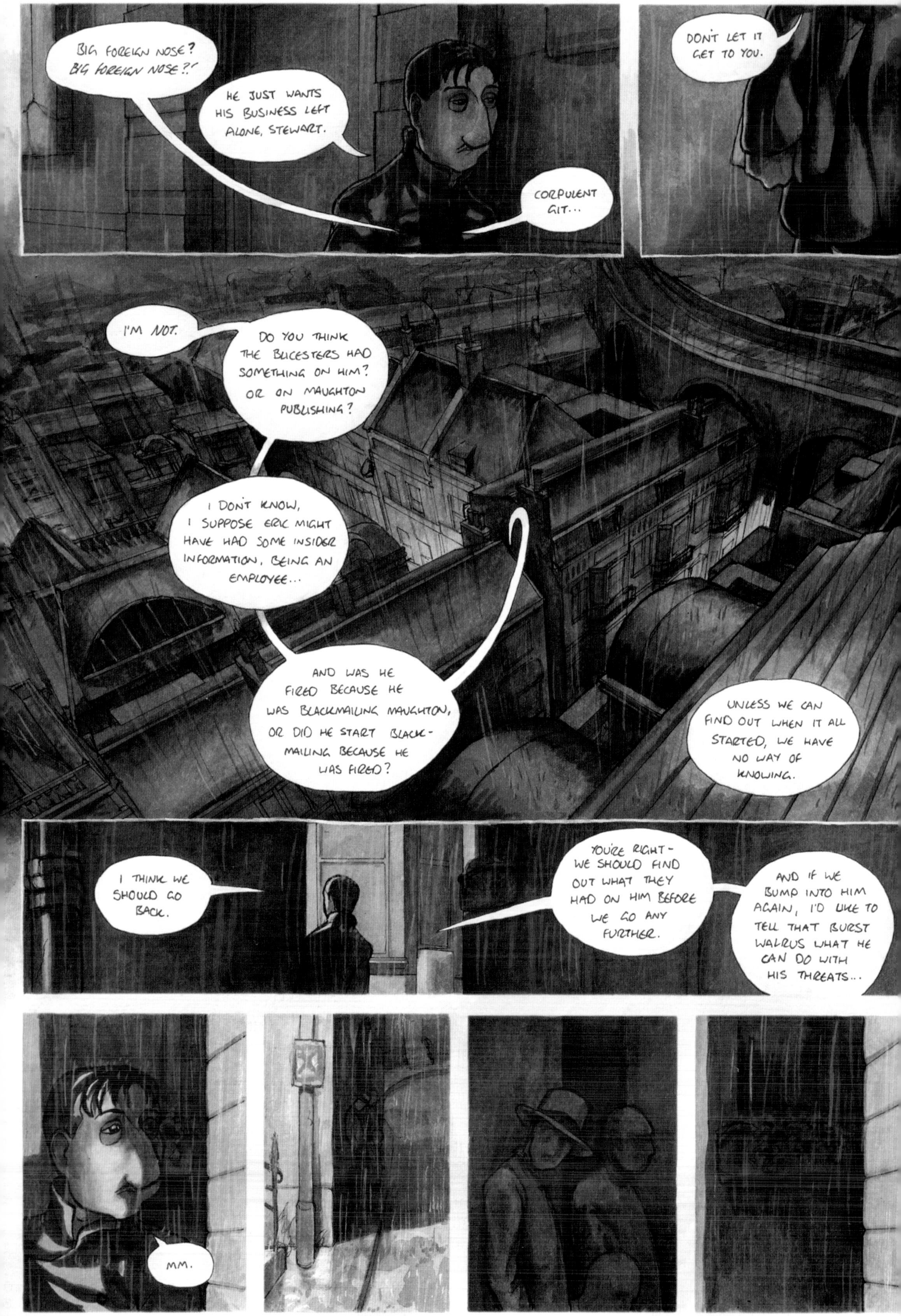
BIG FOREIGN NOSE? BIG FOREIGN NOSE?!
HE JUST WANTS HIS BUSINESS LEFT ALONE, STEWART.
CORPULENT GIT...
DON'T LET IT GET TO YOU.
I'M NOT.
DO YOU THINK THE BLICESTERS HAD SOMETHING ON HIM? OR ON MAUGHTON PUBLISHING?
I DON'T KNOW, I SUPPOSE ERIC MIGHT HAVE HAD SOME INSIDER INFORMATION, BEING AN EMPLOYEE...
AND WAS HE FIRED BECAUSE HE WAS BLACKMAILING MAUGHTON, OR DID HE START BLACK-MAILING BECAUSE HE WAS FIRED?
UNLESS WE CAN FIND OUT WHEN IT ALL STARTED, WE HAVE NO WAY OF KNOWING.
I THINK WE SHOULD GO BACK.
YOU'RE RIGHT- WE SHOULD FIND OUT WHAT THEY HAD ON HIM BEFORE WE GO ANY FURTHER.
AND IF WE BUMP INTO HIM AGAIN, I'D LIKE TO TELL THAT BURST WALRUS WHAT HE CAN DO WITH HIS THREATS...
MM.

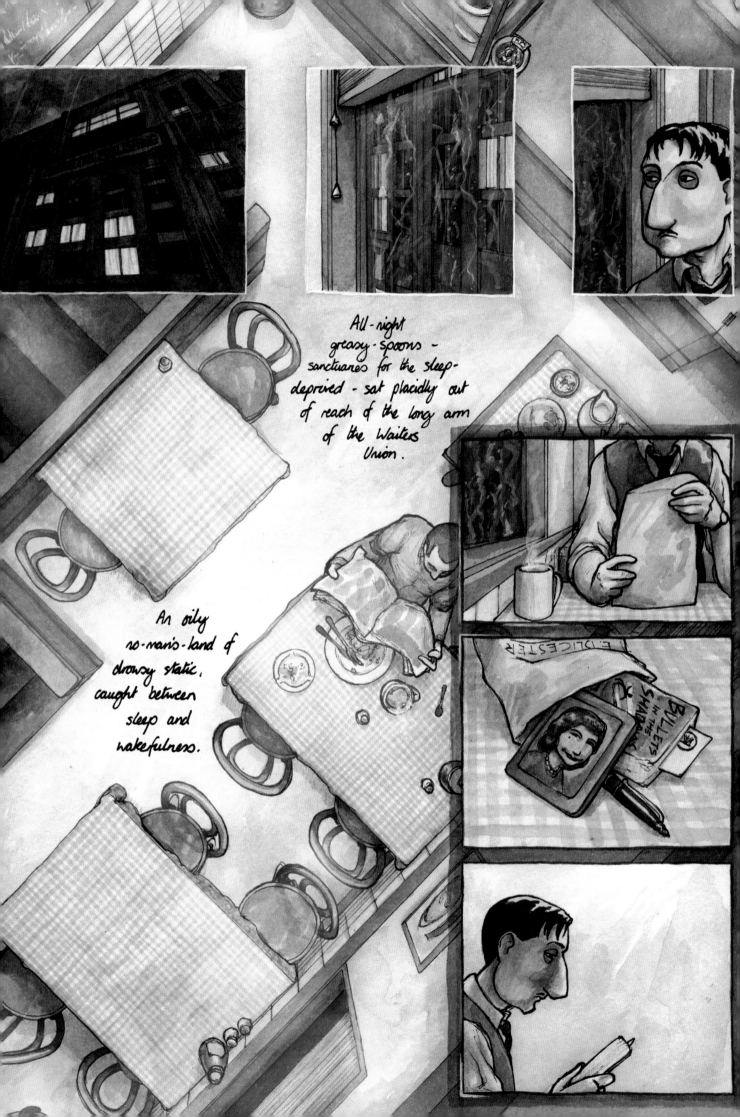

All-night greasy-spoons — sanctuaries for the sleep-deprived — sat placidly out of reach of the long arm of the Waiters Union.

An oily no-man's-land of drowsy static, caught between sleep and wakefulness.

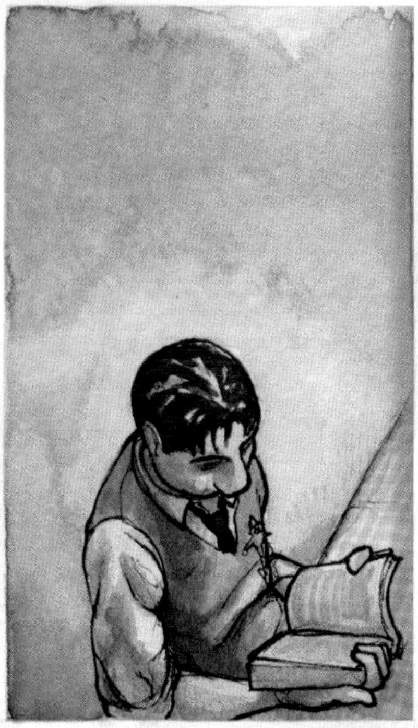

"Blast it, Hamish! Don't you think of anyone but yourself?!"

She stood there, her head cocked like my .45 Colt, and I realised we were playing Russian roulette with the conversation. It was my turn, and I don't like playing games with women. Lack of logic makes them dangerous.

"I think of Janet."

"Janet?" Her laugh refreezes the ice in my drink. "What do you care for Janet?"

"I care enough to see her steer clear of Eisenburgh and his cronies. So if you're after an apology, you'd better take a ticket and join the queue."

Her dainty left hand turns to iron and slaps me hard in the face. I was surprised, but not enough to drop my glass. It was a good scotch. The bracelets on her wrists jangle as she bristles with rage.

"You're a cold, cruel, good-for-nothing bum. Mallery should have left you breathing Pacific while he had the chance!"

"Easy, Dolores, I still got a heart."

She curls her lip like a theatre curtain and treats me to the front row of her snarl.

"If you had a heart I'd see it there on your sleeve next to your cheap cufflinks."

She grinds my doormat under her heel as she storms out of my office, leaving in her wake the scent of rose petals and malice. If this were another time and another place, she'd be alright.

Hell, maybe I'd even love her.

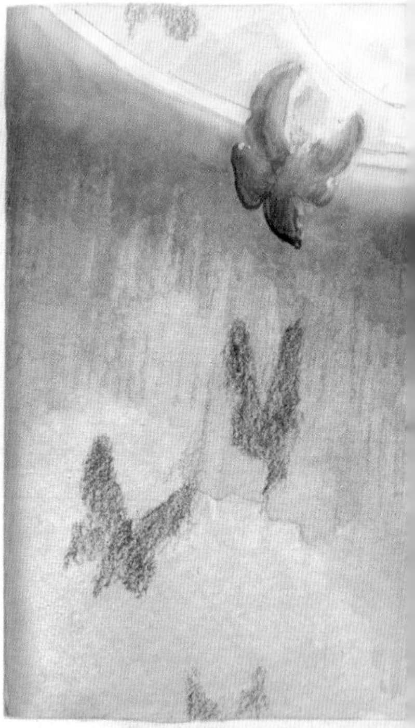

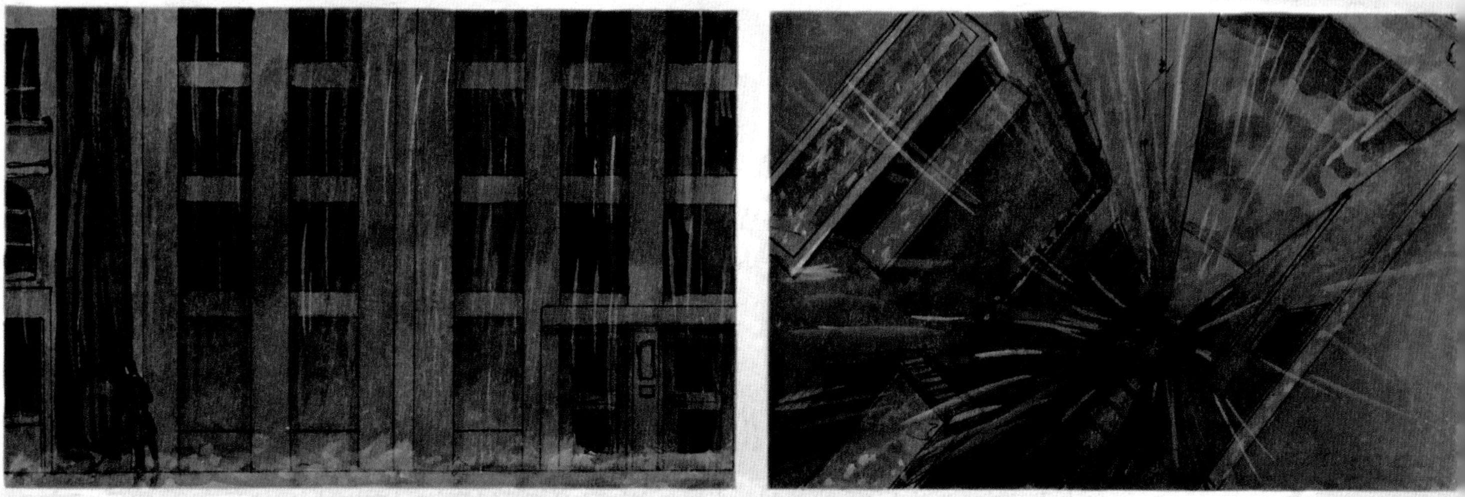

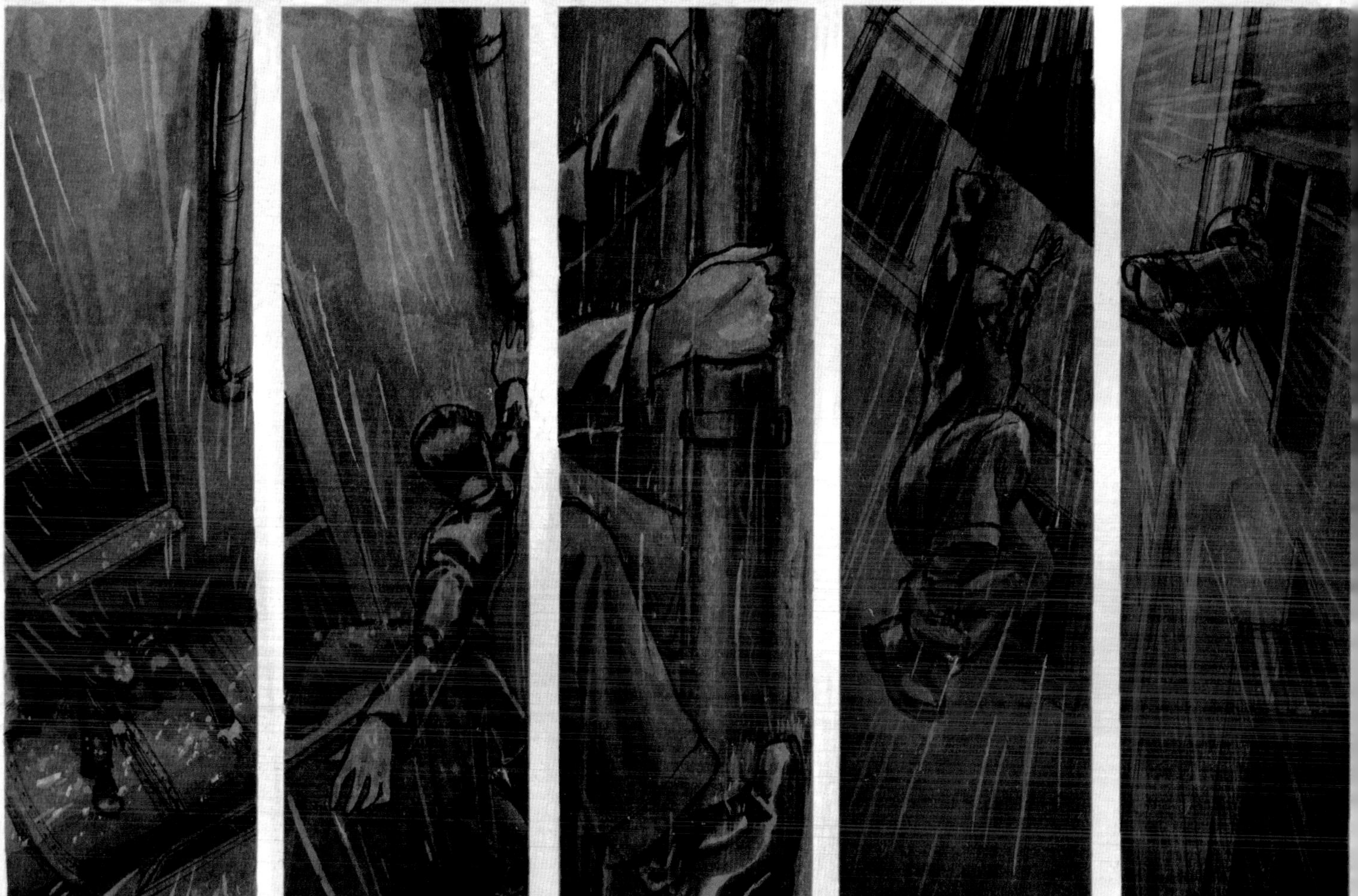

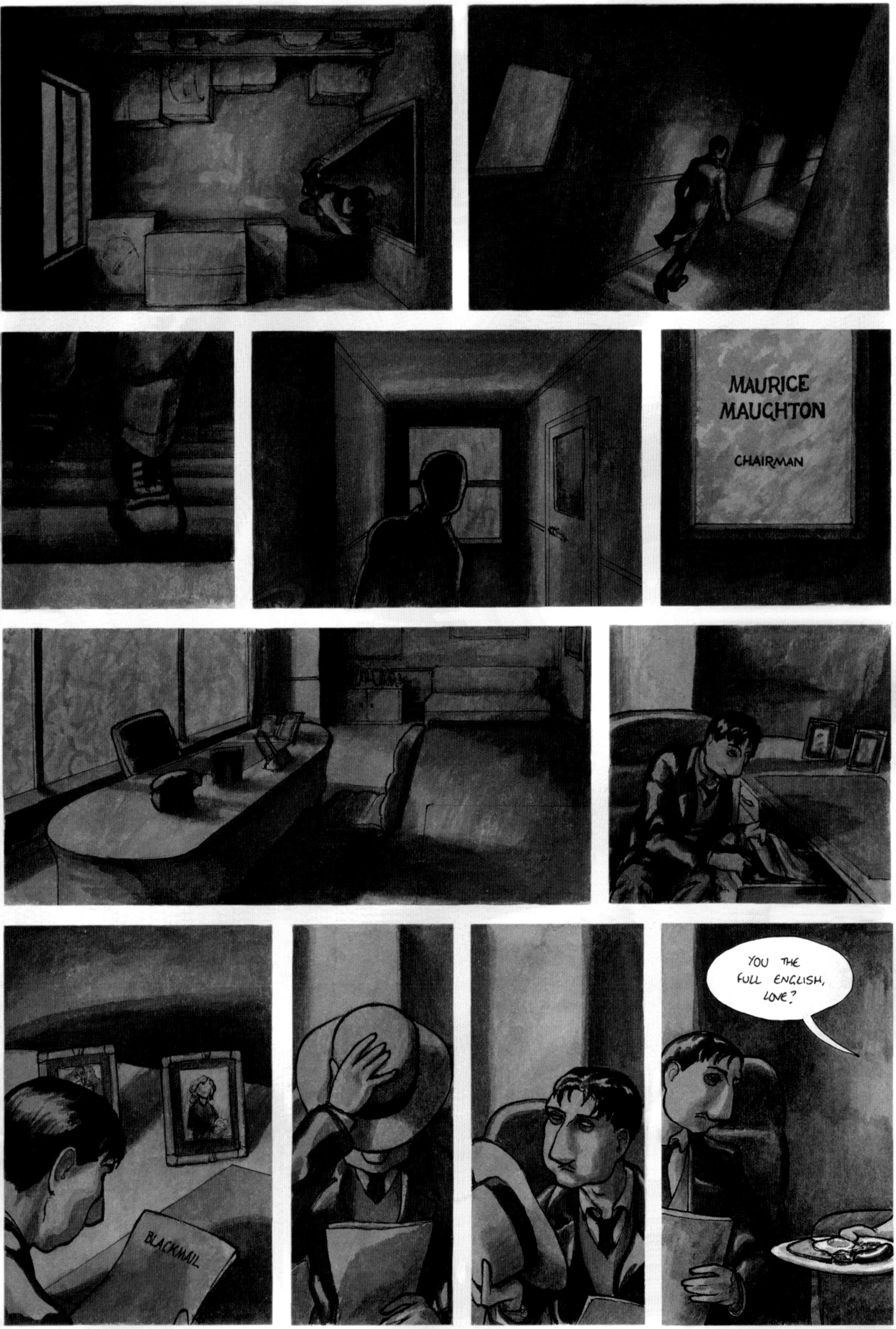
MAURICE
MAUGHTON
CHAIRMAN
BLACKMAIL
YOU THE
FULL ENGLISH,
LOVE?

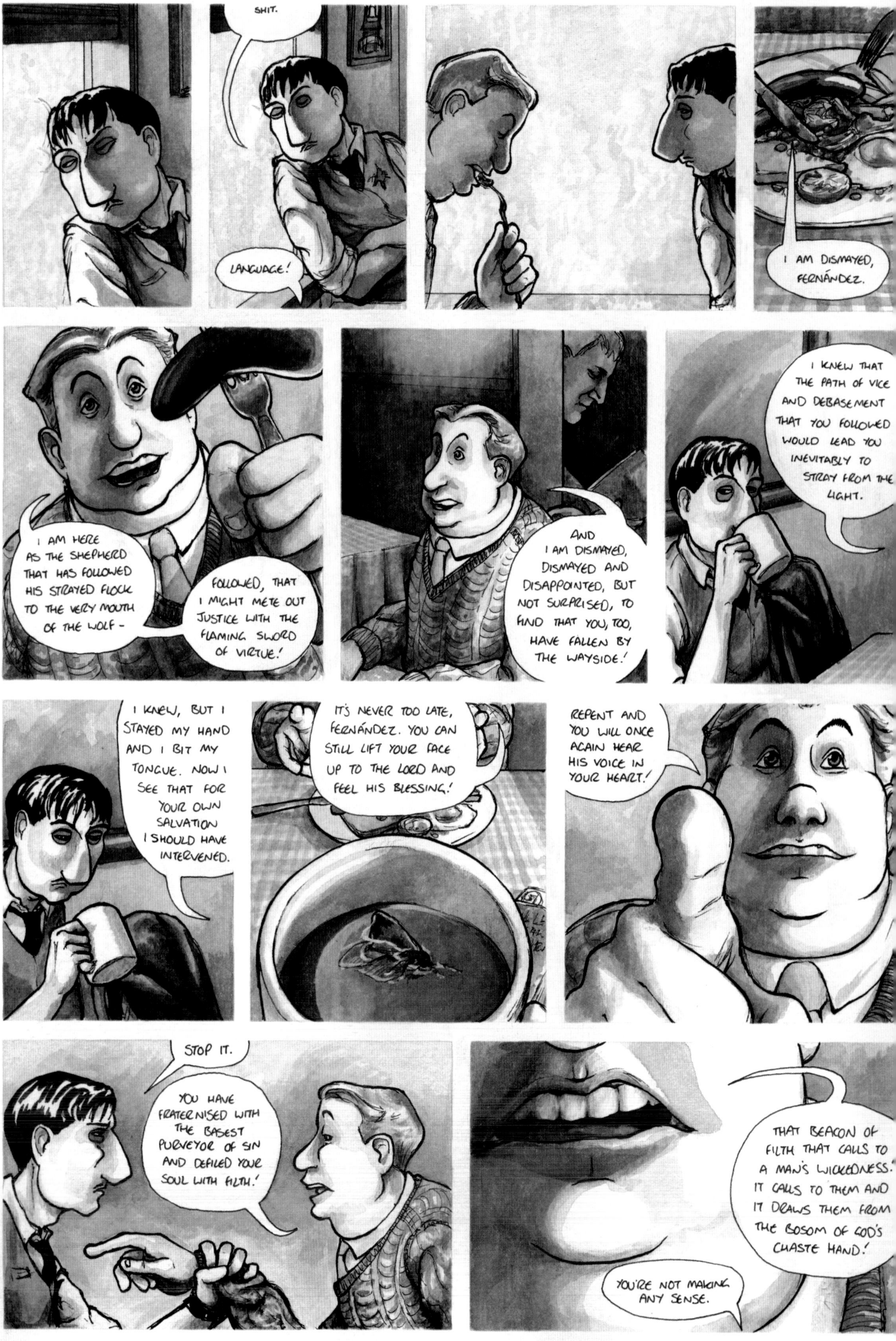
SHIT.
LANGUAGE!
I AM DISMAYED, FERNÁNDEZ.
I AM HERE AS THE SHEPHERD THAT HAS FOLLOWED HIS STRAYED FLOCK TO THE VERY MOUTH OF THE WOLF -
FOLLOWED, THAT I MIGHT METE OUT JUSTICE WITH THE FLAMING SWORD OF VIRTUE!
AND I AM DISMAYED, DISMAYED AND DISAPPOINTED, BUT NOT SURPRISED, TO FIND THAT YOU, TOO, HAVE FALLEN BY THE WAYSIDE!
I KNEW THAT THE PATH OF VICE AND DEBASEMENT THAT YOU FOLLOWED WOULD LEAD YOU INEVITABLY TO STRAY FROM THE LIGHT.
I KNEW, BUT I STAYED MY HAND AND I BIT MY TONGUE. NOW I SEE THAT FOR YOUR OWN SALVATION I SHOULD HAVE INTERVENED.
IT'S NEVER TOO LATE, FERNÁNDEZ. YOU CAN STILL LIFT YOUR FACE UP TO THE LORD AND FEEL HIS BLESSING!
REPENT AND YOU WILL ONCE AGAIN HEAR HIS VOICE IN YOUR HEART!
STOP IT.
YOU HAVE FRATERNISED WITH THE BASEST PURVEYOR OF SIN AND DEFILED YOUR SOUL WITH FILTH!
THAT BEACON OF FILTH THAT CALLS TO A MAN'S WICKEDNESS! IT CALLS TO THEM AND IT DRAWS THEM FROM THE BOSOM OF GOD'S CHASTE HAND!
YOU'RE NOT MAKING ANY SENSE.

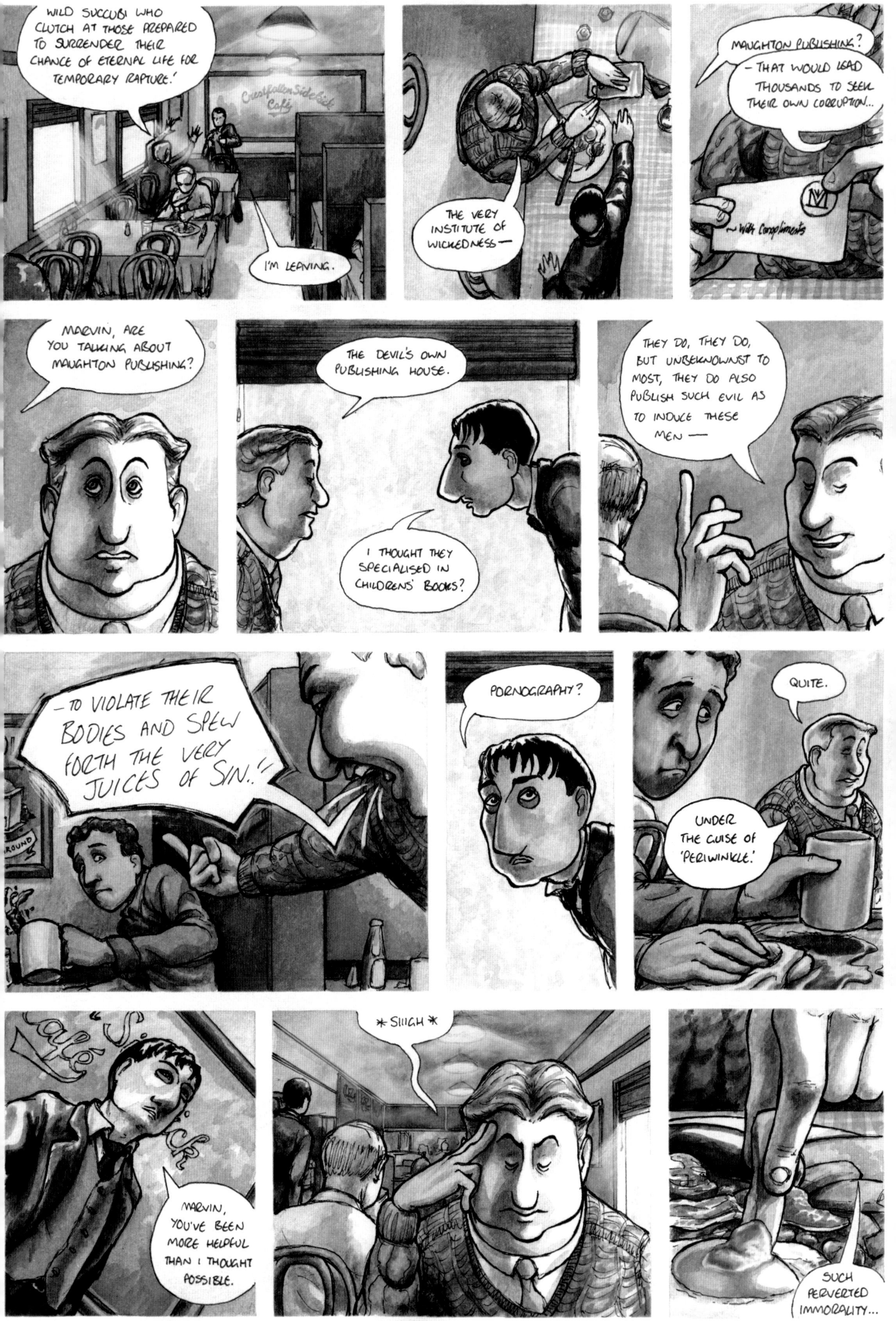
WILD SUCCUBI WHO CLUTCH AT THOSE PREPARED TO SURRENDER THEIR CHANCE OF ETERNAL LIFE FOR TEMPORARY RAPTURE.'
Crestfallen Sidekick Café
I'M LEAVING.
THE VERY INSTITUTE OF WICKEDNESS—
MAUGHTON PUBLISHING?
—THAT WOULD LEAD THOUSANDS TO SEEK THEIR OWN CORRUPTION...
~ With Compliments
MARVIN, ARE YOU TALKING ABOUT MAUGHTON PUBLISHING?
THE DEVIL'S OWN PUBLISHING HOUSE.
I THOUGHT THEY SPECIALISED IN CHILDRENS' BOOKS?
THEY DO, THEY DO, BUT UNBEKNOWNST TO MOST, THEY DO ALSO PUBLISH SUCH EVIL AS TO INDUCE THESE MEN—
—TO VIOLATE THEIR BODIES AND SPEW FORTH THE VERY JUICES OF SIN..!
PORNOGRAPHY?
QUITE.
UNDER THE GUISE OF 'PERIWINKLE.'
MARVIN, YOU'VE BEEN MORE HELPFUL THAN I THOUGHT POSSIBLE.
SIIIGH
SUCH PERVERTED IMMORALITY...

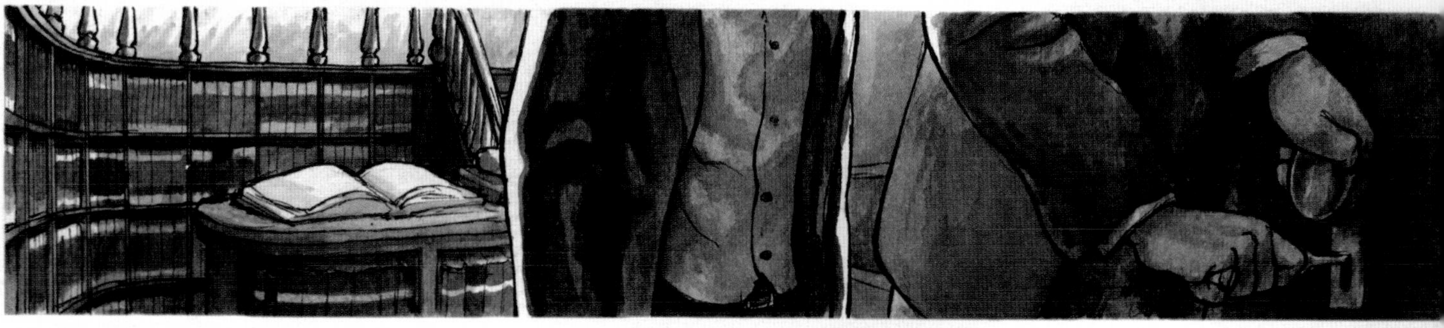

Some careful and discreet questions in some careful and discreet establishments eventually led to Maughton Publishing's other lines of publication.

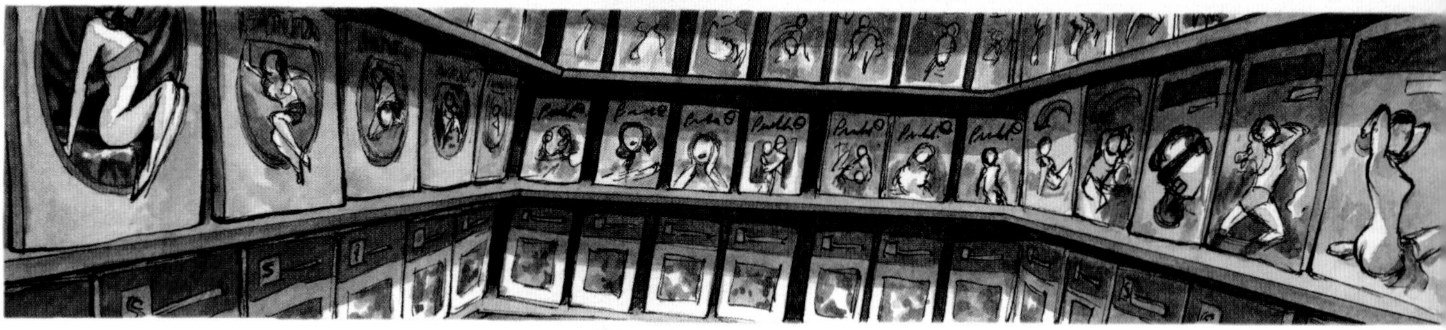

Lines that wouldn't sit well with their usual readership.

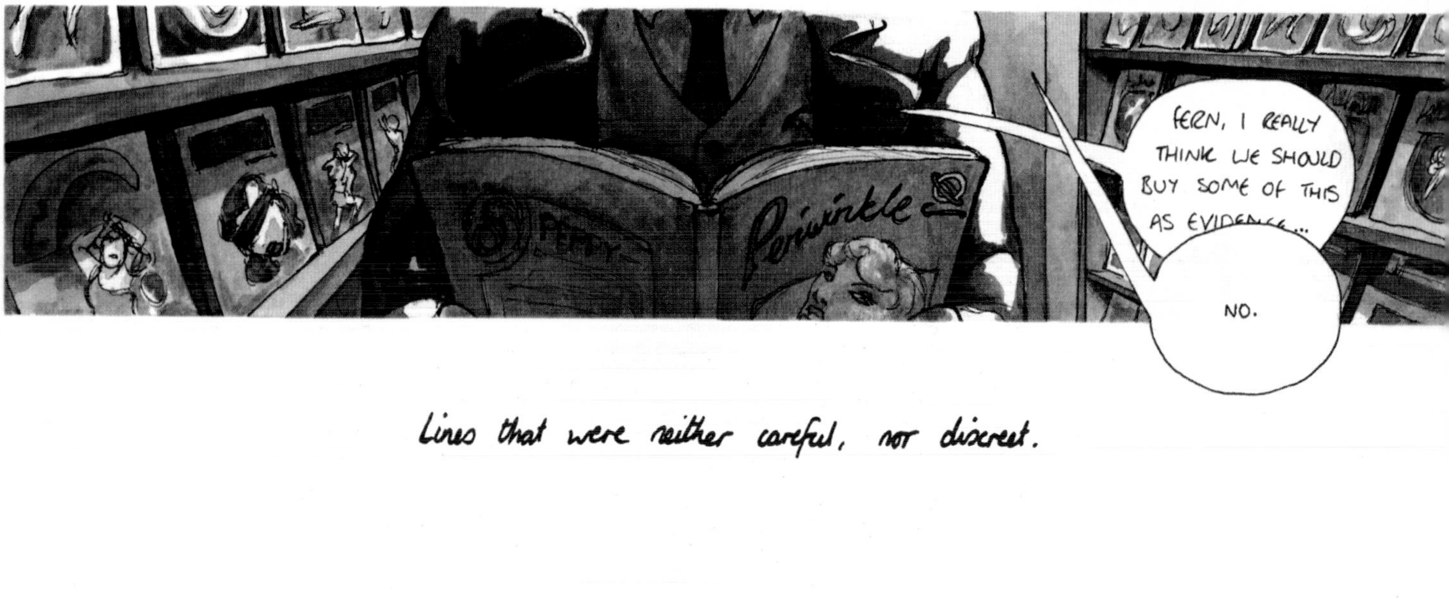
Periwinkle
FERN, I REALLY THINK WE SHOULD BUY SOME OF THIS AS EVID
NO.

Lines that were neither careful, nor discreet.

OBVIOUSLY NOBODY *WANTS* TO HEAR THAT THEIR FIANCÉ WAS KILLED BY A DISGRUNTLED EX-CO-WORKER WIELDING DETAILS OF THEIR FATHER'S DEALINGS WITH PORNOGRAPHY...

IT'S PROBABLY NOT WHAT SHE'S EXPECTING, BUT IT'S GOT TO BE A STEP UP FROM INEXPLICABLE SUICIDE, DON'T YOU THINK?

ON THE SCALE OF THINGS?

MM.

HA HA! AH— FILTHY MAURICE...

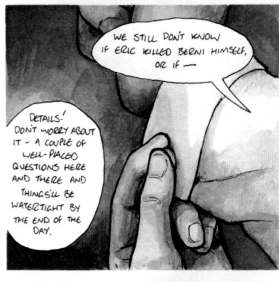

WE STILL DON'T KNOW IF ERIC KILLED BERNI HIMSELF, OR IF—

DETAILS! DON'T WORRY ABOUT IT - A COUPLE OF WELL-PLACED QUESTIONS HERE AND THERE AND THINGS'LL BE WATERTIGHT BY THE END OF THE DAY.

IT'LL BE A WALK IN THE PARK!

I SAY WE TIE UP A COUPLE OF LOOSE ENDS, MAKE OUR WAY TO CHARLOTTE MAUGHTON'S WITH THE NEWS, LET HER SMOTHER US IN GRATITUDE, THEN GET BACK IN TIME FOR THE EARLY EVENING SHOWING OF **'THE MARVELS OF VENUS'** STARRING SYLVETTA SWIFT

I KNOW WHAT YOU'RE THINKING AND HONESTLY I JUST ADMIRE HER FOR HER ACTING SKILLS.

STEWART, THIS HAS ALL SLOTTED INTO PLACE FAR TOO EASILY...

IF THERE'S ONE THING THAT CAN BE RELIED UPON IT'S THE CHAOTIC NATURE OF ALL THINGS...

OH PLEASE, *PLEASE* NOT THIS AGAIN.

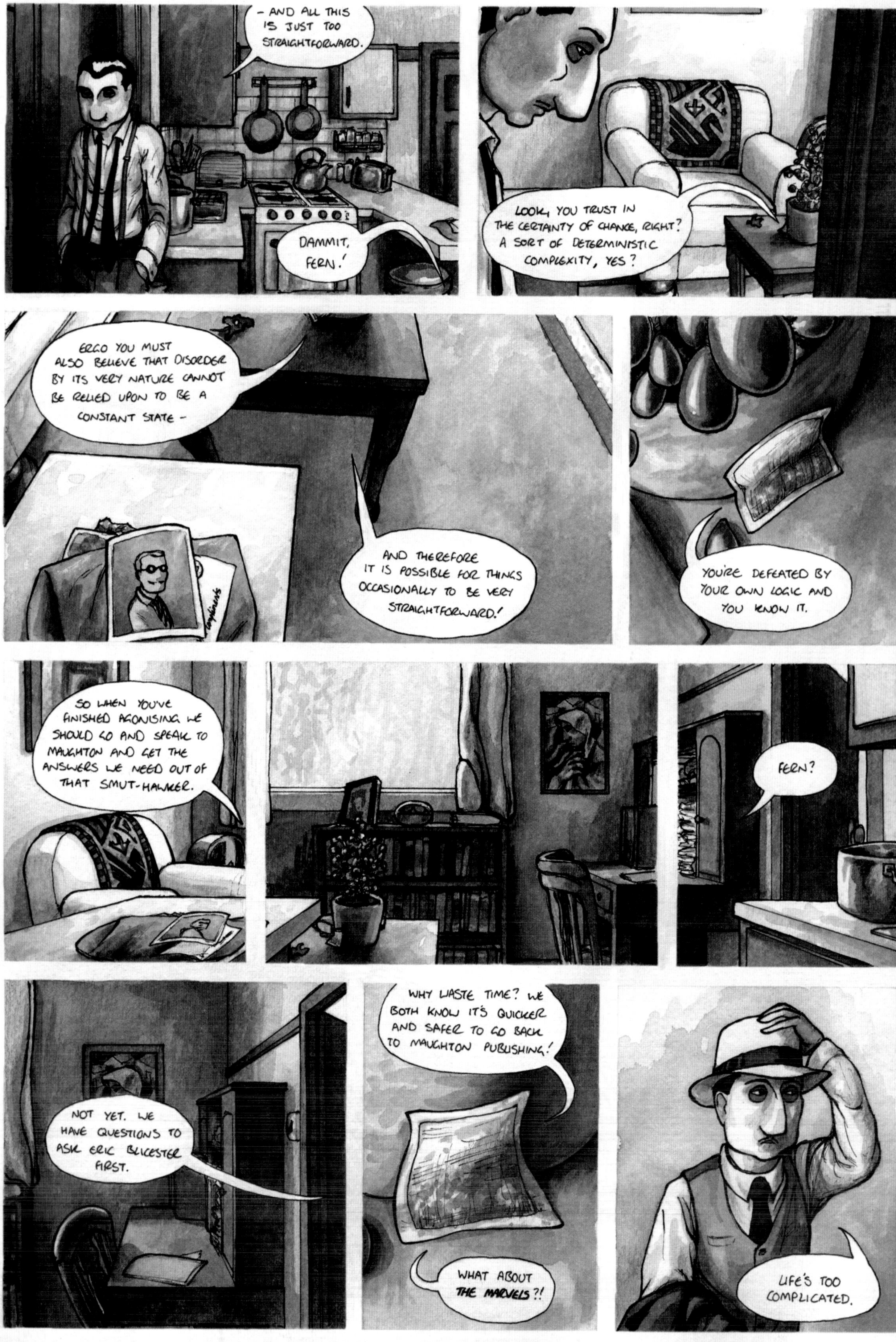
- AND ALL THIS IS JUST TOO STRAIGHTFORWARD.
DAMMIT, FERN!
LOOK, YOU TRUST IN THE CERTAINTY OF CHANCE, RIGHT? A SORT OF DETERMINISTIC COMPLEXITY, YES?
ERGO YOU MUST ALSO BELIEVE THAT DISORDER BY ITS VERY NATURE CANNOT BE RELIED UPON TO BE A CONSTANT STATE -
AND THEREFORE IT IS POSSIBLE FOR THINGS OCCASIONALLY TO BE VERY STRAIGHTFORWARD!
YOU'RE DEFEATED BY YOUR OWN LOGIC AND YOU KNOW IT.
SO WHEN YOU'VE FINISHED AGONISING WE SHOULD GO AND SPEAK TO MAUGHTON AND GET THE ANSWERS WE NEED OUT OF THAT SMUT-HAWKER.
FERN?
NOT YET. WE HAVE QUESTIONS TO ASK ERIC BLICESTER FIRST.
WHY WASTE TIME? WE BOTH KNOW IT'S QUICKER AND SAFER TO GO BACK TO MAUGHTON PUBLISHING!
WHAT ABOUT THE MARVELS?!
LIFE'S TOO COMPLICATED.

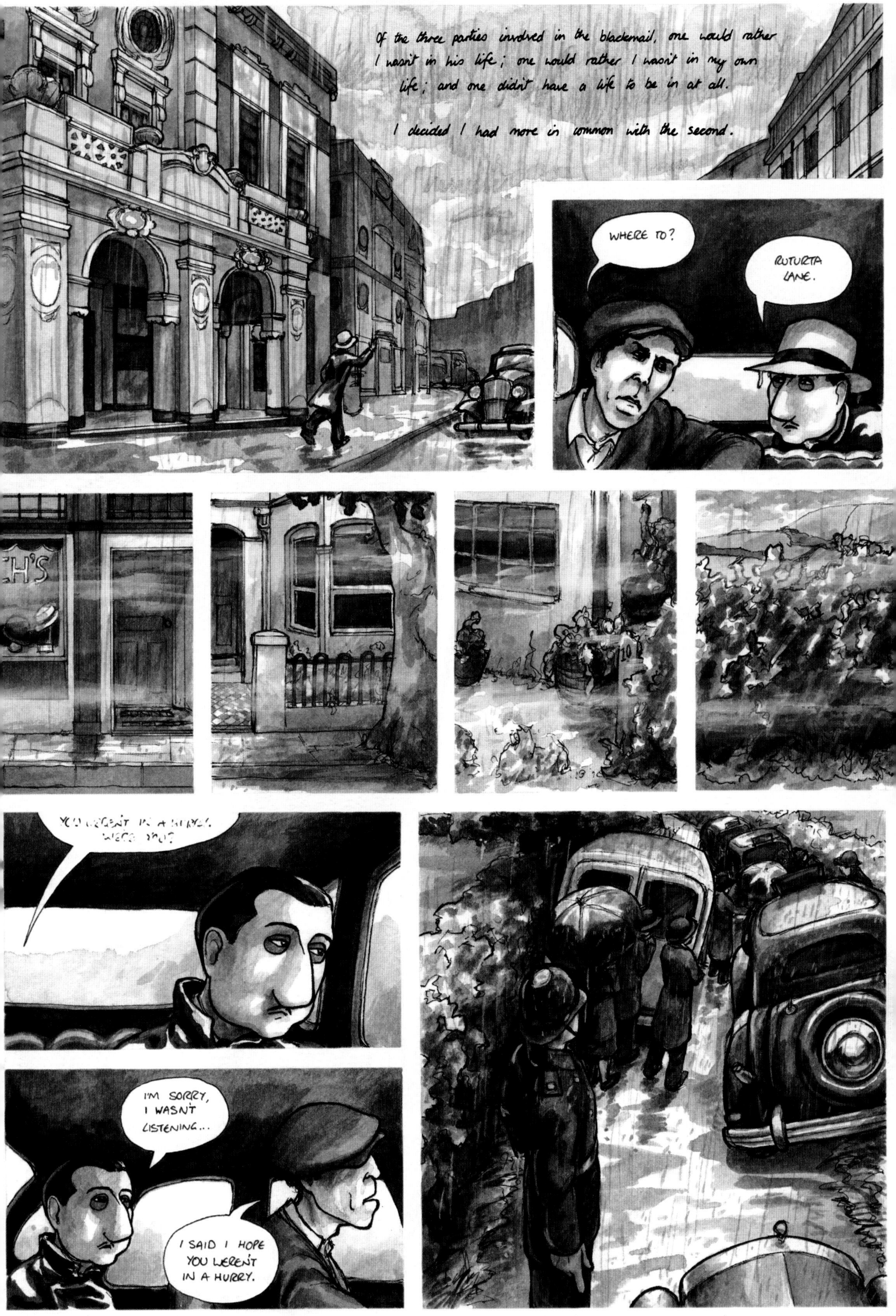
Of the three parties involved in the blackmail, one would rather I wasn't in his life; one would rather I wasn't in my own life; and one didn't have a life to be in at all.
I decided I had more in common with the second.
WHERE TO?
RUTURTA LANE.
YOU WEREN'T IN A HURRY, WERE YOU?
I'M SORRY, I WASN'T LISTENING...
I SAID I HOPE YOU WEREN'T IN A HURRY.

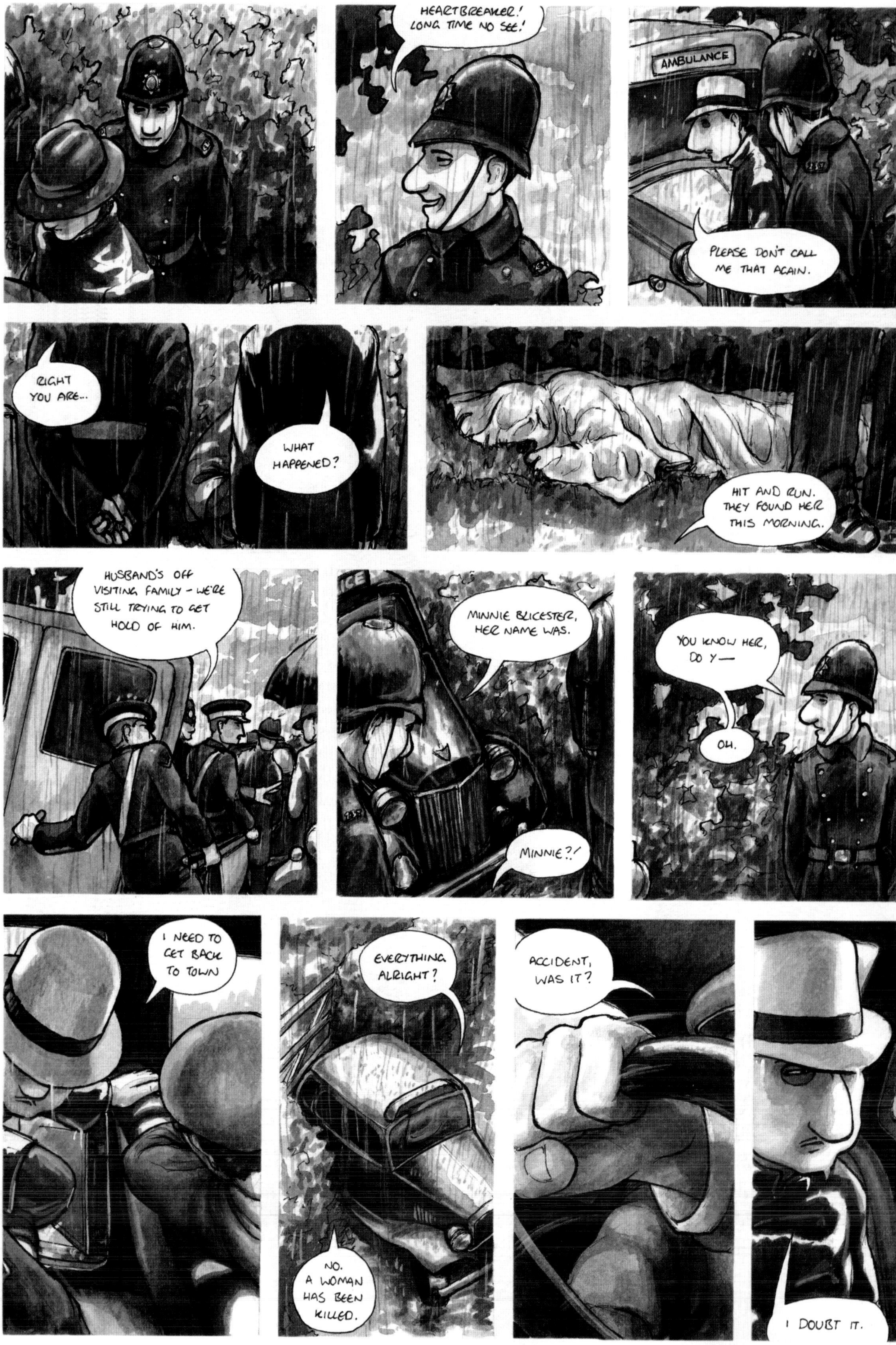
HEARTBREAKER! LONG TIME NO SEE!
AMBULANCE
PLEASE DON'T CALL ME THAT AGAIN.
RIGHT YOU ARE...
WHAT HAPPENED?
HIT AND RUN. THEY FOUND HER THIS MORNING.
HUSBAND'S OFF VISITING FAMILY - WE'RE STILL TRYING TO GET HOLD OF HIM.
MINNIE BLICESTER, HER NAME WAS.
MINNIE?!
YOU KNOW HER, DO Y—
OH.
I NEED TO GET BACK TO TOWN
EVERYTHING ALRIGHT?
NO. A WOMAN HAS BEEN KILLED.
ACCIDENT, WAS IT?
I DOUBT IT.

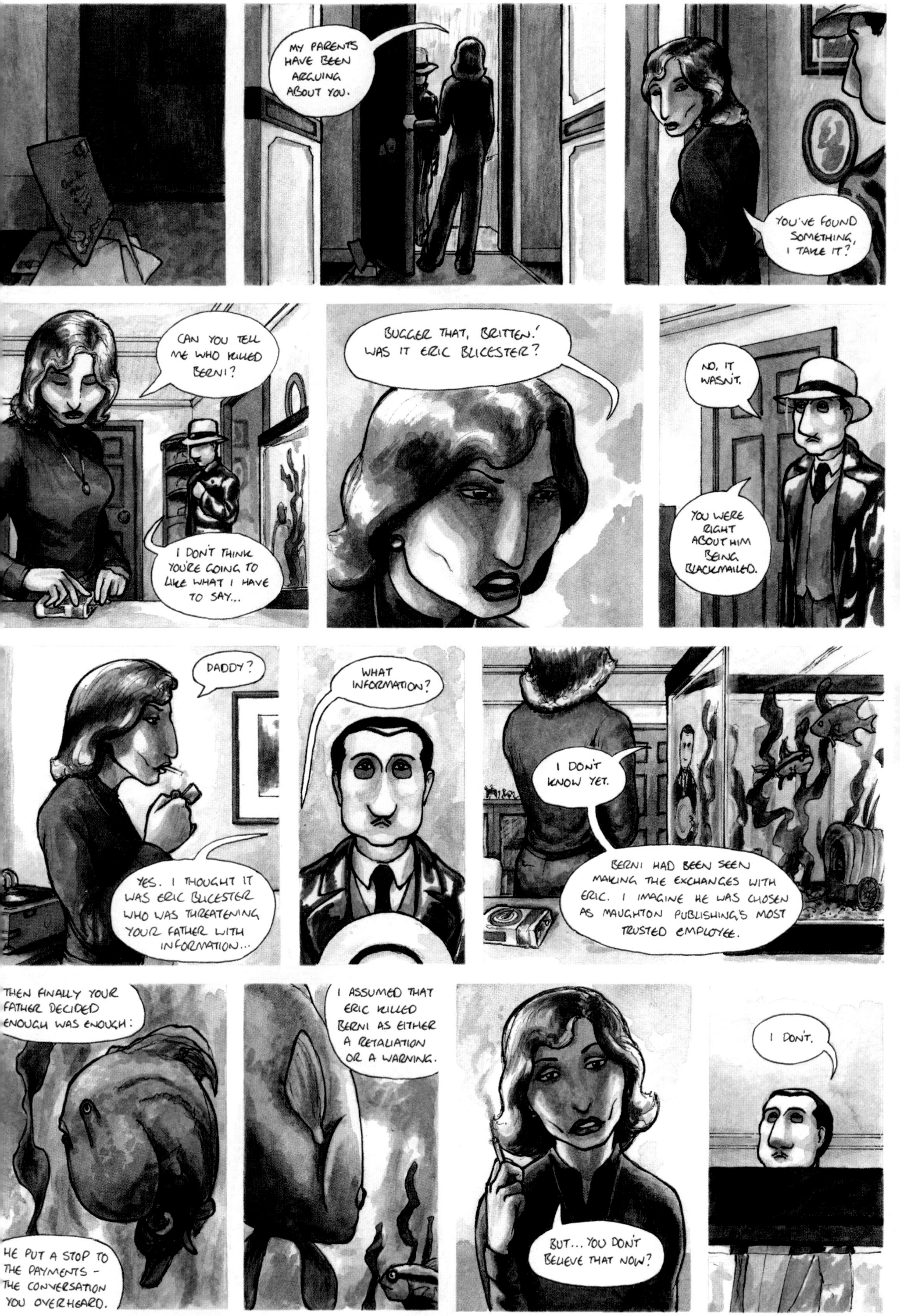
MY PARENTS HAVE BEEN ARGUING ABOUT YOU.
YOU'VE FOUND SOMETHING, I TAKE IT?
CAN YOU TELL ME WHO KILLED BERNI?
I DON'T THINK YOU'RE GOING TO LIKE WHAT I HAVE TO SAY...
BUGGER THAT, BRITTEN! WAS IT ERIC BLICESTER?
NO, IT WASN'T.
YOU WERE RIGHT ABOUT HIM BEING BLACKMAILED.
DADDY?
YES. I THOUGHT IT WAS ERIC BLICESTER WHO WAS THREATENING YOUR FATHER WITH INFORMATION...
WHAT INFORMATION?
I DON'T KNOW YET.
BERNI HAD BEEN SEEN MAKING THE EXCHANGES WITH ERIC. I IMAGINE HE WAS CHOSEN AS MAUGHTON PUBLISHING'S MOST TRUSTED EMPLOYEE.
THEN FINALLY YOUR FATHER DECIDED ENOUGH WAS ENOUGH:
HE PUT A STOP TO THE PAYMENTS - THE CONVERSATION YOU OVERHEARD.
I ASSUMED THAT ERIC KILLED BERNI AS EITHER A RETALIATION OR A WARNING.
BUT... YOU DON'T BELIEVE THAT NOW?
I DON'T.

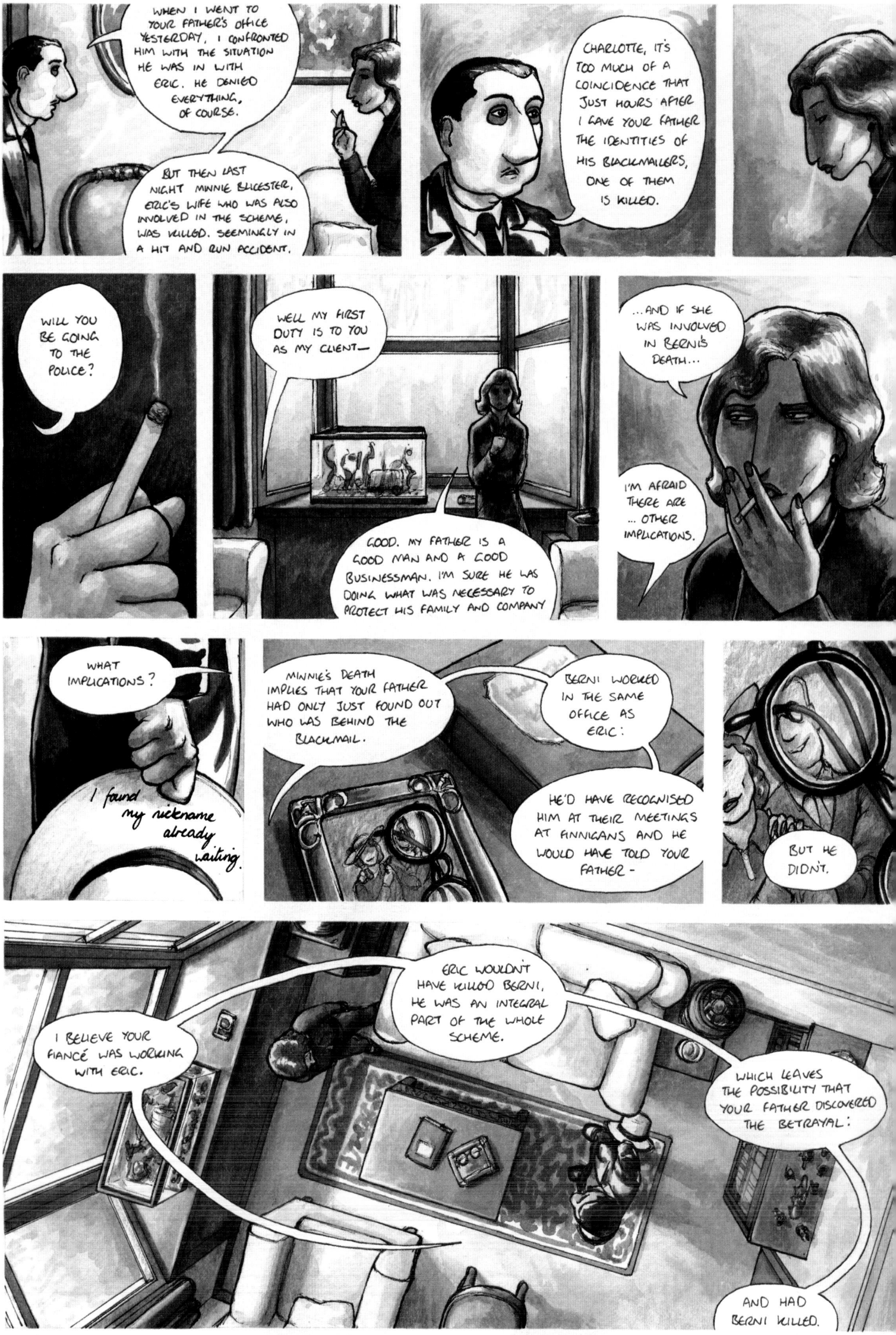
WHEN I WENT TO YOUR FATHER'S OFFICE YESTERDAY, I CONFRONTED HIM WITH THE SITUATION HE WAS IN WITH ERIC. HE DENIED EVERYTHING, OF COURSE.
BUT THEN LAST NIGHT MINNIE BLICESTER, ERIC'S WIFE WHO WAS ALSO INVOLVED IN THE SCHEME, WAS KILLED. SEEMINGLY IN A HIT AND RUN ACCIDENT.
CHARLOTTE, IT'S TOO MUCH OF A COINCIDENCE THAT JUST HOURS AFTER I GAVE YOUR FATHER THE IDENTITIES OF HIS BLACKMAILERS, ONE OF THEM IS KILLED.
WILL YOU BE GOING TO THE POLICE?
WELL MY FIRST DUTY IS TO YOU AS MY CLIENT—
GOOD. MY FATHER IS A GOOD MAN AND A GOOD BUSINESSMAN. I'M SURE HE WAS DOING WHAT WAS NECESSARY TO PROTECT HIS FAMILY AND COMPANY
...AND IF SHE WAS INVOLVED IN BERNI'S DEATH...
I'M AFRAID THERE ARE ... OTHER IMPLICATIONS.
WHAT IMPLICATIONS?
I found my nickname already waiting.
MINNIE'S DEATH IMPLIES THAT YOUR FATHER HAD ONLY JUST FOUND OUT WHO WAS BEHIND THE BLACKMAIL.
BERNI WORKED IN THE SAME OFFICE AS ERIC:
HE'D HAVE RECOGNISED HIM AT THEIR MEETINGS AT FINNIGANS AND HE WOULD HAVE TOLD YOUR FATHER -
BUT HE DIDN'T.
I BELIEVE YOUR FIANCÉ WAS WORKING WITH ERIC.
ERIC WOULDN'T HAVE KILLED BERNI, HE WAS AN INTEGRAL PART OF THE WHOLE SCHEME.
WHICH LEAVES THE POSSIBILITY THAT YOUR FATHER DISCOVERED THE BETRAYAL:
AND HAD BERNI KILLED.

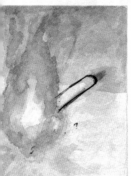

GET OUT.

I'M SORRY...

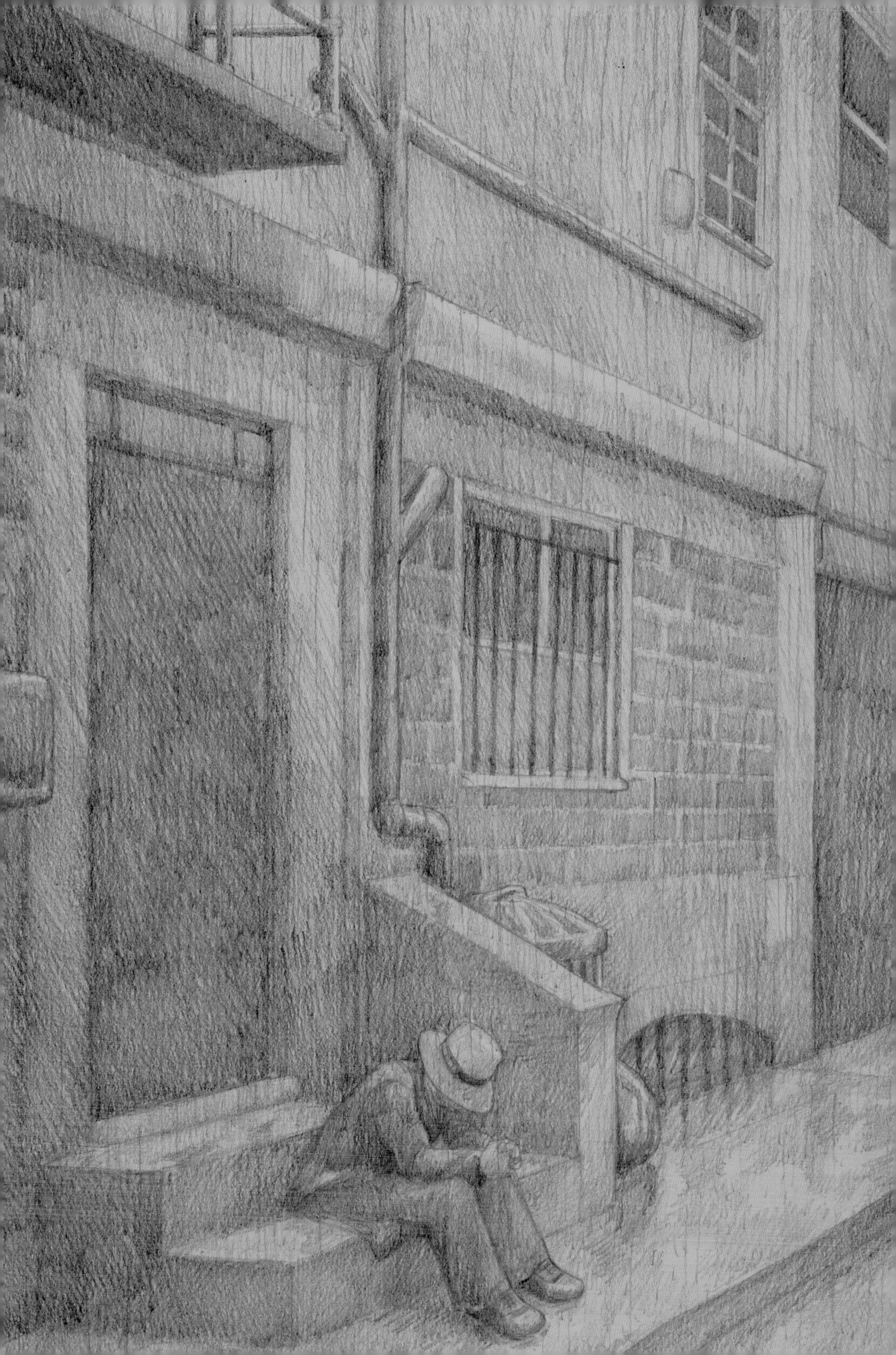

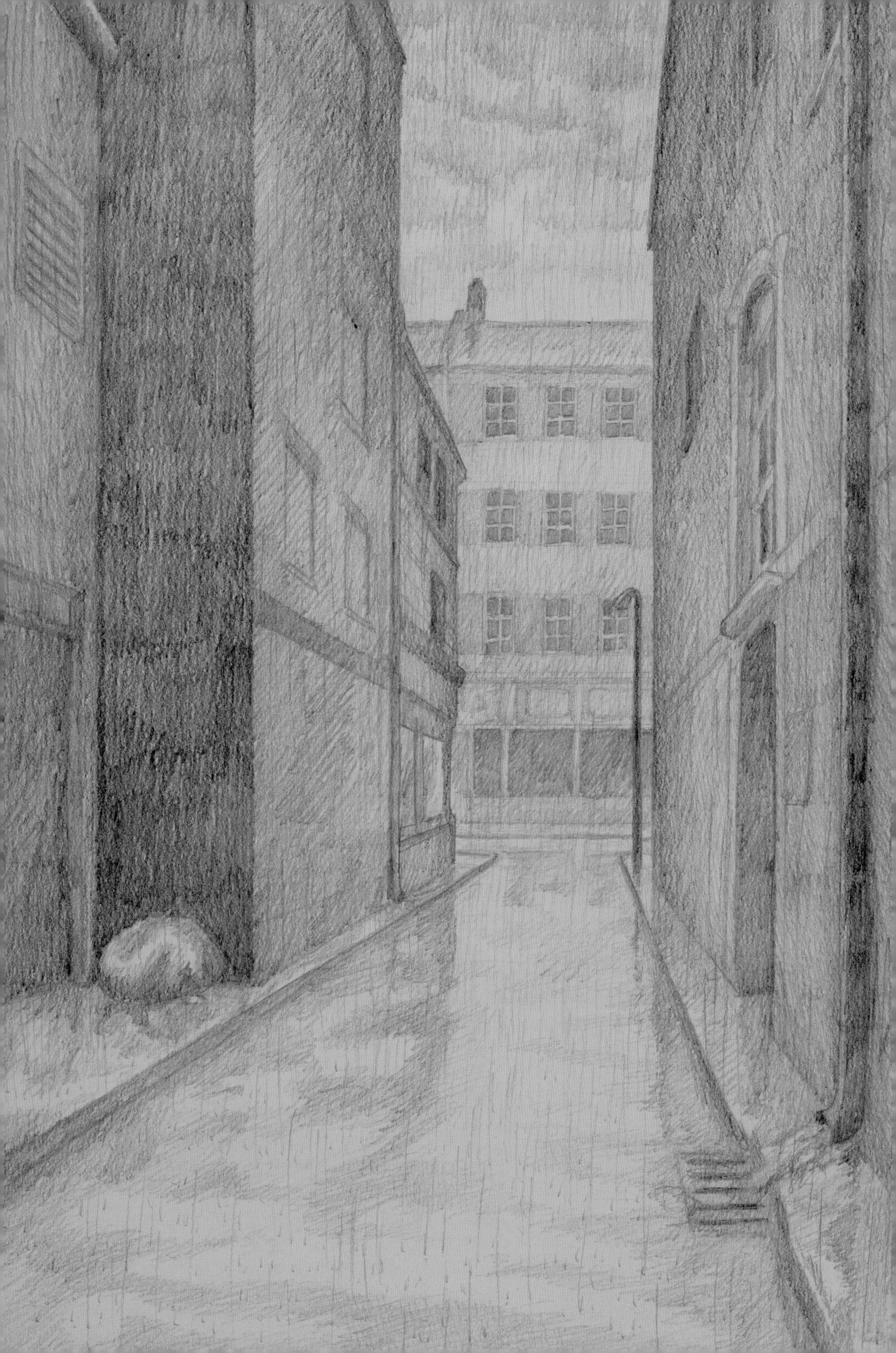

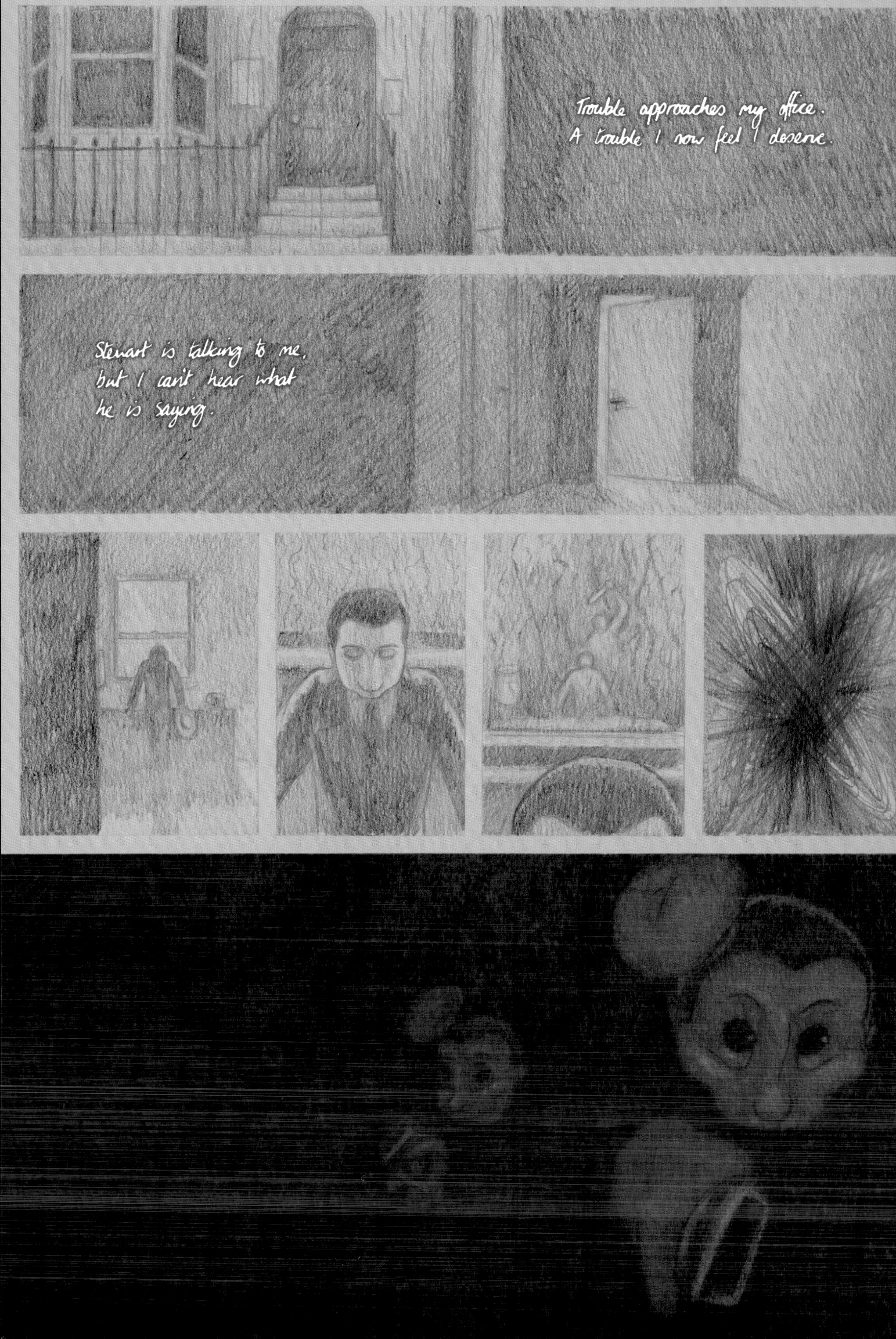
Trouble approaches my office.
A trouble I now feel I deserve.
Stewart is talking to me,
but I can't hear what
he is saying.

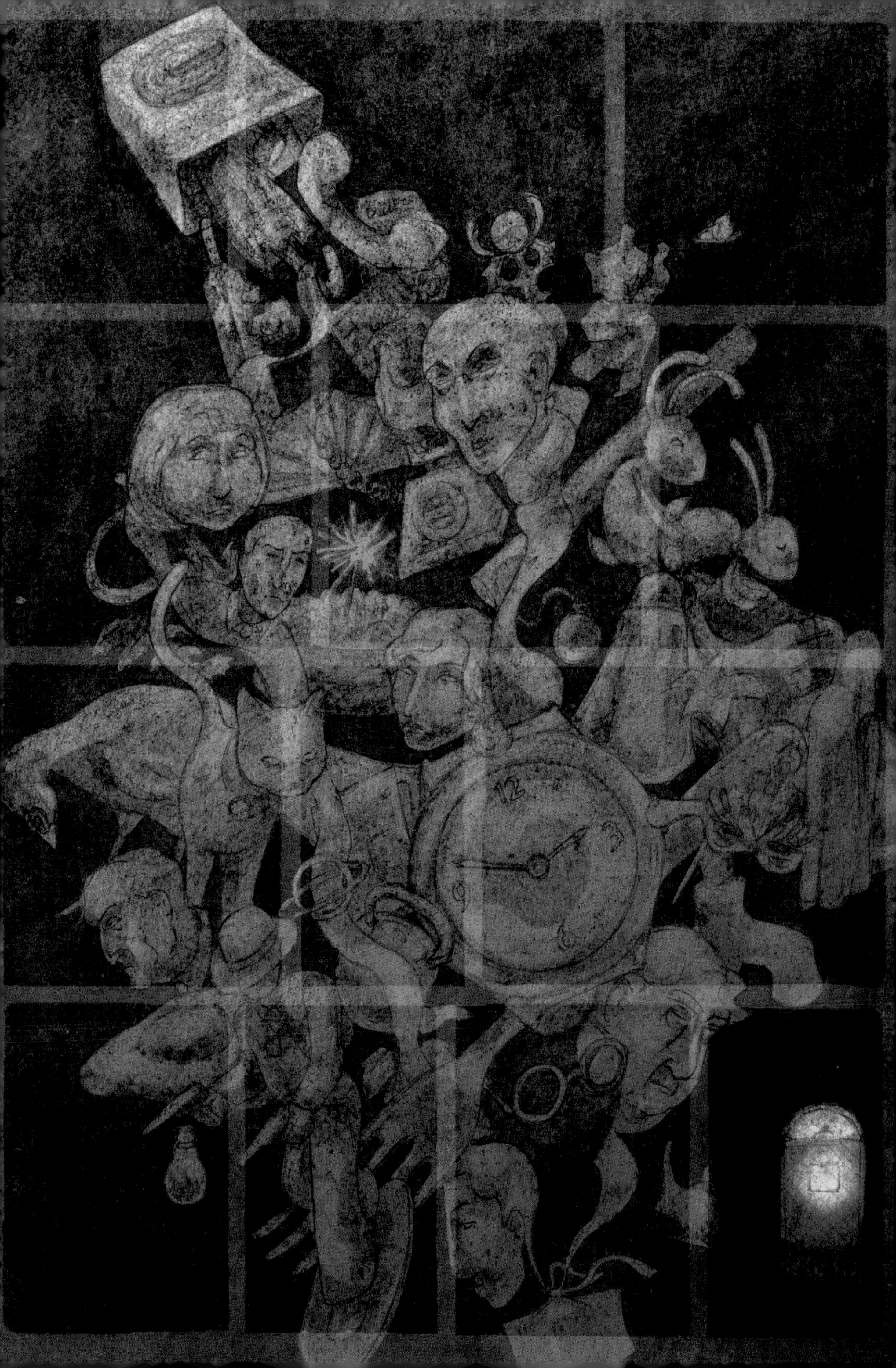

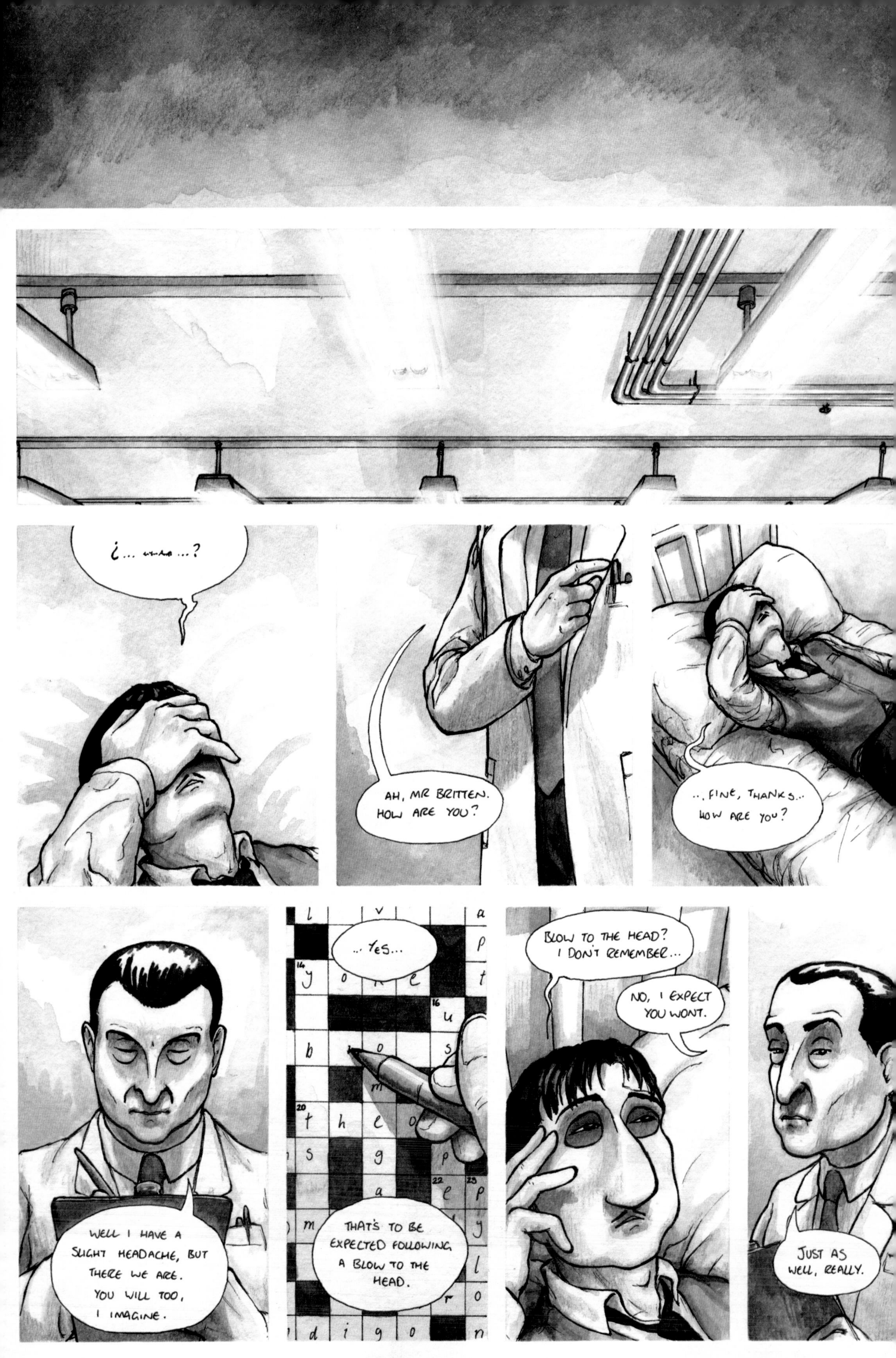
¿... ...?
AH, MR BRITTEN. HOW ARE YOU?
... FINE, THANKS... HOW ARE YOU?
WELL I HAVE A SLIGHT HEADACHE, BUT THERE WE ARE. YOU WILL TOO, I IMAGINE.
... YES...
THAT'S TO BE EXPECTED FOLLOWING A BLOW TO THE HEAD.
BLOW TO THE HEAD? I DON'T REMEMBER...
NO, I EXPECT YOU WONT.
JUST AS WELL, REALLY.

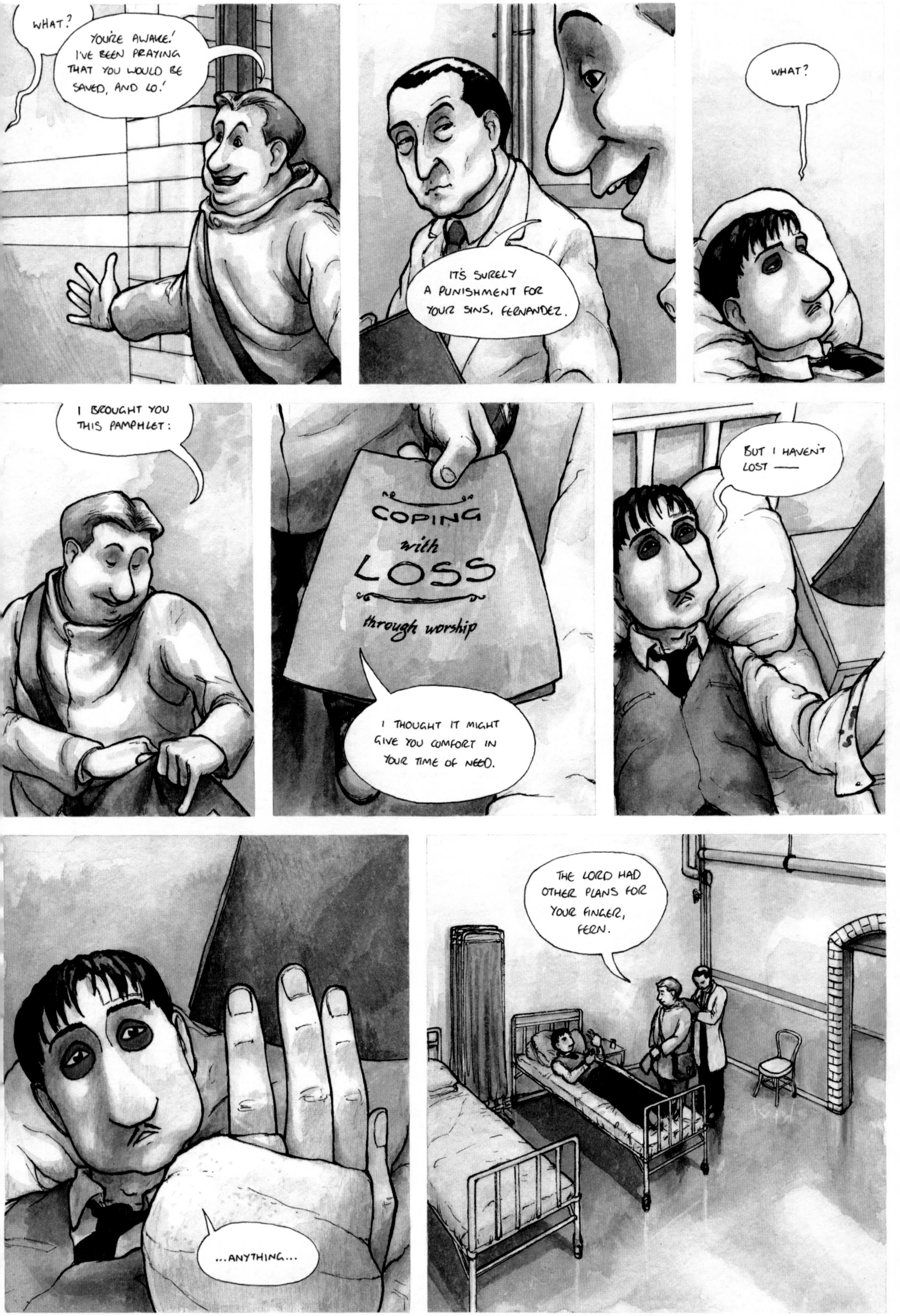
WHAT?
YOU'RE AWAKE! I'VE BEEN PRAYING THAT YOU WOULD BE SAVED, AND LO!
IT'S SURELY A PUNISHMENT FOR YOUR SINS, FERNANDEZ.
WHAT?
I BROUGHT YOU THIS PAMPHLET:
COPING with LOSS through worship
I THOUGHT IT MIGHT GIVE YOU COMFORT IN YOUR TIME OF NEED.
BUT I HAVEN'T LOST —
...ANYTHING...
THE LORD HAD OTHER PLANS FOR YOUR FINGER, FERN.

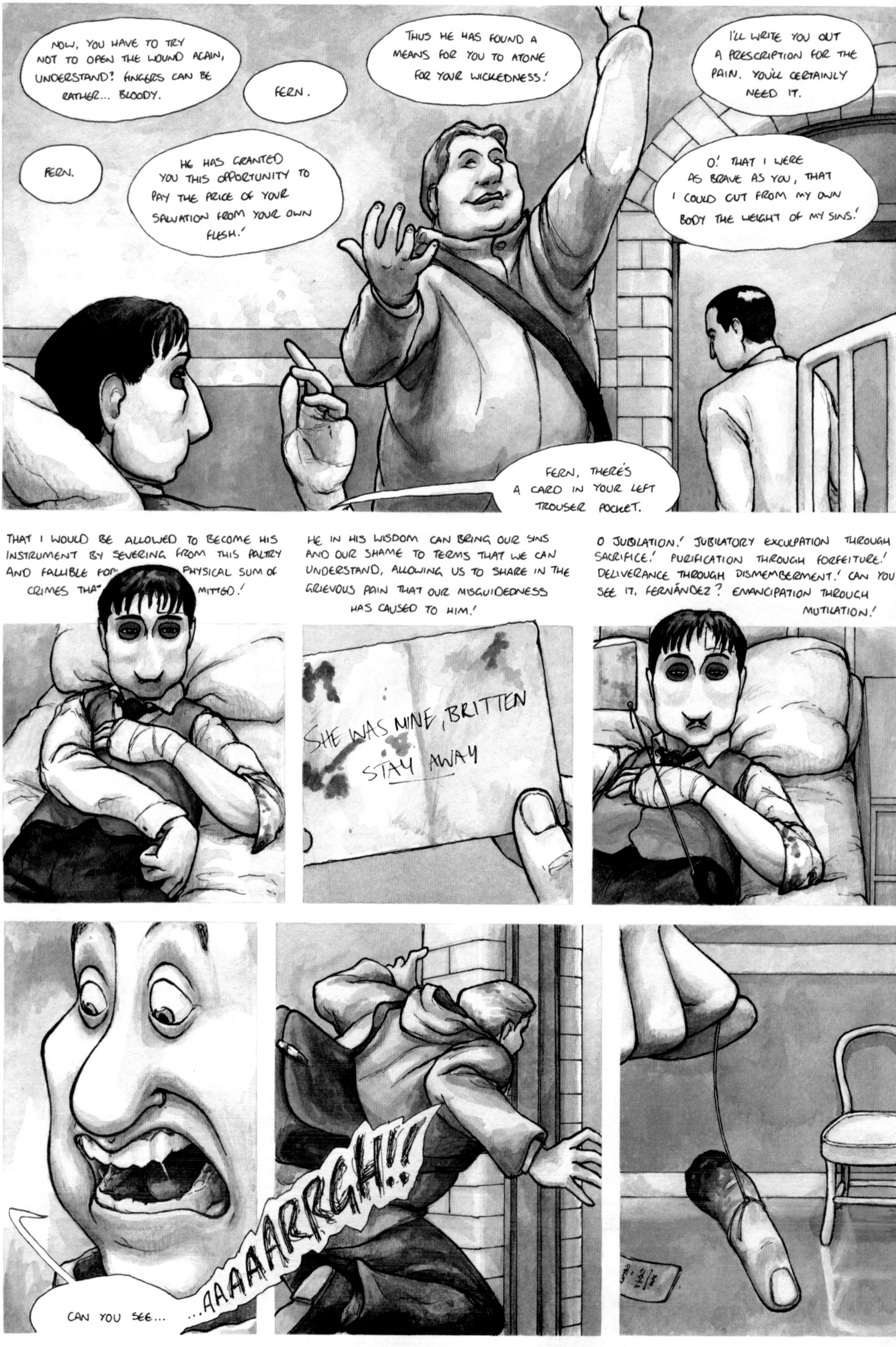
NOW, YOU HAVE TO TRY NOT TO OPEN THE WOUND AGAIN, UNDERSTAND? FINGERS CAN BE RATHER... BLOODY.
FERN.
THUS HE HAS FOUND A MEANS FOR YOU TO ATONE FOR YOUR WICKEDNESS!
I'LL WRITE YOU OUT A PRESCRIPTION FOR THE PAIN. YOU'LL CERTAINLY NEED IT.
FERN.
HE HAS GRANTED YOU THIS OPPORTUNITY TO PAY THE PRICE OF YOUR SALVATION FROM YOUR OWN FLESH!
O! THAT I WERE AS BRAVE AS YOU, THAT I COULD CUT FROM MY OWN BODY THE WEIGHT OF MY SINS!
FERN, THERE'S A CARD IN YOUR LEFT TROUSER POCKET.
THAT I WOULD BE ALLOWED TO BECOME HIS INSTRUMENT BY SEVERING FROM THIS PALTRY AND FALLIBLE FOR PHYSICAL SUM OF CRIMES THA MITTED!
HE IN HIS WISDOM CAN BRING OUR SINS AND OUR SHAME TO TERMS THAT WE CAN UNDERSTAND, ALLOWING US TO SHARE IN THE GRIEVOUS PAIN THAT OUR MISGUIDEDNESS HAS CAUSED TO HIM!
O JUBILATION! JUBILATORY EXCULPATION THROUGH SACRIFICE! PURIFICATION THROUGH FORFEITURE! DELIVERANCE THROUGH DISMEMBERMENT! CAN YOU SEE IT, FERNÁNDEZ? EMANCIPATION THROUGH MUTILATION!
SHE WAS MINE, BRITTEN
STAY AWAY
CAN YOU SEE...
...AAAAARRGH!!

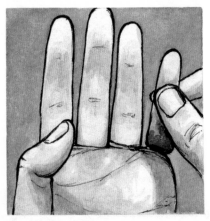

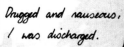
Drugged and nauseous, I was discharged.

The lingering ache, a dull requiem for my chances of ever becoming a concert pianist.

I didn't know who had taken it upon themselves to mutilate me, but I suspected the recently bereaved Eric Bicester.

He needn't have worried about my further involvement, though:

His act was a bloody punctuation mark at the end of a regrettable career.

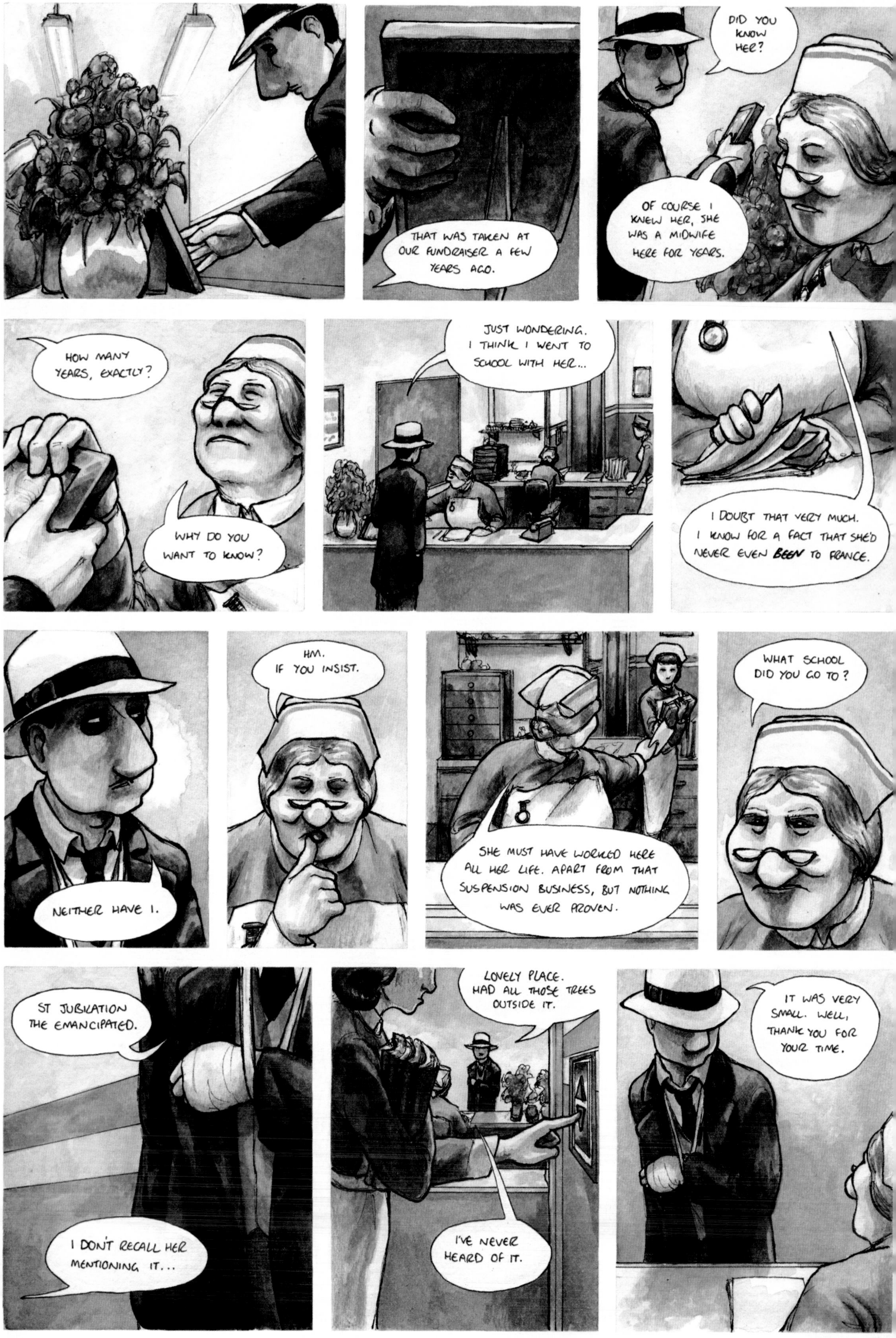
THAT WAS TAKEN AT OUR FUNDRAISER A FEW YEARS AGO.
DID YOU KNOW HER?
OF COURSE I KNEW HER, SHE WAS A MIDWIFE HERE FOR YEARS.
HOW MANY YEARS, EXACTLY?
WHY DO YOU WANT TO KNOW?
JUST WONDERING. I THINK I WENT TO SCHOOL WITH HER...
I DOUBT THAT VERY MUCH. I KNOW FOR A FACT THAT SHE'D NEVER EVEN BEEN TO FRANCE.
NEITHER HAVE I.
HM. IF YOU INSIST.
SHE MUST HAVE WORKED HERE ALL HER LIFE. APART FROM THAT SUSPENSION BUSINESS, BUT NOTHING WAS EVER PROVEN.
WHAT SCHOOL DID YOU GO TO?
ST JUBILATION THE EMANCIPATED.
I DON'T RECALL HER MENTIONING IT...
LOVELY PLACE. HAD ALL THOSE TREES OUTSIDE IT.
I'VE NEVER HEARD OF IT.
IT WAS VERY SMALL. WELL, THANK YOU FOR YOUR TIME.

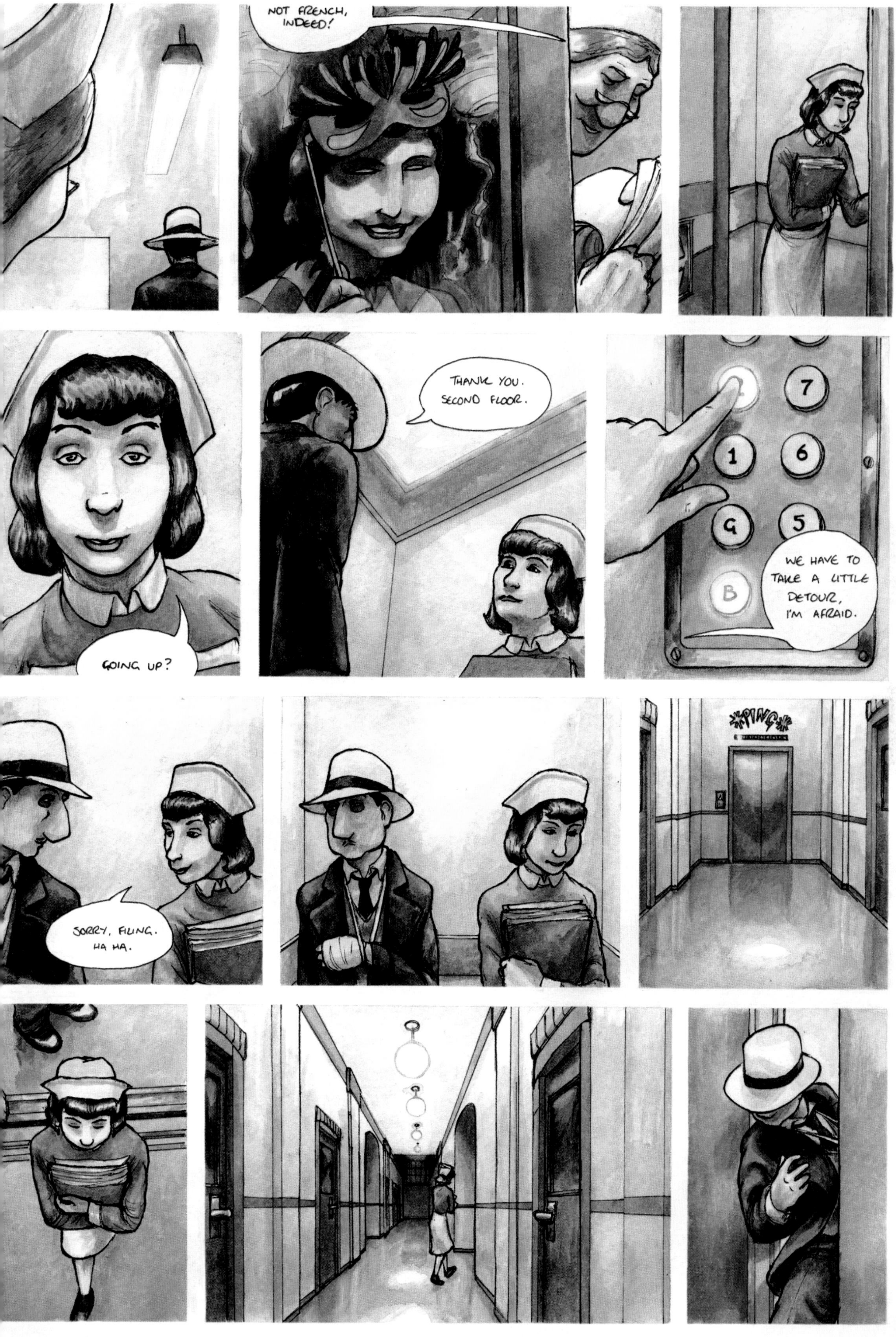
NOT FRENCH, INDEED!
GOING UP?
THANK YOU. SECOND FLOOR.
7
1
6
G
5
B
WE HAVE TO TAKE A LITTLE DETOUR, I'M AFRAID.
SORRY, FILLING. HA HA.
PING

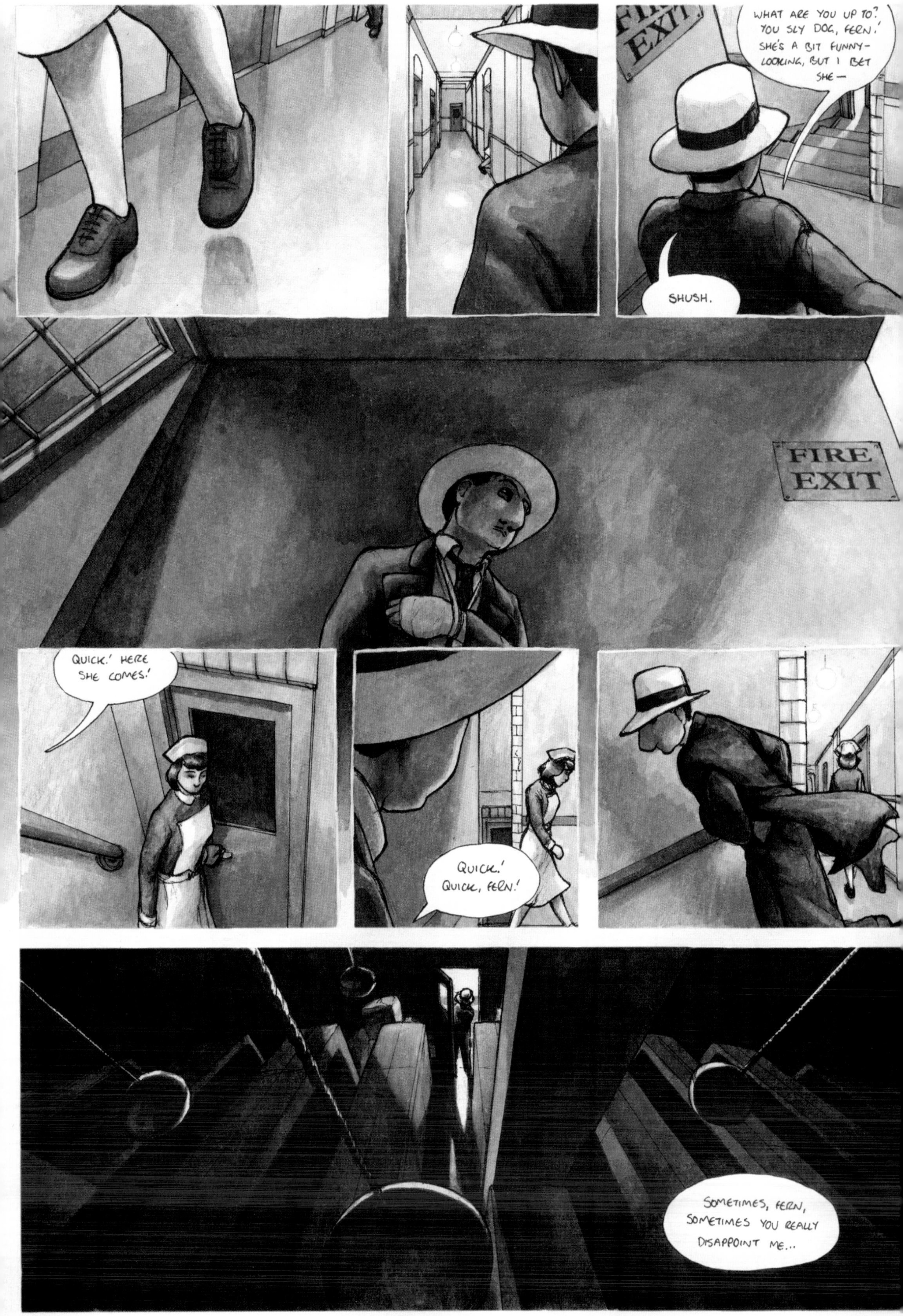

FIRE EXIT
WHAT ARE YOU UP TO? YOU SLY DOG, FERN! SHE'S A BIT FUNNY-LOOKING, BUT I BET SHE—
SHUSH.
FIRE EXIT
QUICK! HERE SHE COMES!
QUICK! QUICK, FERN!
SOMETIMES, FERN, SOMETIMES YOU REALLY DISAPPOINT ME...

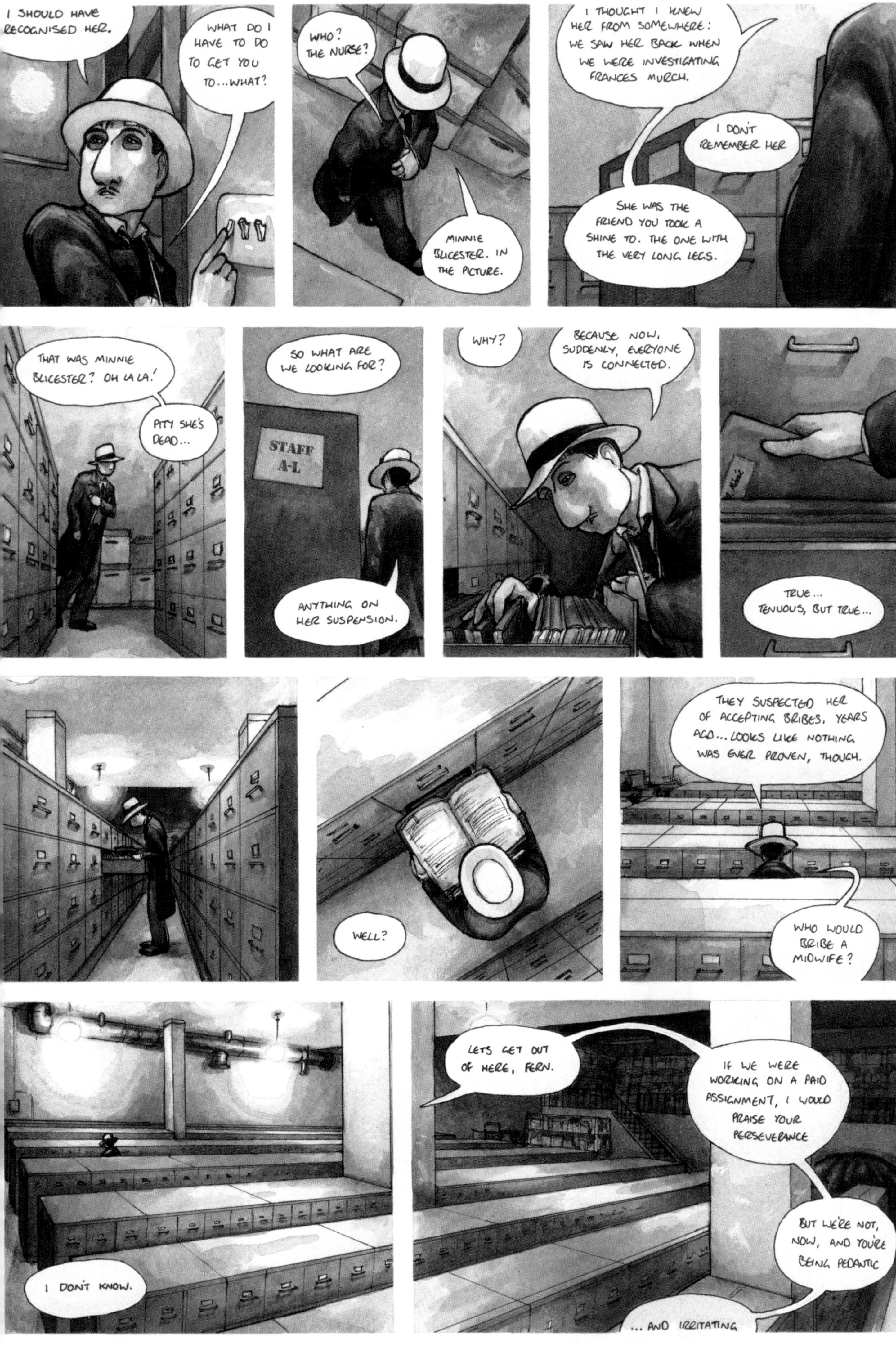
I SHOULD HAVE RECOGNISED HER.
WHAT DO I HAVE TO DO TO GET YOU TO...WHAT?
WHO? THE NURSE?
MINNIE BLICESTER. IN THE PICTURE.
I THOUGHT I KNEW HER FROM SOMEWHERE: WE SAW HER BACK WHEN WE WERE INVESTIGATING FRANCES MURCH.
I DON'T REMEMBER HER
SHE WAS THE FRIEND YOU TOOK A SHINE TO. THE ONE WITH THE VERY LONG LEGS.
THAT WAS MINNIE BLICESTER? OH LA LA!
PITY SHE'S DEAD...
SO WHAT ARE WE LOOKING FOR?
STAFF A-L
ANYTHING ON HER SUSPENSION.
WHY?
BECAUSE NOW, SUDDENLY, EVERYONE IS CONNECTED.
TRUE... TENUOUS, BUT TRUE...
WELL?
THEY SUSPECTED HER OF ACCEPTING BRIBES, YEARS AGO... LOOKS LIKE NOTHING WAS EVER PROVEN, THOUGH.
WHO WOULD BRIBE A MIDWIFE?
I DON'T KNOW.
LETS GET OUT OF HERE, FERN.
IF WE WERE WORKING ON A PAID ASSIGNMENT, I WOULD PRAISE YOUR PERSEVERANCE
BUT WE'RE NOT, NOW, AND YOU'RE BEING PEDANTIC
...AND IRRITATING

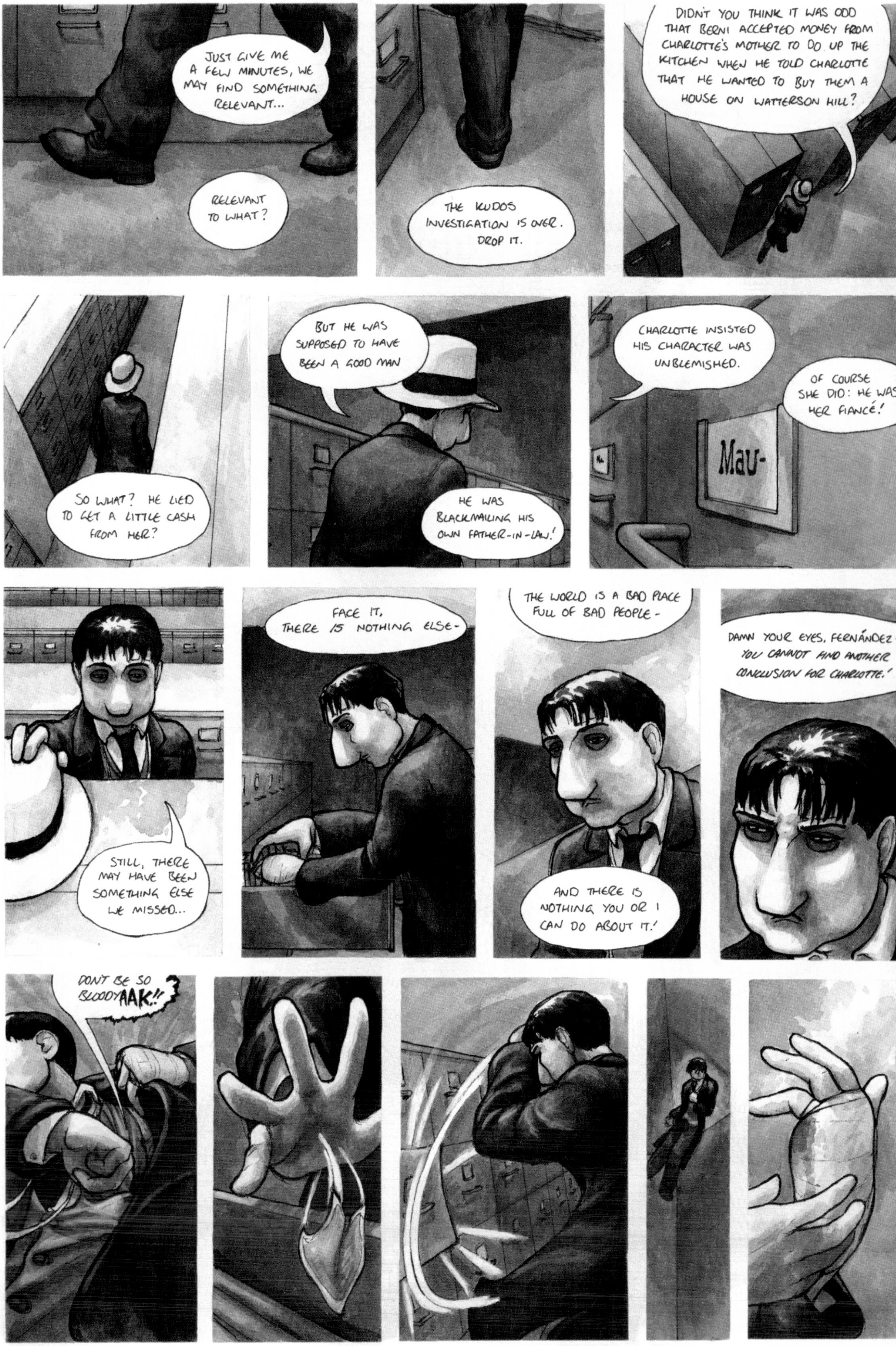
JUST GIVE ME A FEW MINUTES, WE MAY FIND SOMETHING RELEVANT...
RELEVANT TO WHAT?
THE KUDOS INVESTIGATION IS OVER. DROP IT.
DIDN'T YOU THINK IT WAS ODD THAT BERNI ACCEPTED MONEY FROM CHARLOTTE'S MOTHER TO DO UP THE KITCHEN WHEN HE TOLD CHARLOTTE THAT HE WANTED TO BUY THEM A HOUSE ON WATTERSON HILL?
SO WHAT? HE LIED TO GET A LITTLE CASH FROM HER?
BUT HE WAS SUPPOSED TO HAVE BEEN A GOOD MAN
HE WAS BLACKMAILING HIS OWN FATHER-IN-LAW!
CHARLOTTE INSISTED HIS CHARACTER WAS UNBLEMISHED.
OF COURSE SHE DID: HE WAS HER FIANCÉ!
Mau-
STILL, THERE MAY HAVE BEEN SOMETHING ELSE WE MISSED...
FACE IT, THERE IS NOTHING ELSE-
THE WORLD IS A BAD PLACE FULL OF BAD PEOPLE-
AND THERE IS NOTHING YOU OR I CAN DO ABOUT IT!
DAMN YOUR EYES, FERNÁNDEZ- YOU CANNOT FIND ANOTHER CONCLUSION FOR CHARLOTTE!
DON'T BE SO BLOODY AAK!!

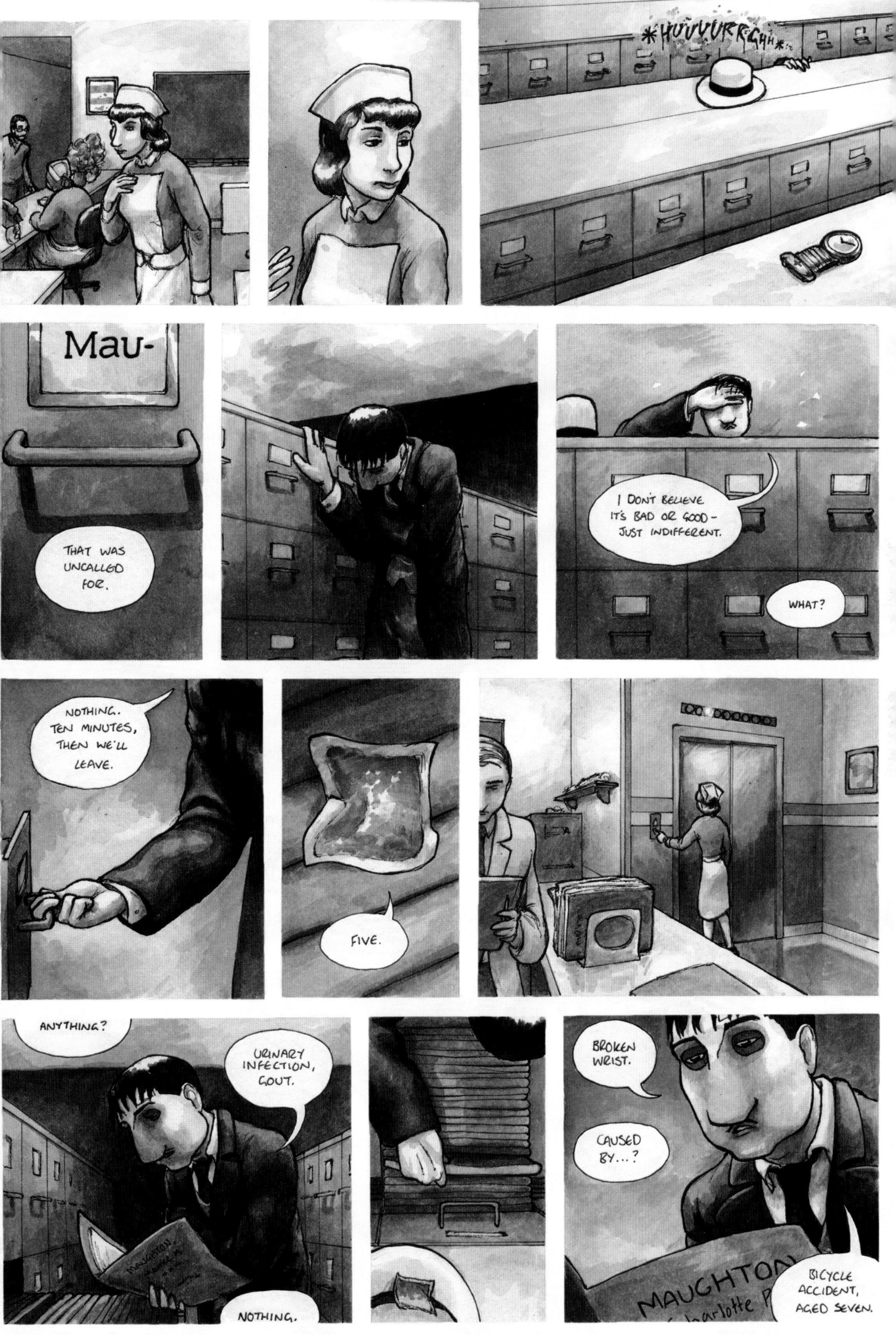
HUVVURRGHH
Mau-
THAT WAS UNCALLED FOR.
I DON'T BELIEVE IT'S BAD OR GOOD - JUST INDIFFERENT.
WHAT?
NOTHING. TEN MINUTES, THEN WE'LL LEAVE.
FIVE.
ANYTHING?
URINARY INFECTION, GOUT.
NOTHING.
BROKEN WRIST.
CAUSED BY...?
MAUGHTON
Charlotte
BICYCLE ACCIDENT, AGED SEVEN.

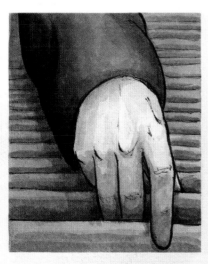

'VIRGINIA MAUGHTON: SCARLET FEVER, MISCARRIAGE, MISCARRIAGE, INFLUENZA, CHARLOTTE'S BIRTH, INFLUENZA.'

SATISFIED?

I'M NOT SURE...

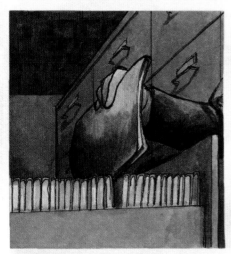

PERHAPS MIDWIFE MINNIE WAS UPSET BY THE MISCARRIAGES AND HELD MAURICE RESPONSIBLE?

DON'T BE FACETIOUS.

TICK TOCK, FERN.

FERN?

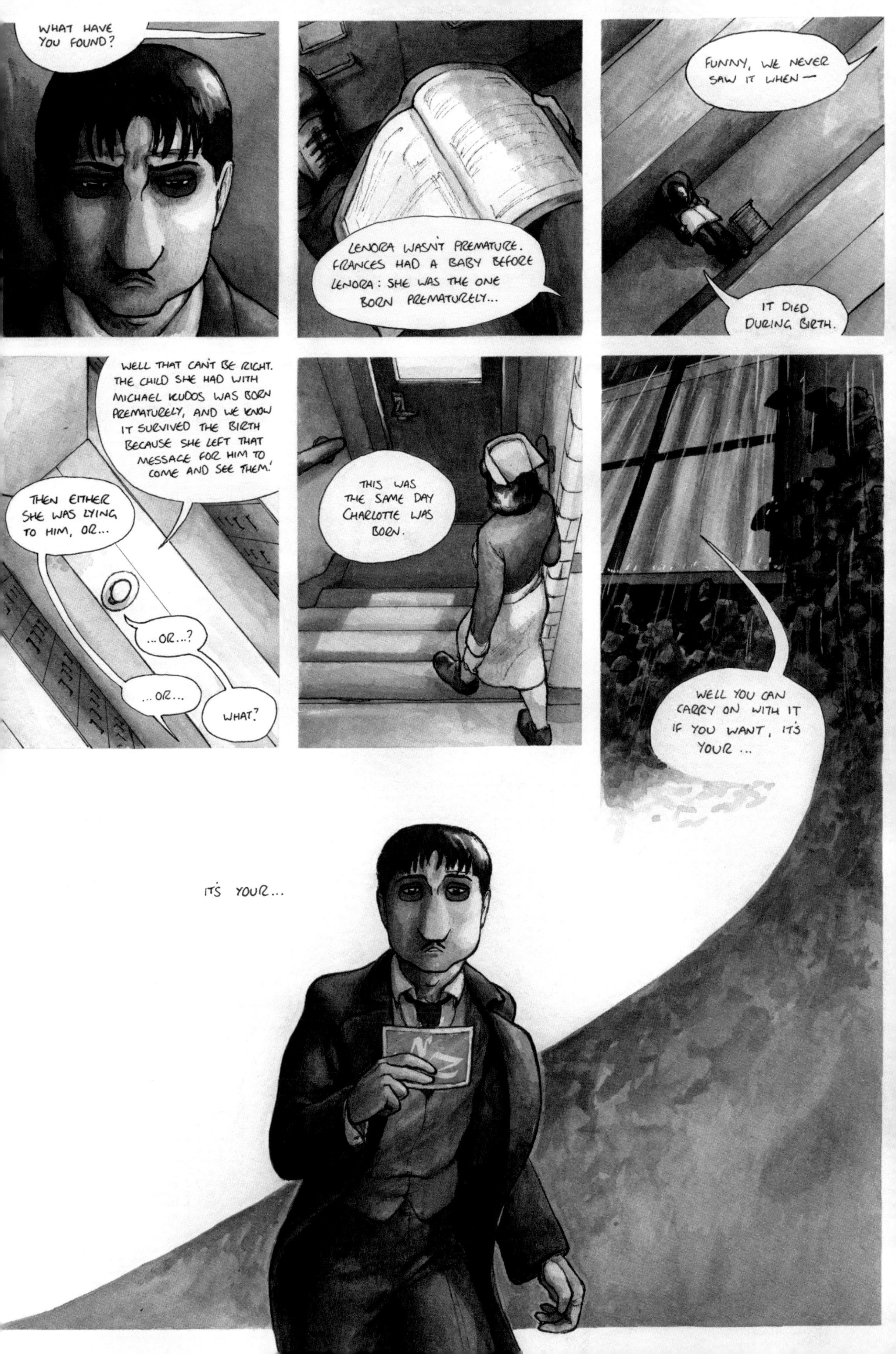
WHAT HAVE YOU FOUND?
LENORA WASN'T PREMATURE. FRANCES HAD A BABY BEFORE LENORA: SHE WAS THE ONE BORN PREMATURELY...
FUNNY, WE NEVER SAW IT WHEN—
IT DIED DURING BIRTH.
WELL THAT CAN'T BE RIGHT. THE CHILD SHE HAD WITH MICHAEL KUDOS WAS BORN PREMATURELY, AND WE KNOW IT SURVIVED THE BIRTH BECAUSE SHE LEFT THAT MESSAGE FOR HIM TO COME AND SEE THEM!
THEN EITHER SHE WAS LYING TO HIM, OR...
...OR...?
...OR...
WHAT?
THIS WAS THE SAME DAY CHARLOTTE WAS BORN.
WELL YOU CAN CARRY ON WITH IT IF YOU WANT, IT'S YOUR...
IT'S YOUR...

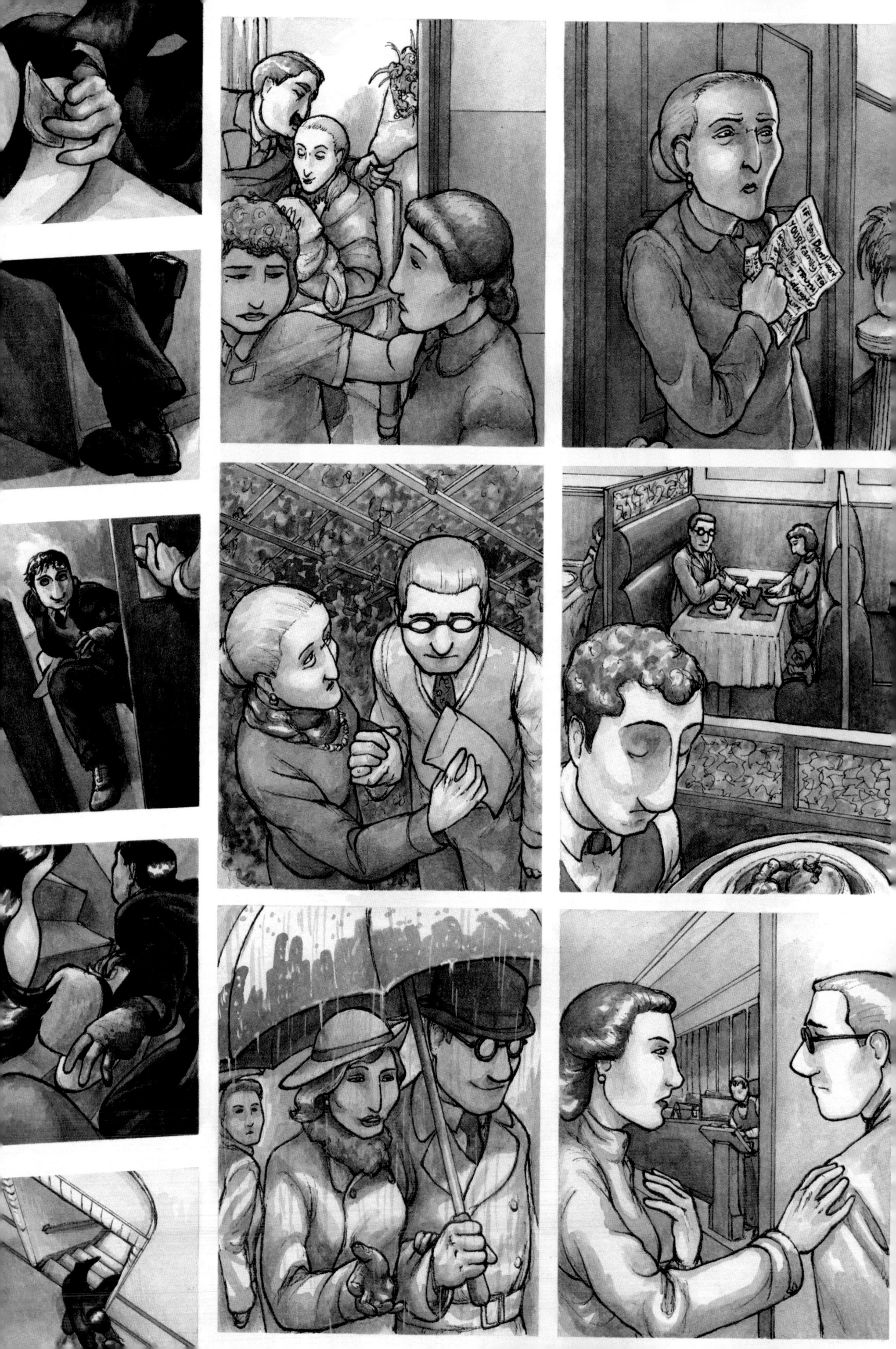
IF you Don't want
YOUR family, TO
know
TRUTH
your daughter

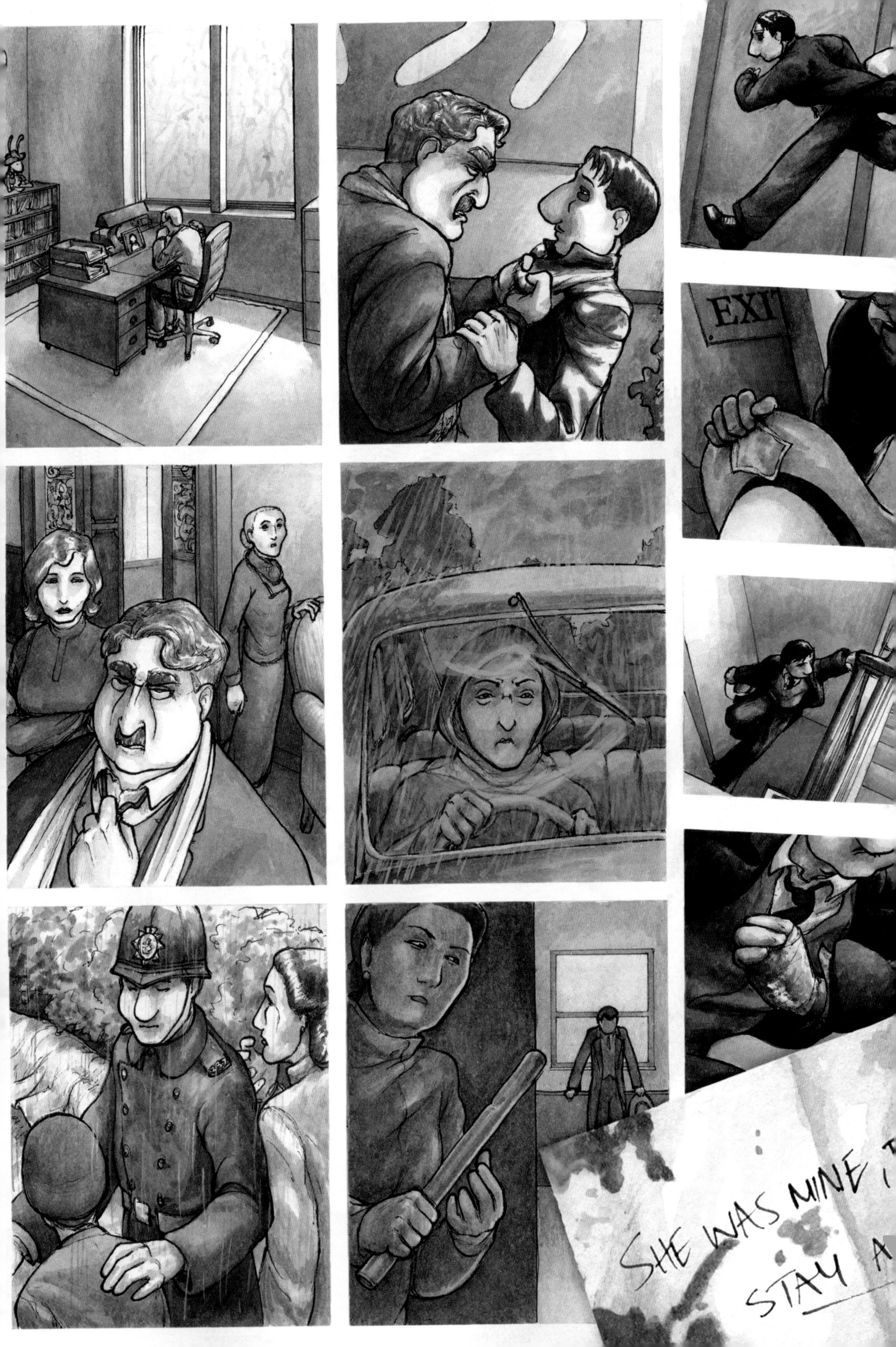
SHE WAS MINE
STAY

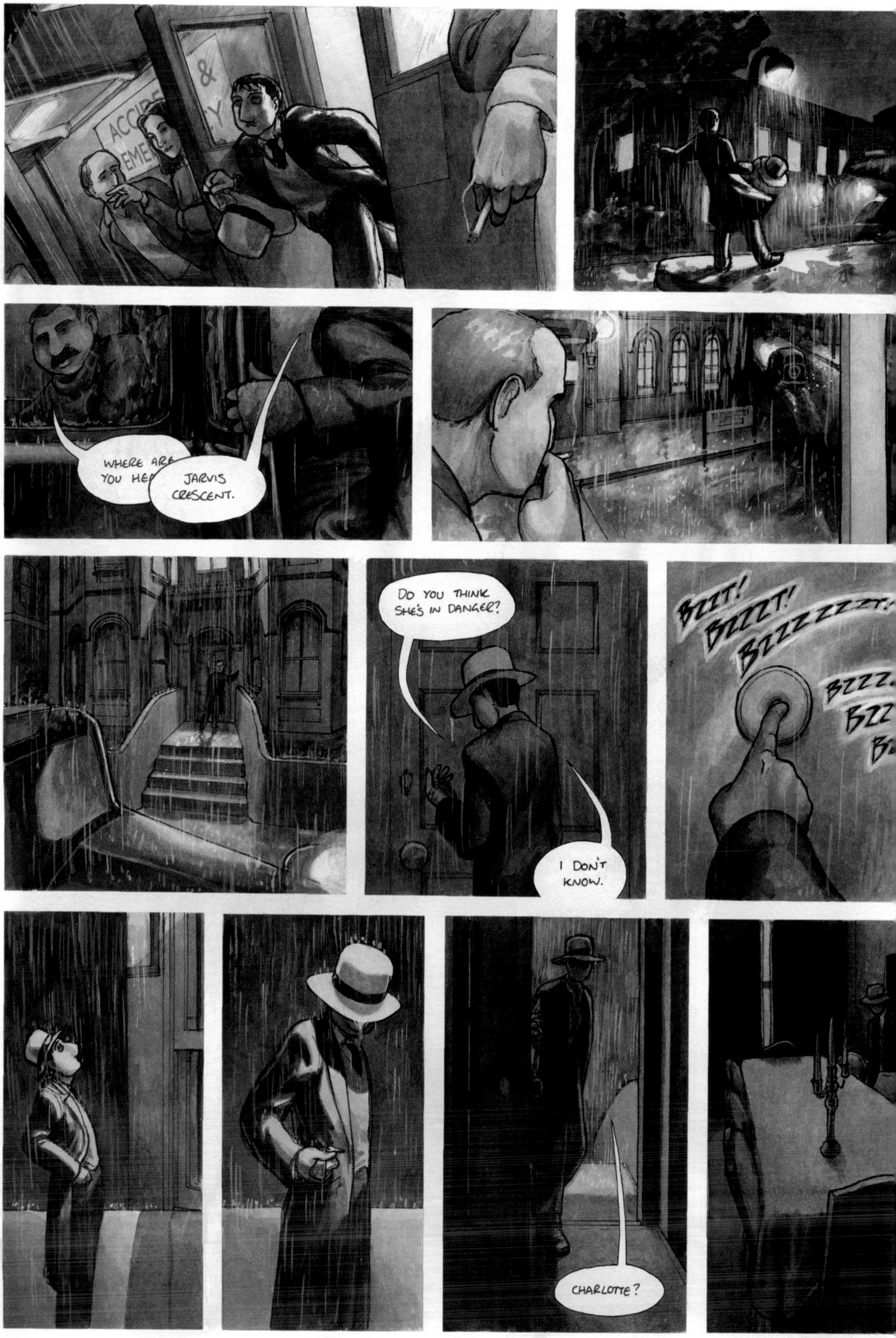
WHERE ARE YOU HEA
JARVIS CRESCENT.
DO YOU THINK SHE'S IN DANGER?
I DON'T KNOW.
BZZT!
BZZZT!
BZZZ.
BZZ
CHARLOTTE?

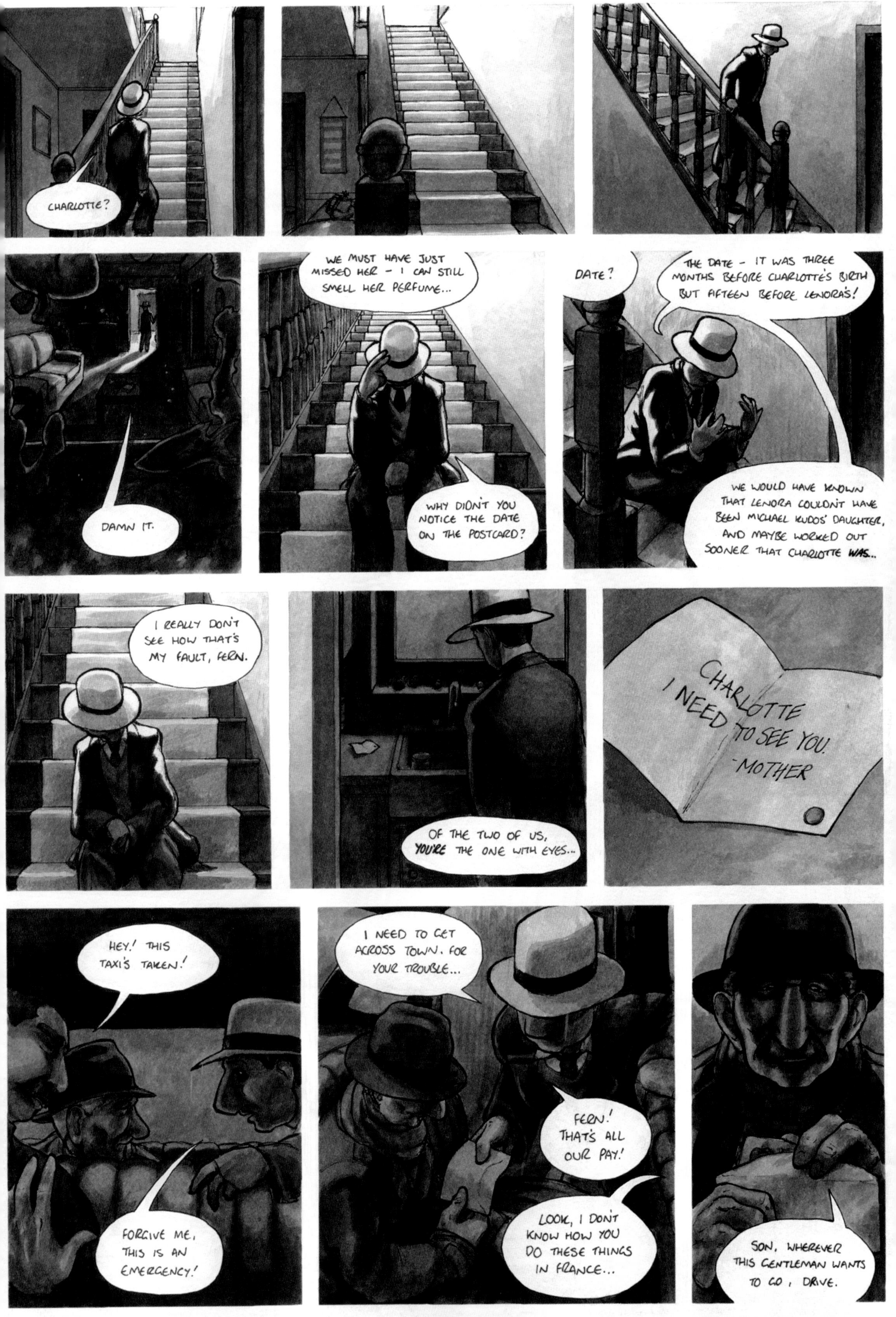
CHARLOTTE?
DAMN IT.
WE MUST HAVE JUST MISSED HER - I CAN STILL SMELL HER PERFUME...
WHY DIDN'T YOU NOTICE THE DATE ON THE POSTCARD?
DATE?
THE DATE - IT WAS THREE MONTHS BEFORE CHARLOTTE'S BIRTH BUT FIFTEEN BEFORE LENORA'S!
WE WOULD HAVE KNOWN THAT LENORA COULDN'T HAVE BEEN MICHAEL KUDOS' DAUGHTER, AND MAYBE WORKED OUT SOONER THAT CHARLOTTE WAS...
I REALLY DON'T SEE HOW THAT'S MY FAULT, FERN.
OF THE TWO OF US, YOU'RE THE ONE WITH EYES...
CHARLOTTE I NEED TO SEE YOU. -MOTHER
HEY! THIS TAXI'S TAKEN!
FORGIVE ME, THIS IS AN EMERGENCY!
I NEED TO GET ACROSS TOWN. FOR YOUR TROUBLE...
FERN! THAT'S ALL OUR PAY!
LOOK, I DON'T KNOW HOW YOU DO THESE THINGS IN FRANCE...
SON, WHEREVER THIS GENTLEMAN WANTS TO GO, DRIVE.

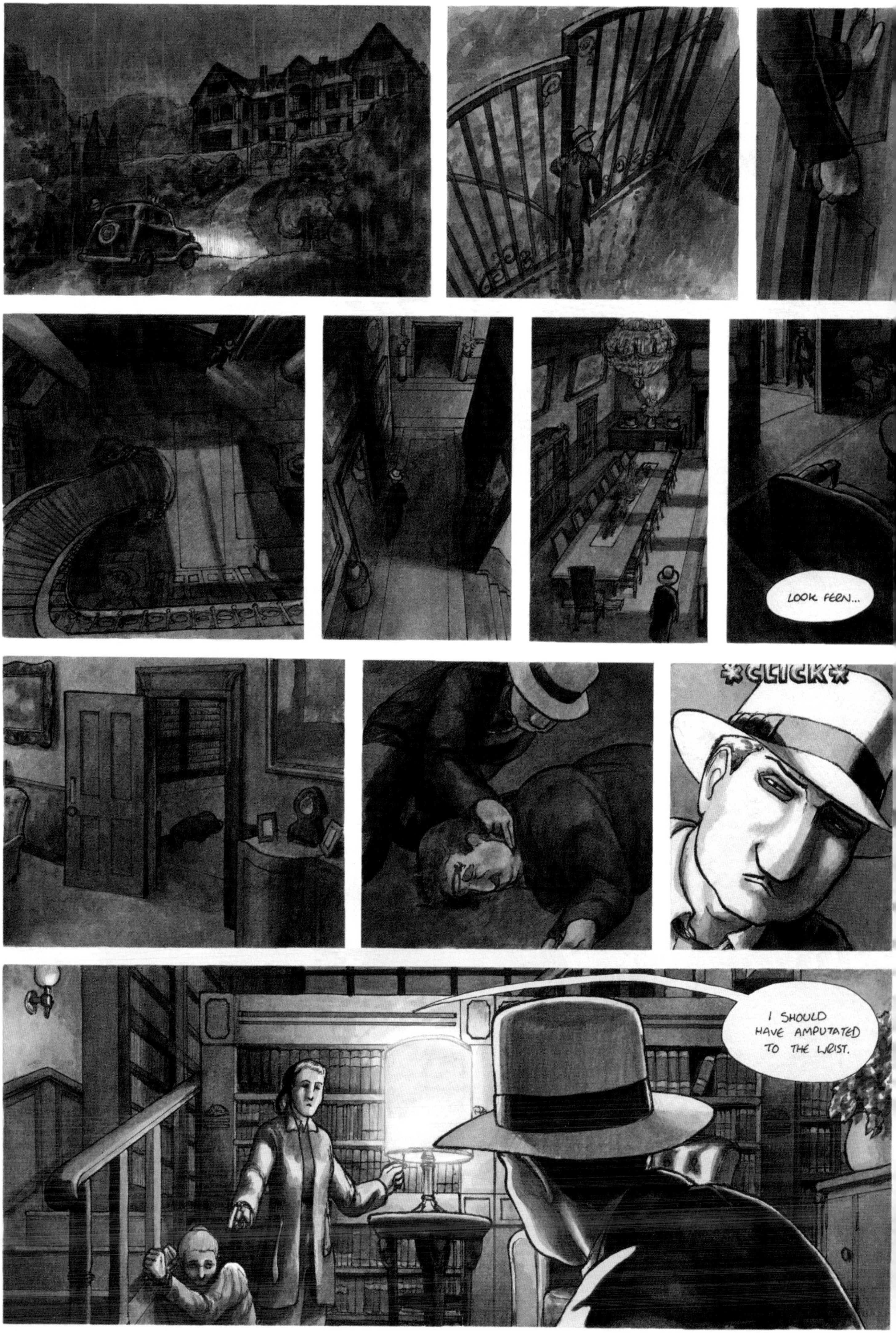
LOOK FERN...
CLICK
I SHOULD HAVE AMPUTATED TO THE WRIST.

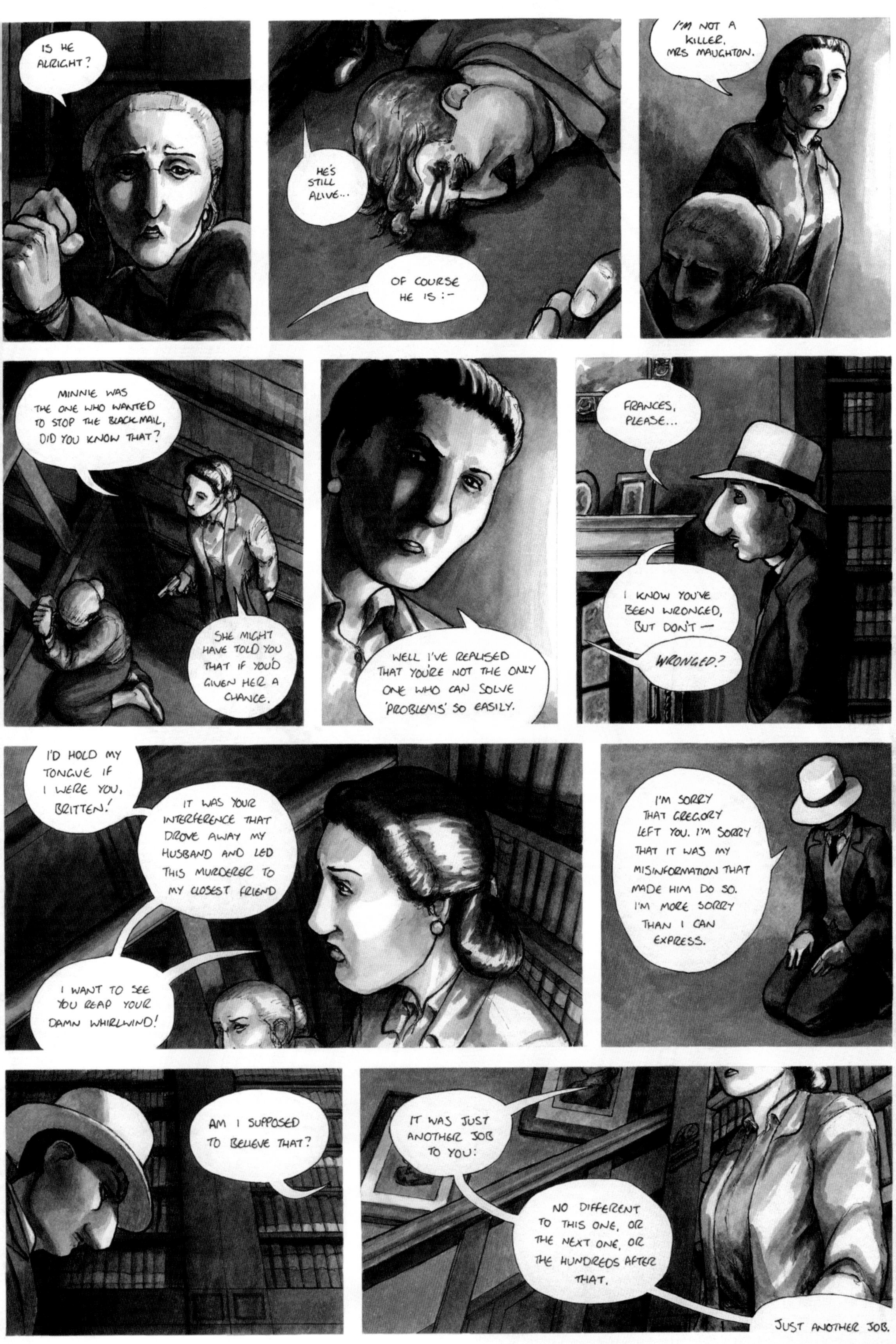
IS HE ALRIGHT?
HE'S STILL ALIVE...
OF COURSE HE IS:-
I'M NOT A KILLER, MRS MAUGHTON.
MINNIE WAS THE ONE WHO WANTED TO STOP THE BLACKMAIL, DID YOU KNOW THAT?
SHE MIGHT HAVE TOLD YOU THAT IF YOU'D GIVEN HER A CHANCE.
WELL I'VE REALISED THAT YOU'RE NOT THE ONLY ONE WHO CAN SOLVE 'PROBLEMS' SO EASILY.
FRANCES, PLEASE...
I KNOW YOU'VE BEEN WRONGED, BUT DON'T—
WRONGED?
I'D HOLD MY TONGUE IF I WERE YOU, BRITTEN!
IT WAS YOUR INTERFERENCE THAT DROVE AWAY MY HUSBAND AND LED THIS MURDERER TO MY CLOSEST FRIEND
I WANT TO SEE YOU REAP YOUR DAMN WHIRLWIND!
I'M SORRY THAT GREGORY LEFT YOU. I'M SORRY THAT IT WAS MY MISINFORMATION THAT MADE HIM DO SO. I'M MORE SORRY THAN I CAN EXPRESS.
AM I SUPPOSED TO BELIEVE THAT?
IT WAS JUST ANOTHER JOB TO YOU:
NO DIFFERENT TO THIS ONE, OR THE NEXT ONE, OR THE HUNDREDS AFTER THAT.
JUST ANOTHER JOB.

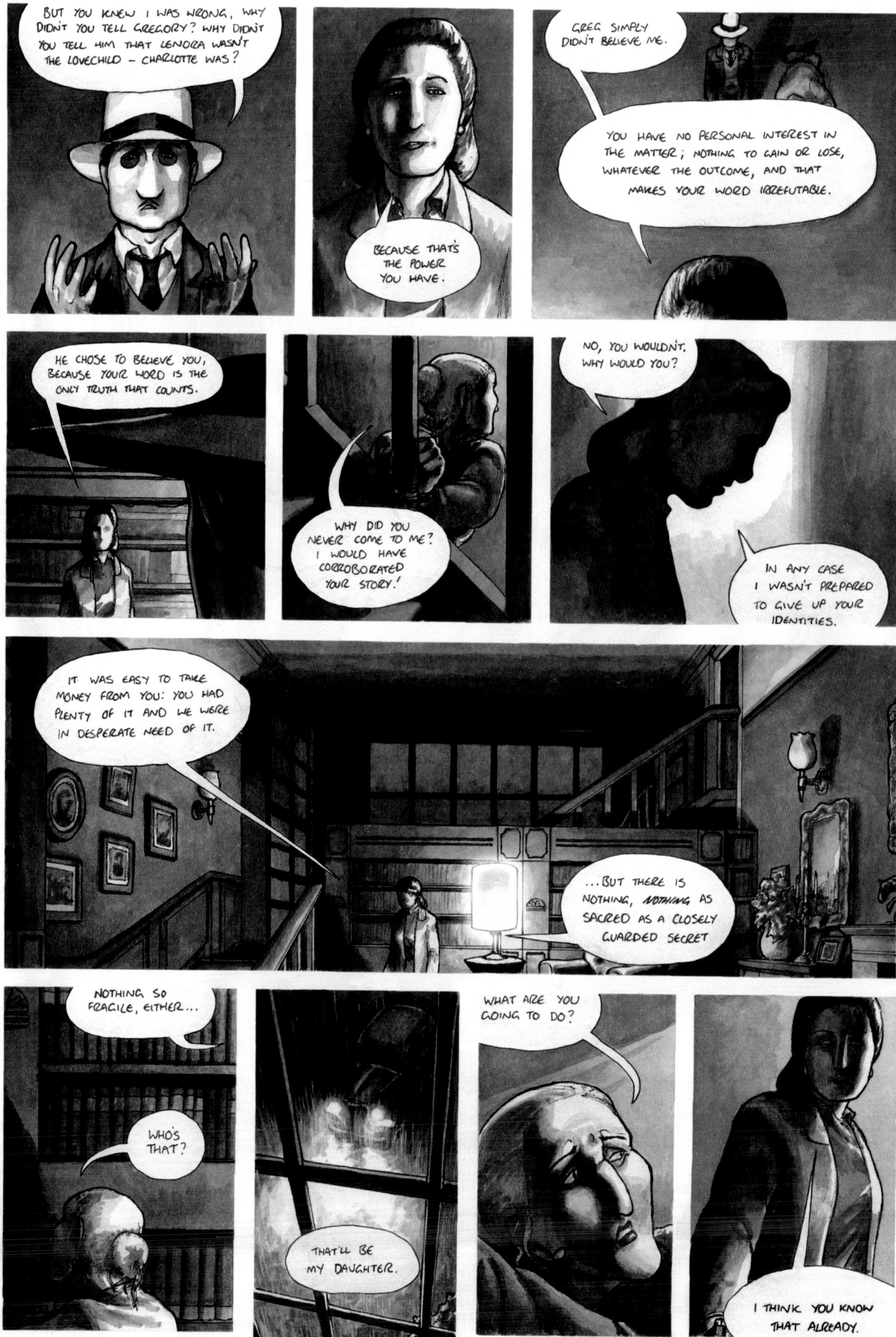
BUT YOU KNEW I WAS WRONG, WHY DIDN'T YOU TELL GREGORY? WHY DIDN'T YOU TELL HIM THAT LENORA WASN'T THE LOVECHILD – CHARLOTTE WAS?
BECAUSE THAT'S THE POWER YOU HAVE.
GREG SIMPLY DIDN'T BELIEVE ME.
YOU HAVE NO PERSONAL INTEREST IN THE MATTER; NOTHING TO GAIN OR LOSE, WHATEVER THE OUTCOME, AND THAT MAKES YOUR WORD IRREFUTABLE.
HE CHOSE TO BELIEVE YOU, BECAUSE YOUR WORD IS THE ONLY TRUTH THAT COUNTS.
WHY DID YOU NEVER COME TO ME? I WOULD HAVE CORROBORATED YOUR STORY!
NO, YOU WOULDN'T. WHY WOULD YOU?
IN ANY CASE I WASN'T PREPARED TO GIVE UP YOUR IDENTITIES.
IT WAS EASY TO TAKE MONEY FROM YOU: YOU HAD PLENTY OF IT AND WE WERE IN DESPERATE NEED OF IT.
...BUT THERE IS NOTHING, NOTHING AS SACRED AS A CLOSELY GUARDED SECRET
NOTHING SO FRAGILE, EITHER...
WHO'S THAT?
THAT'LL BE MY DAUGHTER.
WHAT ARE YOU GOING TO DO?
I THINK YOU KNOW THAT ALREADY.

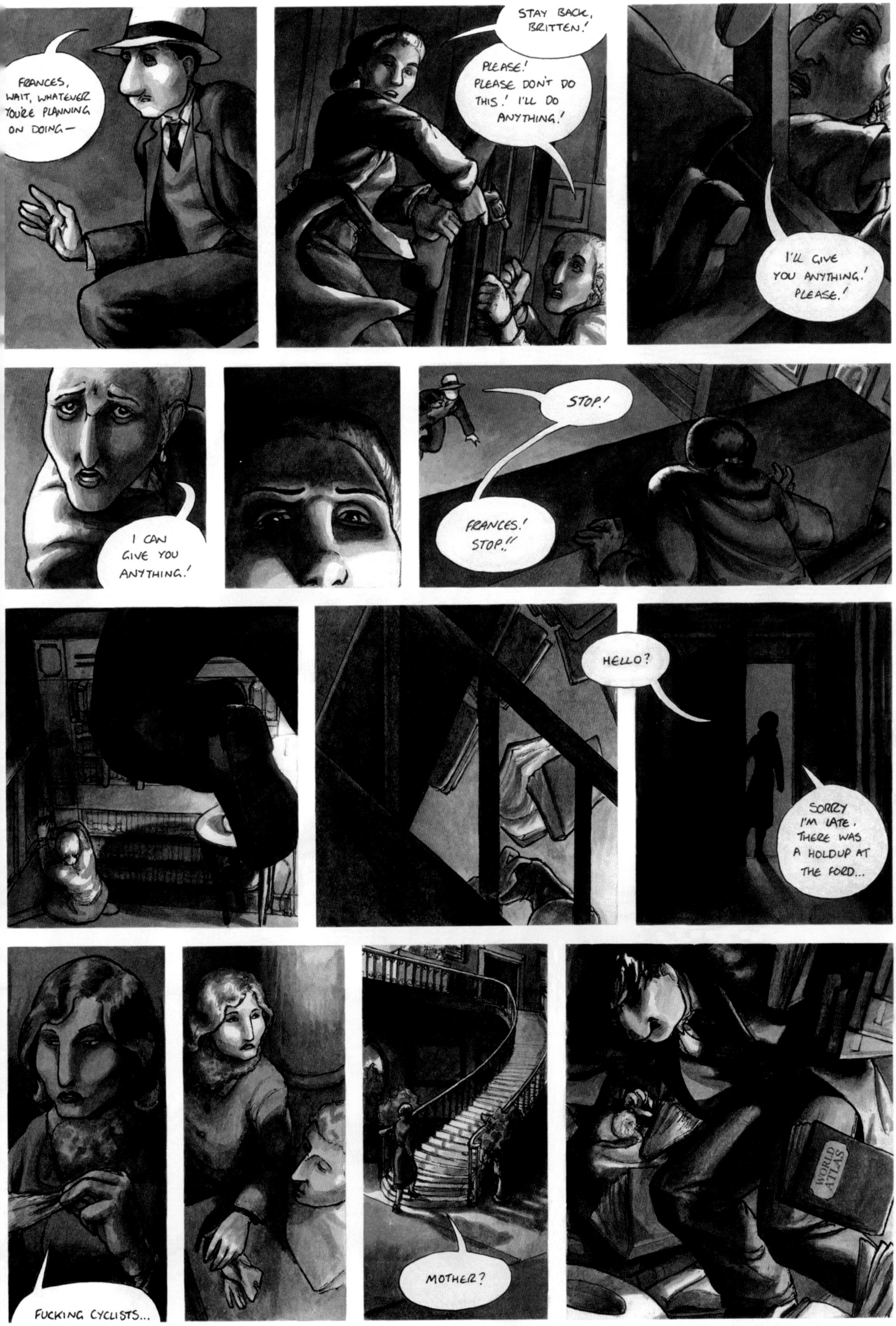
FRANCES, WAIT, WHATEVER YOU'RE PLANNING ON DOING—
STAY BACK, BRITTEN!
PLEASE! PLEASE DON'T DO THIS! I'LL DO ANYTHING!
I'LL GIVE YOU ANYTHING! PLEASE!
I CAN GIVE YOU ANYTHING!
STOP!
FRANCES! STOP!!
HELLO?
SORRY I'M LATE. THERE WAS A HOLDUP AT THE FORD...
FUCKING CYCLISTS...
MOTHER?
WORLD ATLAS

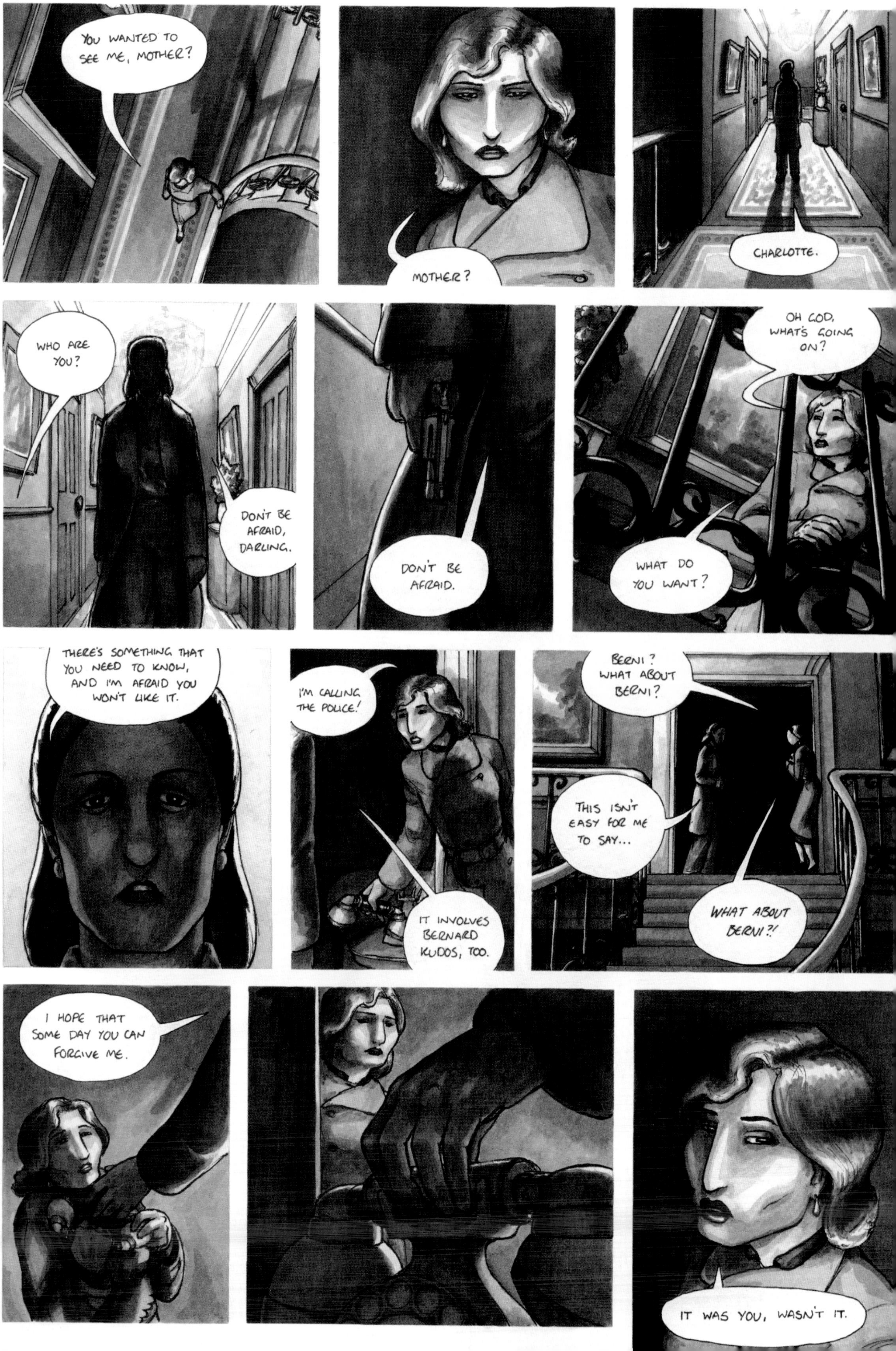
YOU WANTED TO SEE ME, MOTHER?
MOTHER?
CHARLOTTE.
WHO ARE YOU?
DON'T BE AFRAID, DARLING.
DON'T BE AFRAID.
OH GOD, WHAT'S GOING ON?
WHAT DO YOU WANT?
THERE'S SOMETHING THAT YOU NEED TO KNOW, AND I'M AFRAID YOU WON'T LIKE IT.
I'M CALLING THE POLICE!
IT INVOLVES BERNARD KUDOS, TOO.
BERNI? WHAT ABOUT BERNI?
THIS ISN'T EASY FOR ME TO SAY...
WHAT ABOUT BERNI?!
I HOPE THAT SOME DAY YOU CAN FORGIVE ME.
IT WAS YOU, WASN'T IT.

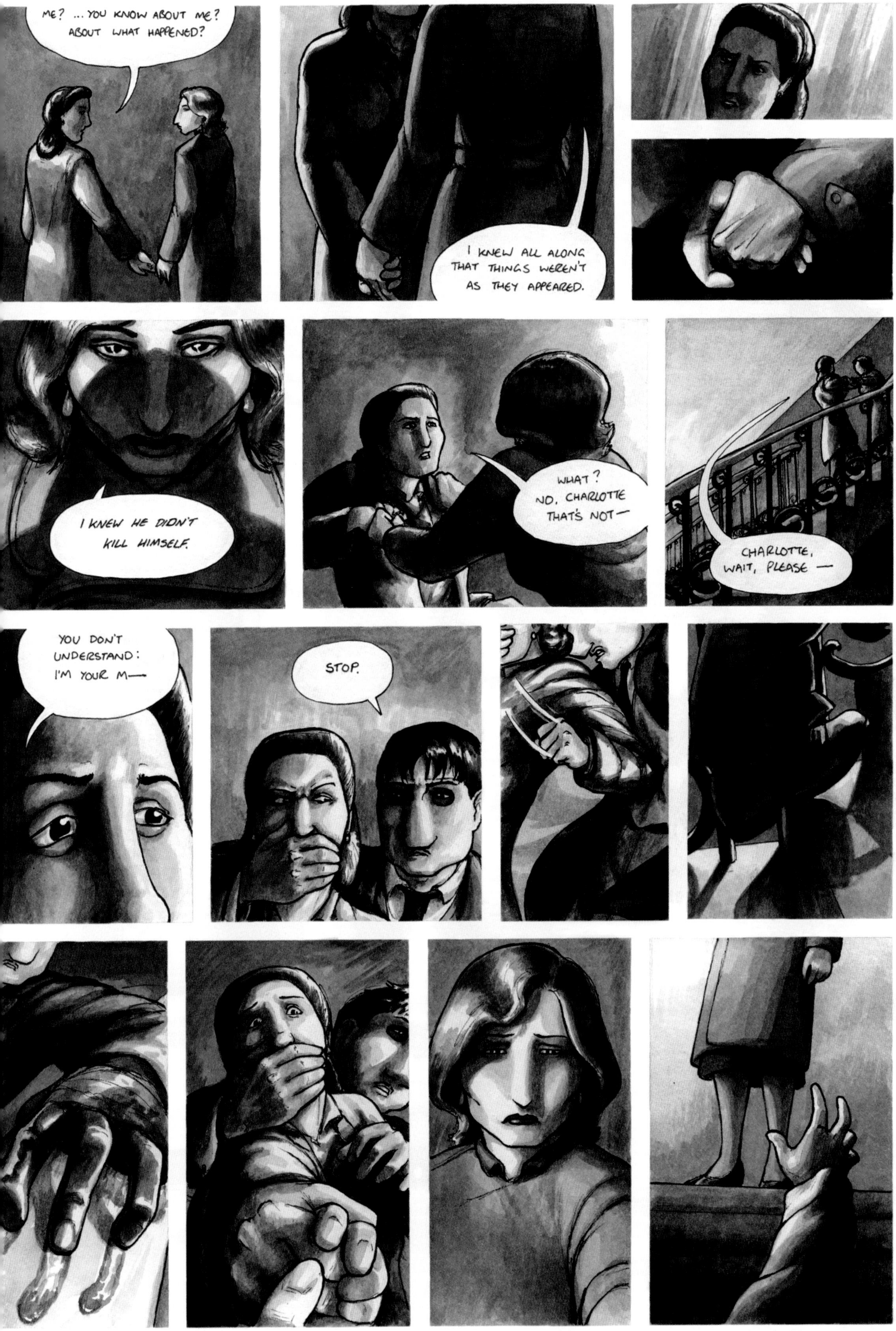
ME? ... YOU KNOW ABOUT ME? ABOUT WHAT HAPPENED?
I KNEW ALL ALONG THAT THINGS WEREN'T AS THEY APPEARED.
I KNEW HE DIDN'T KILL HIMSELF.
WHAT? NO, CHARLOTTE THAT'S NOT—
CHARLOTTE, WAIT, PLEASE —
YOU DON'T UNDERSTAND: I'M YOUR M—
STOP.

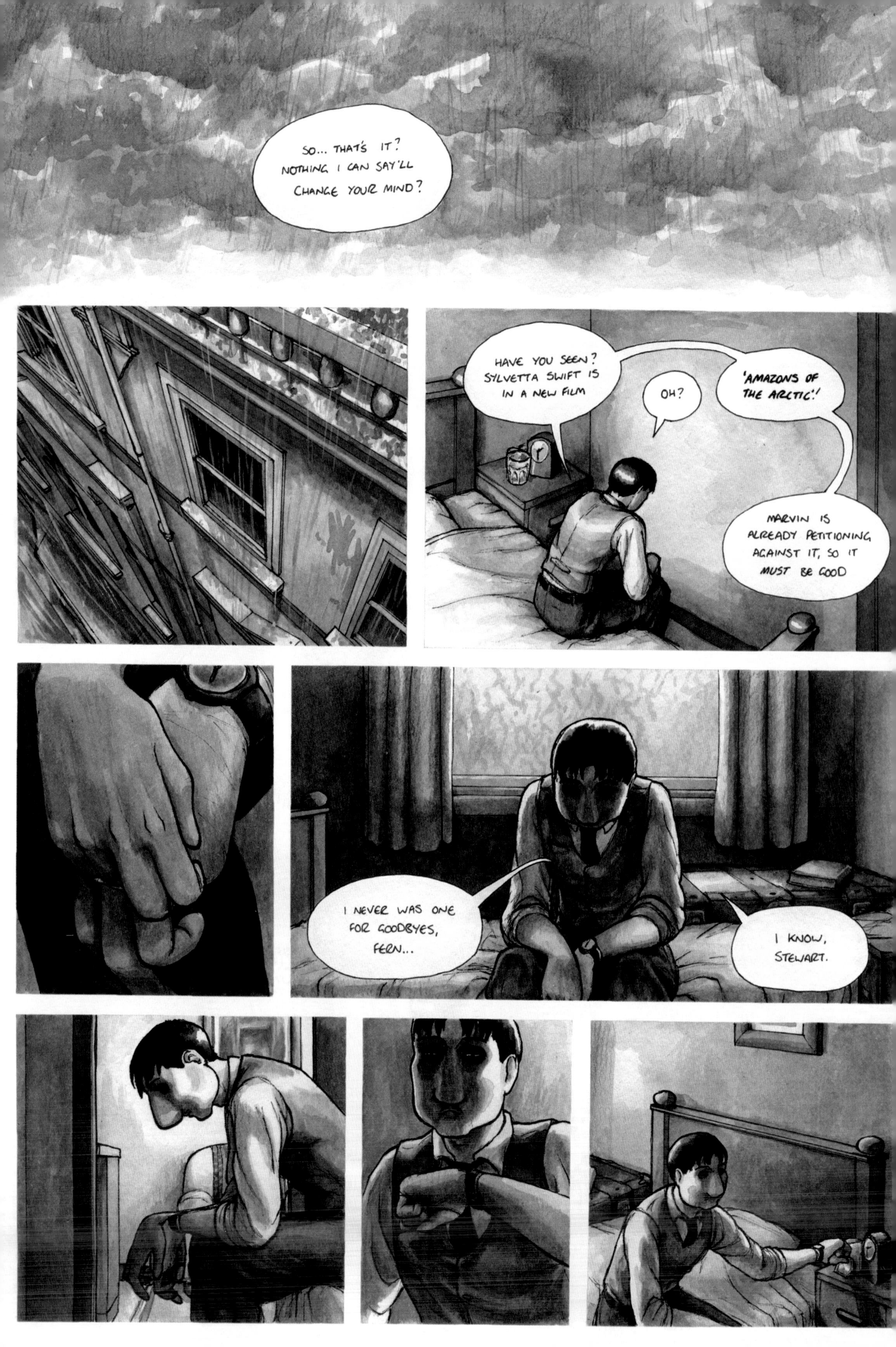
SO... THAT'S IT? NOTHING I CAN SAY'LL CHANGE YOUR MIND?
HAVE YOU SEEN? SYLVETTA SWIFT IS IN A NEW FILM
OH?
'AMAZONS OF THE ARCTIC'!
MARVIN IS ALREADY PETITIONING AGAINST IT, SO IT MUST BE GOOD
I NEVER WAS ONE FOR GOODBYES, FERN...
I KNOW, STEWART.

I knew that there were casualties, of course. I knew that Ginny should have been held accountable for Minnie's death. I knew that Eric deserved to know what had happened to his wife, and that Lenora — poor Lenora — as an innocent bystander should never have had this much suffering thrust upon her.

I knew this, yet I did nothing to set the record straight. Perched precariously on top of this ugly hill of lies and deceit was Charlotte's oblivious peace of mind. She was my client, she came to me for help, and I had a responsibility to her. Absolute morality is a luxury for the short-sighted.

By the time the police had arrived, Frances was long dead — her neck broken during the fall. The Maughtons evidently had powerful friends, as no investigation ever took place.

Charlotte concluded, when told about Michael Kudos leaving Frances alone to bear his illegitimate child, that Frances must have killed Berni out of cold-blooded revenge. I didn't redirect her: she was partly right in her conclusion.

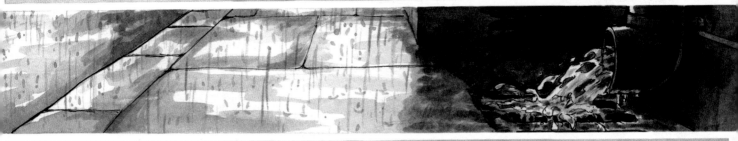

In telling him that his fiancée was his own brother's daughter, Frances left Berni trapped with an incredible, undeniable truth. Forced to choose between his incestuous marriage and a revelation that would destroy both the family that had accepted him so readily and the girl he was devoted to, he took his own life.

After I left the Naughtons' house for the last time, I went
 to my office and destroyed the file, burning it to ashes.
Once I'd started, there seemed no reason to stop. My other cases;
my life's work; files and files and every one a compilation of
wretched misery, a window onto infinite sadness...
 I burned them all.

 I have wielded the truth for sixteen long years, the name
 'Heartbreaker' perched on my shoulder like a vulture. The grand
 finale I naively waited for never came, and the absolution
 I was so desperate to find has eluded me to the end.

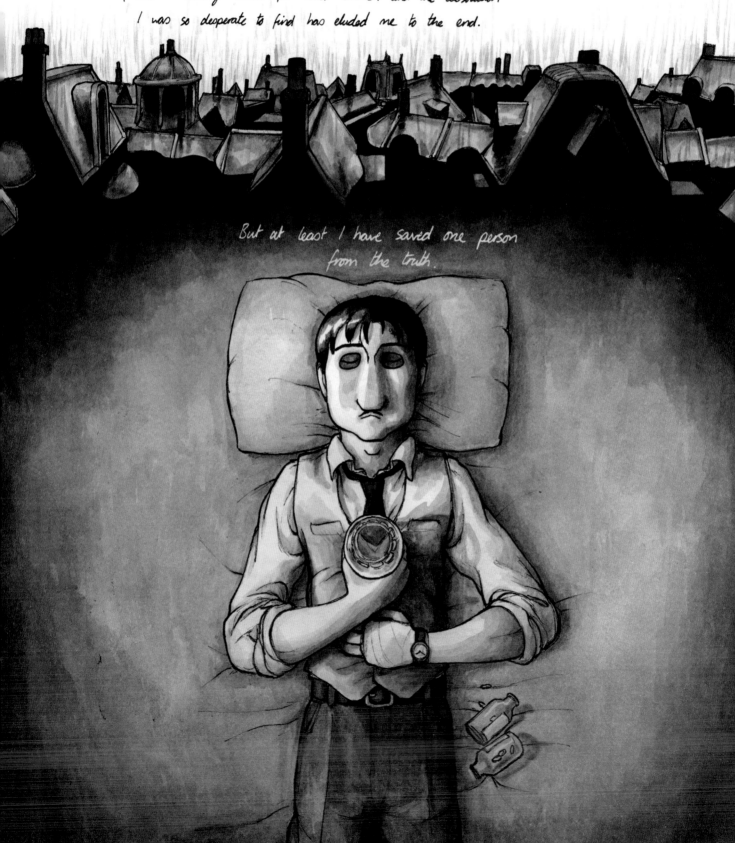

But at least I have saved one person
from the truth.

THE FOLLOWING PEOPLE DESERVE ACKNOWLEDGMENT

NIGEL BALDWIN, the man who encouraged me to write and rewrite and rewrite until my ears bled, for being right every time; EMILY GRAVETT, for providing a discerning eye, a sympathetic ear, and beans on toast; MUM, DAD, and CHRIS, for unconditional (and often undeserved) love and support; and all those other good friends who know who they are and will forgive me for not naming them for fear of accidental omission. You are, all of you, a tribute to humanity.

This book was also assisted by a grant from THE AUTHORS' FOUNDATION, for which I am extremely grateful.